EXPLAINING NATO
ENLARGEMENT

Of Related Interest

Turkey: Anglo-American Security Interests, 1945–1952: The First Enlargement of NATO
by Ekavi Athanasopoulou

NATO in the Twenty-First Century
edited by Ted Galen Carpenter

Critical Reflections on Security and Change
edited by Stuart Croft and Terry Terriff

Reviewing the Cold War: Approaches, Interpretations, Theory
edited by Odd Arne Westad

Precision and Purpose: Debating Robert A Pape's Bombing to Win
edited by Benjamin Frankel

Culture and Security: Multilateralism, Arms Control and Security Building
edited by Keith R. Krause

Stability and Security in the Baltic Sea Region
edited by Olav F. Knudsen

Preventing the Use of Weapons of Mass Destruction
edited by Eric Herring

Twenty-First Century Weapons Proliferation
edited by Henry Sokolski

Arms Control: New Approaches to Theory and Policy
edited by Nancy W. Gallagher

EXPLAINING NATO ENLARGEMENT

Editor

ROBERT W. RAUCHHAUS

University of California at Berkeley

FRANK CASS
LONDON • PORTLAND, OR

First published in 2001 in Great Britain by
FRANK CASS PUBLISHERS
Newbury House, 900 Eastern Avenue
London, IG2 7HH

and in the United States of America by
FRANK CASS PUBLISHERS
c/o ISBS, 5824 N.E. Hassalo Street
Portland, Oregon 97213-3644

Copyright © 2001 Frank Cass & Co. Ltd.

Website: www.frankcass.com

British Library Cataloguing in Publication Data

Explaining NATO enlargement
   1. North Atlantic Treaty Organization
   2. Security, International
   I. Rauchhaus, Robert W.
   355'.031'091821

      ISBN 0-7146-5127-3 (cloth)
      ISBN 0-7146-8153-9 (paper)

Library of Congress Cataloging-in-Publication Data

Explaining NATO enlargement / editor, Robert W. Rauchaus.
   p. cm.
  Includes bibliographical references and index.
  ISBN 0-7146-5127-3 – ISBN 0-7146-8153-9
  1. North Atlantic Treaty Organization – Europe, Eastern.
  2. Europe – Defenses. 3. Europe, Eastern – Defenses.
  I. Rauchaus, Robert W., 1971–
  UA646.5.E85 E97 2000
  355'. 031091821 – dc 21   00-047498

This group of studies first appeared as a special issue of *Contemporary Security Policy*,
ISSN 1352-3260, Vol.21, No.2 (August 2000) published by Frank Cass and Co. Ltd.

Printed in Great Britain by
Antony Rowe Ltd, Chippenham, Wilts

Contents

Acknowledgements

This volume is a collective effort and represents the contributions of many people and organizations. In the spring of 1998, the Friedrich Ebert Foundation, the University of California Center for German and European Studies, and the Center for Slavic and East European Studies sponsored a conference on NATO enlargement at the University of California at Berkeley. At the time the conference was held, there were no plans to present or publish papers, but by the end of the conference it was clear that the issues raised by the participants were worth pursuing further.

Without the generous financial support of the Friedrich Ebert Foundation, this never would have happened. Dieter Dettke and Peter Schulze deserve special mention for ensuring that this project received funding and intellectual direction. The Center for German and European Studies also provided financial support, and Gia White expertly co-ordinated the conference held at Berkeley. Special thanks go to Beverly Crawford whose valuable suggestions and advice shaped this project at every stage.

This volume also benefited from the intellectual support of a number of other individuals. The participants at the NATO enlargement conference helped provoke thought and stimulate debate on many important issues. Although not all of the conference participants have essays in this volume, their ideas influenced many of the contributors. Two anonymous reviewers provided helpful advice on the structure and organization of the volume as well as on many of the individual essays. Stuart Croft of *Contemporary Security Policy* and Jonathan Manley of Frank Cass Publishers also provided valuable advice and comments.

ROBERT W. RAUCHHAUS
Berkeley, California

PART 1: INTRODUCTION

Marching NATO Eastward: Can International Relations Theory Keep Pace?

ROBERT W. RAUCHHAUS[1]

> Today we recognize in fact what has always been true in spirit. Today we confirm through our actions that the lands of King Stephen and Cardinal Mindszenty, Charles the Fourth and Vaclav Havel, Copernicus and Pope John Paul II reside fully and irrevocably within the Atlantic community for freedom. And to that I say, to quote an old central European expression, 'Hallelujah'.
>
> **Madeleine Albright**

The North Atlantic Treaty Organization (NATO) is currently experiencing a renaissance. Following the collapse of the Soviet Union and the end of the Cold War, many expected the alliance to wither away or, at best, to stagnate and decline in importance. More than a decade later, it is clear that these earlier predictions were wrong. Not only is the transatlantic alliance alive and well, but, since the end of the Cold War, its mission and capabilities have grown. Of the many significant changes to the organization, two decisions, the enlargement of NATO and the airstrikes against Yugoslavia, stand out as the most crucial. While the long-term consequences of NATO's actions in Yugoslavia remain to be seen, we can say for certain that the enlargement of NATO will remain an important topic in the years to come. The decision to expand the alliance, reached in Madrid at a summit of NATO countries during the summer of 1997, did more than extend membership to three new countries – it initiated a larger process that will require NATO members to make more decisions about enlargement in the future. While there is considerable disagreement as to whether expansion will have positive or negative effects, both proponents and opponents of the policy believe that it will have far-reaching consequences for the alliance and for European security.

There are several good reasons either to support or to oppose the expansion of NATO. Advocates of the policy focus on a number of issues, including how NATO enlargement may help the domestic reform efforts of eastern European post-communist countries. It is hoped that NATO membership – or perhaps just the prospect of NATO membership – will create strong incentives for eastern European countries to improve their civil–military relations, resolve ongoing border disputes, and guarantee the fair treatment of national minorities.[2] In addition to providing new members with economic and political aid, proponents of the policy also hope that an Article 5 security guarantee (see Appendix 1) will allow new members to focus more of their attention on domestic matters. If eastern European states do not receive a security guarantee, there is concern that these countries will be forced to build up their militaries and engage in costly security competition with Russia or other neighbouring states. As the history of the twentieth century demonstrates, the region is a tinderbox; irredentist claims and long-standing ethnic hatreds have caused local, regional, and even world wars. Also, recent events in Bosnia show that dire consequences may result if NATO and the West fail to prevent the outbreak of hostilities.[3] While enlargement is financially costly in the short run, in the long run it may help prevent the outbreak of conflicts, which would be much more costly, not only financially but also in terms of lives.[4]

Critics of the policy warn that expanding NATO into eastern Europe will undermine European security. Regardless of whether enlargement accomplishes much of what its proponents hope it will, critics warn that the costs of enlargement are too high, and that the policy is too risky and may have unintended consequences. One of the main concerns for critics is whether NATO expansion will negatively affect the fragile domestic political balance in Russia.[5] Critics worry that Russians may perceive the expansion of NATO as a threat, which may increase nationalist sentiment, thereby strengthening the position of the anti-West, non-democratic opposition. The uncertainty stemming from a post-Yeltsin Russia only heightens this concern. Critics also worry that NATO enlargement will undermine Russia's willingness to co-operate with the West on a number of important issues. For example, if enlargement threatens progress on START III, or prevents other arms control efforts, then is it really worth pursuing? Critics conclude that expansion is ultimately counterproductive, and that it will reduce, not increase, European security.[6]

In the months leading up to the Madrid summit, both critics and advocates of the policy believed that the decision to enlarge NATO would have far-reaching consequences. While this claim may, at present, seem a bit exaggerated, it may only be premature. It is of course unlikely that the decision to offer membership to the Visegrad Three – Poland, Hungary and the Czech Republic – will have any significant consequences, either positive or negative. These three nations did not have pressing security issues, and their admission did not pose a serious threat to Russia. However, while admitting these three countries may not have many negative consequences, it may not have many positive consequences either. Given that these three countries already had a high level of political and economic development, NATO membership provides them with few new benefits.

It is important to remember, however, that the admission of these three countries only marks the beginning of a much larger process. As President Clinton and his foreign policy team have stated on a number of occasions, the question of future rounds of NATO enlargement is 'no longer whether, but rather when and whom'.[7] In 2001, NATO will once again take up this contentious issue and decide whether to expand NATO further eastward. There is a long list of NATO hopefuls in eastern Europe, including Bulgaria, Romania, Slovenia, Slovakia and the Baltic states. The next wave of applicants will generate even more controversy than the last one. Unlike the Visegrad Three, some of the countries in question still face a number of political and economic challenges, and they have more precarious situations with national minorities. Some of the countries also pose a legitimate security concern for Russia, and would bring NATO to another one of Russia's western borders, but this time even closer to Moscow.

Future rounds of enlargement will require NATO to make some difficult choices. The Baltic states, for example, fit all the criteria for membership, but due to their proximity to Russia, NATO probably will not offer them membership in the next round. In contrast, Romania, which has more domestic problems and fewer historic ties with the West, may be one of the next countries admitted. What is the strategic rationale for including Romania but not Estonia? These kinds of dilemmas are certain to pose real problems for policy-makers, and they guarantee that the next round of enlargement will generate even more controversy.

NATO'S UNEXPECTED TURNAROUND

The initial decision to offer NATO membership to eastern European countries caught most observers by surprise. This fact, in retrospect, is often overlooked since by the time the formal decision to enlarge NATO was reached in July 1997, everyone knew enlargement would happen. However, it is important to recall that only a few years prior to the decision to enlarge the alliance, no one thought that such a bold initiative was possible. While today analysts and scholars debate why NATO is thriving and whether the alliance should expand further eastward, less than a decade ago, many of these same individuals were debating whether the alliance could survive at all.[8]

In the early 1990s, the conventional wisdom about NATO's future was very pessimistic. Most policy-makers and political pundits believed the historical record offered strong evidence that alliances collapse shortly after the defeat of a common enemy. Several leading international relations (IR) theories also caused pessimism among academics and scholars. Some versions of neorealism, for example, expected that in the absence of an external threat, NATO would lose its cohesion and sense of purpose.[9] Other neorealists went a step further. They argued that even if the alliance did not collapse from atrophy or disuse, the dissolution of the Soviet Union and the subsequent creation of a gross asymmetry in the international distribution of power would create internal rivalry within the alliance. Because of unipolarity, European member states would actively begin balancing against the United States, thereby causing the alliance's demise.[10]

Scholars familiar with the domestic politics of key NATO members were often equally pessimistic. It seemed reasonable that the legislatures and publics of NATO members would become reluctant to bear the costs of alliance membership.[11] The United States, for example, has a long history of reverting to isolationism after fighting wars against states that have hegemonic ambitions.[12] There was also worry that France, no longer in need of an American security guarantee, would build on the momentum generated by recent advances in European integration and create a European security organization that excluded the United States. Another concern was that German reunification might pose new problems for the alliance. Would a reunified Germany remain in NATO? Could the German government continue to withstand pressure from domestic groups critical of low-flying US warplanes and the many other costs associated with the stationing of more than 300,000 foreign troops on German soil? These issues and the domestic politics of other key NATO members provided analysts with a number of reasons to believe that the end of the Cold War could also mean the end of NATO.

However, not all analysts were equally pessimistic about NATO's prospects. There was a group of 'optimists' who believed the alliance could transform itself into something new and survive beyond its original purpose. They argued that given NATO's popularity and proven track record, it would make more sense for NATO members to modify and adapt the organization, rather than pursue risky or costly alternatives. Creating a new organization, or addressing European security issues in an *ad hoc* manner, would involve a considerable gamble.

In addition to the lack of good alternatives to NATO, there was also reason to believe that NATO, owing to its own qualities, could and would survive. Although NATO began life as a military alliance, over the course of 40 years, the alliance had evolved into something bigger and better. At minimum, NATO had evolved into a formal organization with a broad set of political and security functions. Perhaps NATO had even helped establish a transatlantic security community, in which it had become firmly embedded.[13] If so, the shared values of members would guarantee the organization's survival.

It is important to note, though, that even the experts who were optimistic about NATO's role in the post-Cold War world had modest expectations. While they believed that NATO would survive and play a role in post-Cold War Europe, they also believed that its capacity and importance would be diminished. The debate, therefore, was not between NATO optimists and NATO pessimists, but rather it was between different individuals with varying degrees of pessimism. Suspiciously absent from the debate was any speculation that the alliance would flourish and prosper, as it has in fact done.

The belief that NATO would not fare too well in a post-Cold War world was confirmed by events in the early 1990s. Following the collapse of the Soviet Union, NATO members began unilaterally cutting defence spending with little or no consultation with allies; in addition, the United States began removing large numbers of troops from Europe; tensions resurfaced between Turkey and Greece over Cyprus; there was also considerable disagreement within the alliance over defining a new post-Cold War mission for NATO; France was building on the momentum of European integration and began pushing for the Western European Union (WEU) as a European-only alternative; NATO was unable to develop a common policy on the Gulf War; and, most importantly, NATO stood by as war raged in Yugoslavia, unable – or at least unwilling – to do anything to stop the fighting and genocide. While the US debated whether

Yugoslavia was an issue of direct national interest, European members had difficulty translating their shared interest into a common policy. Even before the outbreak of full-scale hostilities, it was clear that the alliance was in for difficult times, with Germany breaking ranks and unilaterally recognizing Croatia.[14] In the early 1990s, things certainly did not look good for NATO.

The organization's turnaround is as remarkable as it was unexpected. Even as late as 1994, it would have been difficult to imagine that NATO would witness a renaissance within the next few years. Once sidelined and immobilized, NATO has now proved that it is the only security organization capable of taking direct action to help stop fighting in the Balkans. Member states have given the organization authority to conduct out-of-area operations; the command and control system has received a significant makeover; and force structure has changed markedly, most notably with the creation of a rapid deployment force.[15] Also, in October 1998, NATO took the unprecedented step of issuing an activation order and threatening to bomb Yugoslavia, a sovereign state, for the treatment of ethnic Albanians in the province of Kosovo. On 24 March 1999, NATO finally made good on its threat and began a 78-day air campaign, which included more than 38,000 sorties and the use of 28,000 bombs and missiles. Today NATO remains the world's premier security organization and stands poised to expand even further eastward.

ORGANIZATION AND PURPOSE OF THIS VOLUME

Of the many important changes to NATO since the end of the Cold War, the decision to expand NATO eastward and the decision to intervene in Yugoslavia are by far the most significant. The long-term effects of actions in Yugoslavia are difficult to predict: have NATO's actions established a new precedent, or will they become an historical anomaly? While analysts have different views on this issue, most agree that the decision to offer membership to former Warsaw Pact countries is critical. NATO members will have to decide whether or not to expand the alliance in the future, and this will undoubtedly lead to another lively debate.

The decision to enlarge NATO raises a number of important questions. Why did the alliance decide to offer membership to its former Cold War adversaries? What are the likely consequences of the decision to expand NATO eastward? Which countries will be admitted in future rounds? Which countries *should* be admitted in future rounds? These questions provide analysts with the perfect opportunity to apply IR theory to an issue that is both current and important.

This volume assembles the essays of a number of distinguished scholars and foreign policy experts. The authors approach NATO enlargement from a variety of perspectives, and shed light on the utility of several leading IR theories, including neorealism, neoliberal institutionalism, organization theory, constructivism and foreign-policy-based approaches.

Substantively, the volume has three main purposes. First, most of the authors apply various theories of international relations to explain why the decision was made to expand NATO. The reasons for the enlargement of NATO are especially interesting from the perspective of IR theory and lead to some important insights about alliances and international institutions. Second, most of the contributors evaluate the pros and cons of enlargement and weigh in on whether enlargement is likely to have positive or negative consequences for the alliance and European security in general. Third, this volume examines an important second-order question: why did IR theory fail to predict NATO enlargement? The answer to this question helps to highlight some of the strengths and weaknesses of how theorists generally try to make sense of and cope with ongoing events.

This volume diverges from previous efforts to examine NATO enlargement in several important ways. Most of the authors in this volume are primarily motivated to explain why the decision to enlarge NATO was made. This is a natural extension of the discourse that followed the end of the Cold War, and cuts to the heart of several debates in IR theory. Because the debate was originally between those who expected NATO to collapse and those who expected the alliance to survive or persist, it is important to ask why the alliance is now thriving and expanding its membership.

Another important difference between the essays in this volume and those in other works is that most of the essays in this volume use IR theory to deal directly with whether enlargement will have positive or negative consequences for the alliance and for European security. While this question has received considerable attention in leading newspapers, news magazines, and policy-oriented journals, there are surprisingly few efforts to apply IR theory directly to the issue.[16] Even when leading IR theorists have participated in the debate, they have been prone to discard their analytic tools, offering *ad hoc* explanations that rest on historical analogies or normatively grounded arguments. In contrast, the essays in this volume that address these issues explicitly use IR theory to inform their explanations of, and recommendations for, NATO enlargement.

From an IR theory perspective, this volume is also unique because all of the contributors are forced to grapple with the same set of empirical issues. The authors do not dodge hard questions by pre-selecting favourable or easy test cases. Consequently, the volume tells us a good deal about the state of IR theory and helps to highlight the strengths and weaknesses of using off-the-shelf theory to make sense of complex, real-world events. The contributors to this volume recognize and explicitly address the truly political nature of the issues at hand. They help identify the hidden assumptions and probabilistic conditions that often plague work that enjoys the benefit of years of hindsight. The volume, therefore, also serves as a guide for how to modify and apply theory to important current events.

This volume is organized into five parts. The next part, Part II, 'Power and Preferences', Kenneth N. Waltz (essay 2) and Beverly Crawford (essay 3) assess how the international distribution of power and US hegemony help explain the decision to enlarge NATO. In Part III, 'Institutions and Choice', Vinod Aggarwal (essay 4), Ernst B. Haas (essay 5), Steven Weber (essay 6) and Gale Mattox (essay 7) examine a number of important issues that stem from NATO's unique organizational attributes. They ask why NATO was preferred to its competitors and expanded, and what still needs to be done in order for enlargement to achieve its goals. Aggarwal's essay focuses on the questions of why NATO is enlarging and why NATO beat out its competitors; Mattox concentrates on why enlargement was the right decision, and what needs to be done to guarantee that the goals of enlargement are met. Haas and Weber examine both of these issues. In Part IV, 'Domestic Politics and National Interests', Charles Kupchan (essay 8) examines how the decision to enlarge NATO was reached in the US; Ronald Bee (essay 9) does the same for several key European states. The conclusion, Part V, 'Explaining NATO Enlargement', ties together the findings of this volume's essays, and assesses whether they collectively offer a coherent and unified explanation, or whether their conclusions are contradictory and irreconcilable.

INTERNATIONAL RELATIONS THEORY AND
NATO ENLARGEMENT

This section reviews several leading theories of international relations. In the process of reviewing these theories, I provide an overview of the essays in this volume and evaluate their contributions to various theories. While I discuss the following essays under the headings of different theories, it is important to note that only a few of the essays fit neatly under a single heading. The main goal of all of the essays in this volume is to address the important issues surrounding NATO enlargement, not to 'prove' or 'disprove' any particular theory. The following essays, therefore, advance arguments that make sense of the facts; they do not force facts to fit with any particular IR theory. Several of the contributors offer arguments that are original and very bold. Indeed, readers may even be surprised by the conclusions that some of the contributors reach when they apply and modify conventional approaches.

Neorealism

At the end of the Cold War, neorealism was one of the few theories to offer clear and unambiguous predictions about NATO's future. Despite the important differences that exist between competing versions of neorealism, it is fair to say that neorealism, as a whole, predicted that NATO would either collapse entirely or, if it survived, would do so in name only. In either case, NATO would cease to play a significant role in international politics.

While this prediction was pessimistic, the assumptions and reasoning from which it stemmed are sound. Alliances are formed as a balance against power or external threats, and when power shifts or threats disappear, so too do the reasons for alliances. For neorealists, the end of the Cold War and the collapse of the Soviet Union eliminated NATO's *raison d'être*. Therefore, without a menacing external threat, NATO members might no longer be inclined to make the types of compromises necessary for maintaining an alliance, and it seemed likely that the disagreements over leadership and burden-sharing, which were previously sidelined, would now take centre-stage.

Some neorealists went a step further, arguing that the end of the Cold War would do more than make small or dormant issues more important – it would also create new ones. For example, when viewed through the lens of balance-of-power theory, the collapse of the Soviet Union does more than simply remove an external threat: it also leaves the United States as the world's only superpower. It therefore follows that the United States, similar to other states that have occupied positions of primacy in the past, would undoubtedly try to establish a post-Cold War order that reflects American values and preferences. This would cause intra-alliance tensions, because 'states balance against hegemons – even those like the United States that seek to maintain their preeminence by employing strategies based more on benevolence than coercion'.[17]

It is clear that neorealists' predictions about NATO were either off the mark or at least a decade or more premature. This legitimately raises the question, is neorealism of any use for understanding the alliance's decision to expand NATO membership? The answer to this question depends on how neorealists respond to NATO's resurgence and growth. There are two types of response: one is useful and places neorealism at the centre of several ongoing debates; the other takes neorealism out of play.

If neorealists try to dodge the issue by claiming that not enough time has elapsed for neorealists' predictions to come true, or if they argue that NATO's survival and enlargement is not important, then neorealists have nothing to contribute to our present debate. Neorealists may ultimately be correct and NATO may indeed collapse in the future but, for the time being, this type of argument is both unpersuasive and self-defeating. Clearly NATO played a significant role in Yugoslavia. And many neorealists have argued that NATO's enlargement may have far-reaching negative consequences for European stability. That said, if neorealism cannot offer any insights on these important ongoing issues, then it has, in effect, removed itself from the debate.

A second way of addressing the issue is more constructive and allows neorealists to make an important and immediate contribution. Rather than condemn neorealism as a whole, perhaps the blame lies with particular strains of neorealism, or how individuals have attempted to apply the theory.

A plausible argument can be made that neorealists, from the start, made several questionable assumptions that led their analyses astray. In particular, many neorealists failed to characterize the function of NATO correctly. By considering NATO a traditional military alliance, neorealists may have applied the wrong set of analytic tools – alliance theory – and failed to understand that NATO was and is a security institution, or perhaps merely a treaty of guarantee.

In essay 2, 'NATO Expansion: A Realist's View', Kenneth N. Waltz helps to explain where neorealists went astray. Unlike most military alliances, NATO is highly institutionalized and deals with a variety of important issues, not simply deterring specific threats. Although NATO's level of institutionalization is important and gives a partial explanation of why NATO is surviving and expanding, the real story is not really its institutionalization *per se*, but rather how the United States managed to use NATO to advance its own agenda. Whereas military alliances emphasize the principle of 'all for one', NATO was from the start more about 'one for all'. NATO was therefore never a traditional military alliance – it more closely resembles a treaty of guarantee, provided by the United States to Europe. Most neorealists underestimated the degree to which the United States was, and still is, NATO. The issue, therefore, is not just whether NATO will deter and defend against external threats, but whether NATO serves America's 'perceived or misperceived interests' in Europe. Today, Washington still finds NATO desirable because it provides a way for 'maintaining and lengthening America's grip on the foreign and military policies of European states'. Given the lack of any coherent foreign or military policy for the European Union, NATO still serves Europe's interests too.

In essay 3, 'The Bosnian Road to NATO Enlargement', Beverly Crawford picks up on the same theme and provides a rich analysis of how the decision to enlarge NATO was made. Security concerns arising from fighting in Bosnia, coupled with Europe's inability to act and Russia's obstructionism, made it clear that US leadership was necessary. The United States and key European countries decided that NATO was best suited for peacekeeping and peace-enforcement operations in Bosnia. NATO held a number of procedural and functional advantages over competing institutions. And in addition to having 'more teeth', NATO could also serve the dual role of maximizing American influence in Europe, while excluding Russia, which was either perceived as a threat, or, at minimum, believed to be a great power with obstructionist tendencies. The war in former Yugoslavia helps explain NATO's resurgence, and the Clinton administration's subsequent decision to enlarge NATO.

Neoliberal Institutionalism

At the end of the Cold War, neoliberal institutionalists were considerably less pessimistic about NATO's future. This stems from their view that NATO differs from traditional military alliances in at least two important ways. First, unlike most military alliances, NATO is highly institutionalized. It provides members with well-defined rules and joint decision-making procedures, and requires them to participate in a unified military command structure. Second, NATO is about much more than just co-ordinating military policy to deter and defend against a common enemy. From its inception, NATO has had the broader goal of enhancing its members' security, which includes promoting stable civil–military relations within member states as well as preventing security competition between them.

The collapse of the Soviet Union may have eliminated one of NATO's primary missions, but a number of other important missions still remain. For example, one of the main purposes of the Atlantic Charter was to ensure that Germany would remain firmly anchored in western Europe, and that the US would maintain a presence in Europe and prevent security competition on the continent. The end of the Cold War and the reunification of Germany only renewed the importance of these missions. For example, Britain and especially France were concerned about how unification would affect German preferences and the balance of power in Europe. The end of the Cold War also produced new types of threats. There was real concern that the zone of economic and political instability to the east might create refugee problems. There was also fear that the fighting and ethnic cleansing in the former Yugoslavia might spill over into a larger regional war. Thus, for old and new reasons alike, European states still needed some method for co-ordinating their foreign and defence policies.

However, it is important to note that there are a number of ways that Europeans can address their common concerns. Will they want to keep NATO and adapt it to meet their post-Cold War needs? Or will they prefer to abandon NATO and unilaterally or multilaterally address issues in an *ad hoc* manner? Perhaps European states may prefer the WEU, which excludes the US and fits better with plans for a unified Europe. Another alternative is a larger, more inclusive security organization, such as the Organization for Security and Co-operation in Europe (OSCE), which includes former Warsaw Pact countries and all of NATO. Do either of these alternatives do a better job of meeting the challenges and needs of post-Cold War Europe than NATO?

Neoliberal institutionalism offers unambiguous answers to some, but not all, of these questions. Neoliberals would certainly expect states to prefer to use institutions rather than the *ad hoc* approach, because institutions can help reduce transaction costs and uncertainty. It also makes sense to adapt existing institutions rather than create new ones, which may entail high start-up costs and a number of risks. New institutions may also require a leader or hegemon that is willing to bear a disproportionate share of the burden. Without a menacing threat, such as the one provided by the Soviet Union, it may prove too difficult to convince states to surrender some of their autonomy and join a new alliance. Using existing institutions, even if they are sub-optimal, makes sense when the alternatives are too costly or risky.[18]

On the issue of which existing institution should win out, neoliberal institutionalism is much more ambiguous. Whether NATO will be preferred to other regional institutions, such as the OSCE or the WEU, depends on a number of factors, including the preferences of key members, NATO's own institutional attributes, and the availability of alternatives.

Two essays address these issues. In essay 4, 'Analysing NATO Expansion: An Institutional Bargaining Approach', Vinod K. Aggarwal offers a game-theoretic analysis of why NATO expanded. Aggarwal takes a step back from the detailed accounts of personalities and groups involved in the decision-making process and instead evaluates the major players' preferences and the alternatives available to them. His essay helps explain why of the four available alternatives – dismantlement, *status quo*, widening and deepening – the widening option was chosen. Aggarwal's analysis is bold and original, and will provide readers with an excellent framework within which they can evaluate NATO's future options.

In essay 7, 'NATO Enlargement: A Step in the Process of Alliance Reform', Gale Mattox explains why NATO enlargement was the correct decision for incorporating post-communist states into the West, and for insuring the stability and security of Europe. As Mattox's essay makes clear, the admission of Hungary, Poland and the Czech Republic marks only the start of a much larger process. For enlargement to achieve NATO's objectives, a lot more needs to be done both within, and outside of, the alliance.

Organization Theory

Viewing NATO through the lens of organization theory highlights several additional issues. Whereas neoliberals and neorealists tend to see institutions as tools used by states, organization theory considers the interests and capabilities of the institutions themselves. Organization theorists would be quick to point out that while NATO began life as a military alliance, it has taken on many new tasks and developed many of the characteristics of a formal organization. NATO is not just a piece of paper or a pledge of common defence. Instead, NATO is an organization comprised of thousands of officials and bureaucrats whose livelihood depends on the organization's survival.[19] These individuals can operate somewhat independently of member states, because NATO has a budget with discretionary funds which allows NATO officials to engage in public relations. These officials can press their concerns in a variety of ways, including publishing monthly bulletins, creating websites, and even directly lobbying policy-makers and legislators in member states.

The interests of NATO officials are not always identical to the interests of member states. Officials are charged with looking out for the collective interest of NATO, and the autonomy that they are granted to achieve this objective allows them to look out for their own jobs as well. Unlike alliances or less formalized international institutions, formal organizations do not simply go out of business when their main objective is reached. The Soviet Union may be gone, but the hundreds of individuals that comprise NATO will use the resources at their disposal to create new goals that justify the organization's continuation.

There is evidence that NATO officials did indeed play an important role in finding a post-Cold War mission for the organization. For example, NATO conducted a number of studies that sought a new post-Cold War purpose for the organization. NATO officials raised awareness about 'threats from the south', and stressed the desirability of keeping NATO alive to deal with the greater uncertainty of the post-Cold War world. In the early 1990s, a slogan heard at NATO headquarters was 'out-of-area or out of business', indicating that if NATO did not adapt to serve new functions, such as peacekeeping, it might no longer have a purpose. Manfred Wörner, the Secretary-General of NATO, was very active in pushing for authorization for NATO to conduct out-of-area operations, about which not all NATO members were enthusiastic. Wörner also took a very active role in criticizing member states for neglecting and abandoning the organization.[20]

While organization theory is a useful framework for examining NATO enlargement and highlights many important issues, as Ernst B. Haas argues in essay 5, it can also lead analysts astray. Haas' essay examines three forms of organization theory – redundancy theory, hierarchical nesting and cognitive nesting – and concludes that these theories are often misused by analysts. The problem lies in the failure of analysts to recognize that international organizations are fundamentally different from organizations operating in the domestic arena. This leads to the improper application of organization theory and causes analysts to reach the wrong conclusions about why NATO is enlarging. Haas then turns his attention to which course NATO should take, and makes a number of theoretically informed recommendations.

Constructivism

Constructivists also view NATO as more of an institution than an alliance, but they focus on a different set of issues. Rather than examining the level of institutionalization or the formal characteristics of an organization, constructivists are interested in how international institutions help teach norms and change state preferences.

Compared to proponents of the three theories examined above, constructivists would be the least surprised by NATO's post-Cold War success and expansion. While NATO was created to deter and defend against a common enemy, over time it helped create a transatlantic security community with shared values. Members of this community are generally democratic and capitalist; they believe in the rule of law, the fair treatment of national minorities, and the peaceful adjudication of international disputes. Constructivists would therefore expect NATO to survive not only because of NATO's own organizational attributes, but because it is nested in a transatlantic security community.[21]

While constructivism is often thought of as a new approach, it builds on and extends arguments that are quite old. This line of thinking was perhaps first best articulated by Immanuel Kant, who believed the republics might band together and create 'pacific federations' (*foedus pacificum*).[22] In the 1950s, Karl Deutsch advanced a similar notion, which was labelled 'pluralistic security communities'.[23] Theorists inclined towards sociological explanations have historically focused on how democracies might create international federations or institutions. An important difference between constructivists and the older traditions of Kant and Deutsch is that constructivists claim the causal arrows are running in both directions. Constructivists are especially interested in how international institutions shape state preferences.

In essay 6, 'A Modest Proposal for NATO Expansion', Steven Weber helps identify NATO's unique mix of military alliance and security community. His essay also explains why IR theory has had such difficulty with the issues associated with NATO's survival and enlargement. Weber discusses how IR theorists must take better care to incorporate a role for chance and unknowns in their analyses, a warning that is important to heed, given that alliance expansion is a project that is still in process. Weber then turns his attention to making some recommendations about which course NATO should take to maximize the benefits of enlargement, while minimizing its negative externalities.

Foreign Policy Approaches

Two essays in the volume deal with domestic politics. In essay 8, 'The Origins and Future of NATO Enlargement', Charles Kupchan provides a compelling explanation of why the US decided to expand NATO. As a former member of the National Security Council (NSC) during the Clinton administration, Kupchan offers a detailed account of the domestic political process that led to the policy. His analysis points to three main factors: the support of key players in the Clinton administration, incentives created by election-year presidential politics, and the efforts of a few key domestic groups that actively lobbied the Clinton administration. Kupchan warns us, though, that the alignment of domestic interests is not enough to explain the outcome. It is also necessary to explain why there was not an effective opposition that could have blocked the policy. In the early days of the policy's formation, most experts expected the US Senate and public opinion to derail the policy. Kupchan points to an unusual coalition of key conservative and liberal supporters that skilfully pushed the policy and packaged it in a way that limited Senate debate and took advantage of public apathy.

In essay 9, 'Boarding the NATO Train: Enlargement and National Interests', Ronald Bee examines the decision-making processes in the United States and several key European member states. Bee points to a combination of the organization's past effectiveness and the desire of key policy-makers to keep the alliance alive. While different NATO members have different motives for wanting the alliance to enlarge, all share a long history of using NATO as the first means for addressing security issues in Europe. Bee details how the preference for enlargement formed in a number of key NATO players, including France and Germany.

SUMMARY

Despite the different approaches taken by the various authors, it is interesting to note that at least one conclusion is almost universally shared: while many factors influenced NATO enlargement, there is a general consensus that the US was the driving force behind the policy, and that the US's preponderance of power is an important part of the explanation. It is interesting to note that while the contributors often disagree over the degree to which NATO's level of institutionalization and specific organizational characteristics matter, there is agreement that they do matter to some extent.

Readers will find that the volume also provides an excellent example of how practically and non-dogmatically to use theory to explain particular political events. None of the contributors to this volume, for instance, is so wedded to a theory that he or she forces the facts to fit. Most of the contributors show a clear willingness to point out the limitations of their own framework rather than lead readers astray. Many of the contributors are forced to extend or supplement their approaches in order to explain why the United States wants NATO to enlarge. Although different approaches are able to offer partial explanations, it seems clear that no single theory could be taken off the shelf and applied without modification.

NOTES

1. For their valuable comments and suggestions, I thank Ashlee Bailey, Beverly Crawford, Kevin Donovan, James M. Goldgeier, Michael Gorges, Kenneth P. Miller, Kenneth N. Waltz and two anonymous reviewers. Special thanks to Richard Andreas for helpful comments on an earlier draft. The views expressed here are those of the author and do not represent the views of any organization with which the author is affiliated.
2. For a key policy maker's assessment of how membership, and even the prospects of membership, will help domestic reform efforts, see Secretary of State Madeleine K. Albright, Testimony before the Senate Armed Services Committee, 23 April 1997, Transcript.
3. On the importance of preventing hot-spots in southern and central Europe from spilling over into broader regional conflict, see Ronald D. Asmus, Richard L. Kugler and Stephen F. Larrabee, 'Building a New NATO', *Foreign Affairs*, Vol.72, No.4 (Sept.–Oct. 1993), p.28.
4. In regard to the estimated financial costs of NATO enlargement, see Amos Perlmutter and Ted Galen Carpenter, 'NATO's Expensive Trip East: The Folly of Enlargement', *Foreign Affairs*, Vol.77, No.1 (Jan.–Feb. 1998), pp.2–6; estimates range from the NATO Secretariat's $2 billion, to the Pentagon's $35 billion over 13 years, and the US Congressional Budget Office's estimate of $125 billion over 15 years; cf. Steven Erlanger, 'A War of Numbers Emerges over Cost of Enlarging NATO', *New York Times*, 13 Oct. 1997.
5. On how NATO enlargement might impact on Russia's domestic reform efforts, see Michael Mandelbaum, 'Preserving the New Peace: The Case against NATO Expansion', *Foreign Affairs*, Vol.74, No.3 (May–June 1995), pp.9–13.
6. On ways in which enlargement might undermine Russia's willingness to co-operate with the West, see Thomas L. Friedman, 'Madeleine's Folly', *New York Times*, 17 Feb. 1998; also see George F. Kennan's widely cited piece, 'NATO: A Fateful Error', *New York Times*, 5 Feb. 1997.
7. President William Jefferson Clinton, Remarks by the President on the National Interest for Enlarging NATO, 20 March 1998, Washington, DC. National security adviser Sandy Berger

and Secretary of State Madeleine Albright have also repeated this statement on a number of occasions.

8. In scholarly journals, the possibility of NATO enlargement was introduced very late. Early efforts to forecast NATO's future did not view enlargement as a feasible option. See, for example, Charles L. Glaser, 'Why NATO Is Still Best: Future Security Arrangements for Europe', *International Security*, Vol.18, No.1 (Summer 1993), pp.5–50. While this article was one of the first to tackle the issue of NATO's post-Cold War role, of the several available options discussed by the author, enlargement was not a realistic option. More recent efforts have not fared much better. See, for example, Robert B. McCalla, 'NATO's Persistence after the Cold War', *International Organization*, Vol.50, No.3 (Summer 1996), pp.445–475. As the title illustrates, the author, like most others, was asking why the organization was 'surviving' or 'persisting'. That the organization might prosper and even flourish was not generally considered an option.

9. See Stephen Walt, *The Origins of Alliances* (Ithaca: Cornell University Press, 1987), pp.26–7.

10. See, for example, John J. Mearsheimer, 'Back to the Future: Instability in Europe after the Cold War', *International Security*, Vol.15, No.1 (Summer 1990) pp.5–56.

11. Joseph Lepgold, 'Does Europe Have a Place in U.S. Foreign Policy? A Domestic Politics Argument', in Douglas T. Stuart and Stephen F. Szabo (eds.), *Discord and Collaboration in a New Europe: Essays in Honor of Arnold Wolfers* (Washington, DC: Johns Hopkins Institute, 1994).

12. See John Gerald Ruggie, 'The Past as Prologue? Interests, Identity, and American Foreign Policy', *International Security*, Vol.21, No.4 (Spring 1997), pp.89–125.

13. Karl W. Deutsch *et al.*, *Political Community and the North Atlantic Area* (Princeton: Princeton University Press, 1957), p.5.

14. Beverly Crawford, 'Explaining Defection from International Cooperation – Germany's Unilateral Recognition of Croatia', *World Politics*, Vol.48, No.4 (1996), pp.482–521.

15. On the adoption of NATO's new military policy, see 'NATO's new strategic concept and command restructuring', *International Defense Review*, 1 Jan. 1992, Vol.25, No.1, p.13.

16. For one of the few previous efforts to apply IR theory to NATO enlargement, see James M. Goldgeier, 'US Security Policy Toward the New Europe: How the Decision to Expand NATO Was Made'. Lecture delivered to the American Political Science Association, Washington, DC, Aug. 1997. Goldgeier mainly focuses on the US decision to enlarge NATO, and therefore theories that explain foreign policy, such as Graham Allison's bureaucratic politics approach. On bureaucratic politics and foreign policy, see Allison's *Essence of a Decision: Explaining the Cuban Missile Crisis* (Boston: Little Brown, 1971).

17. Christopher Layne, 'The Unipolar Illusion: Why New Great Powers Will Rise', *International Security*, Vol.17, No.4 (Spring 1993), p.7.

18. For a good review of these issues, see Robert Keohane, *International Institutions and State Power: Essays in International Relations Theory* (Boulder: Westview, 1989), pp.101–2.

19. Peter M. Blau and Marshall W. Meyer, *Bureaucracy in Modern Society*, 3rd ed. (New York: Random House, 1987), pp.106–9.

20. Willaim Drozdiak, 'NATO Seeks New Identity in Europe; Cooperation with East Seen Ensuring Stability', *Washington Post*, 4 Oct. 1991.

21. For a constructivist interpretation of NATO's post-Cold War role, see Thomas Risse-Kappen, 'Collective Identity in a Democratic Community', in Peter J. Katzenstein (ed.), *The Culture of National Security: Norms and Identity In World Politics* (New York: Columbia University Press, 1996), pp.357–92.

22. Immanuel Kant, 'Eternal Peace', *Eternal Peace and Other International Essays*, W. Hastie, trans. (Boston: World Peace Foundation, 1914).

23. Deutsch, *Political Community and the North Atlantic Area*, p.5.

PART II: POWER AND PREFERENCES

NATO Expansion: A Realist's View[1]

KENNETH N. WALTZ

The purpose of this paper is both to ask how well non-realist approaches to international politics serve us and to show how realist theory helps one to understand international–political events and changes. One of the charges hurled at realist theory is that it fails to explain the failure of a new balance of power to form since the end of the Cold War. Another charge is that the survival and flourishing of the North Atlantic Treaty Organization (NATO) defeats realists' expectations.

With the demise of the Soviet Union, the international–political system became unipolar. In the light of structural theory, unipolarity appears as the least durable of international configurations. This is so for two main reasons. One is that dominant powers take on too many tasks beyond their own borders, thus weakening themselves in the long run. Ted Robert Gurr, after examining 336 polities, reaches the same conclusion that Robert G. Wesson had reached earlier: 'Imperial decay is … primarily a result of the misuse of power which follows inevitably from its concentration'.[2] The other reason for the short duration of unipolarity is that even if a dominant power behaves with moderation, restraint and forbearance, weaker states will worry about its future behaviour. America's founding fathers warned against the perils of power in the absence of checks and balances. Is unbalanced power less of a danger in international than in national politics? Throughout the Cold War, what the United States and the Soviet Union did, and how they interacted, were dominant factors in international politics. The two countries, however, constrained each other. Now the United States is alone in the world. As nature abhors a vacuum, so international politics abhors unbalanced power. Faced by unbalanced power, some states try to increase their own strength or they ally with others to bring the international distribution of power into balance. The reactions of other states to the drive for dominance of Charles V

Hapsburg ruler of Spain, of Louis XIV and Napoleon I of France, of Wilhelm II and Adolf Hitler of Germany, illustrate the point.

Will the preponderant power of the United States elicit similar reactions? Unbalanced power, whoever wields it, is a potential danger to others. The powerful state may, and the United States does, think of itself as acting for the sake of peace, justice and well-being in the world. These terms, however, are defined to the liking of the powerful, which may conflict with the preferences and interests of others. In international politics, overwhelming power repels and leads others to try to balance against it. With benign intent, the United States has behaved, and until its power is brought into balance, will continue to behave in ways that sometimes frighten others.

For almost half a century, the constancy of the Soviet threat produced a constancy of American policy. Other countries could rely on the United States for protection because protecting them seemed to serve US security interests. Even so, beginning in the 1950s western European countries, and beginning in the 1970s, Japan had increasing doubts about the reliability of the American nuclear deterrent. As Soviet strength increased, western European countries began to wonder whether America could be counted on to use its deterrent on their behalf, thus risking its own cities. When President Carter moved to reduce American troops in Korea, and later when the Soviet Union invaded Afghanistan and strengthened its forces in the Far East, Japan developed similar worries.

With the disappearance of the Soviet Union, the United States no longer faces a major threat to its security. As General Colin Powell said when he was chairman of the Joint Chiefs of Staff: 'I'm running out of demons. I'm running out of enemies. I'm down to Castro and Kim Il Sung.'[3] Constancy of threat produces constancy of policy; absence of threat permits policy to become capricious. When few if any vital interests are endangered, a country's policy becomes sporadic and self-willed.

The absence of serious threats to American security gives the United States wide latitude in making foreign policy choices. A dominant power acts internationally only when the spirit moves it. One example is enough to show this. When Yugoslavia's collapse was followed by genocidal war in successor states, the United States failed to respond until Senator Robert Dole moved to make Bosnia's peril an issue in the forthcoming presidential election; and it acted not for the sake of its own security but to maintain its leadership position in Europe. American policy was generated not by external security interests but by internal political pressure and national ambition.

Aside from specific threats it may pose, unbalanced power leaves weaker states feeling uneasy and gives them reason to strengthen their positions. The United States has a long history of intervening in weak states, often with the intention of bringing democracy to them. American behaviour over the past century in central America provides little evidence of self-restraint in the absence of countervailing power. Contemplating our history and measuring our capabilities, other countries may well wish for ways to fend off our benign ministrations. Concentrated power invites distrust because it is so easily misused. To understand why some states want to bring power into a semblance of balance is easy, but, with power so sharply skewed, what country or group of countries has the material capability and the political will to bring the 'unipolar moment' to an end? The expectation that following victory in a great war a new balance of power will form is firmly grounded in both history and theory. The last four grand coalitions (two against Napoleon and one in each of the world wars of the twentieth century) collapsed once victory was achieved. Victories in major wars leave the balance of power badly skewed. The winning side emerges as a dominant coalition. The international equilibrium is broken; theory leads one to expect its restoration.

Clearly something has changed. Some believe that America is so nice that, despite the dangers of unbalanced power, others do not feel the fear that would spur them to action. Michael Mastanduno, among others, believes this to be so, although he ends his essay with the thought that 'eventually power will check power'.[4] Others believe that the leaders of states have learned that playing the game of power politics is costly and unnecessary. Instead the explanation for sluggish balancing is a simple one. In the aftermath of earlier great wars, the materials for constructing a new balance were readily at hand. Previous wars left a sufficient number of great powers standing to permit a new balance to be rather easily constructed. Theory enables one to say that a new balance of power will form but not to say how long it will take. International conditions determine that.

Those who refer to the unipolar moment are right. In our perspective, the new balance is emerging slowly; in historical perspectives, it will come in the blink of an eye.

I ended a 1993 article this way: 'one may hope that America's internal preoccupations will produce not an isolationist policy, which has become impossible, but a forbearance that will give other countries at long last the chance to deal with their own problems and make their own mistakes. But I would not bet on it.'[5] I should think that few would do so now. Charles Kegley has said, sensibly, that if the world becomes multipolar once again, realists will be vindicated.[6] Seldom do signs of vindication appear so promptly.

The candidates for becoming the next great powers, and thus restoring a balance, are the European Union, China and Japan. Since the Cold War's end, the policies and behaviours of western European states lead one to believe that for the first time in modern history the new balance of power will be made in the East rather than in the West.

The countries of the European Union have been remarkably successful in integrating their national economies. The achievement of a large measure of economic integration without a corresponding political unity is an accomplishment without historical precedent. On questions of foreign and military policy, however, the European Union can act only with the consent of its members, making bold or risky action impossible. The European Union has all the tools – population, resources, technology and military capabilities – but lacks the organizational ability and the collective will to use them. As Jacques Delors said when he was President of the European Commission: 'It will be for the European Council, consisting of heads of state and government ..., to agree on the essential interests they share and which they will agree to defend and promote together.'[7] Policies that must be arrived at by consensus can be carried out only when they are fairly inconsequential. Inaction as Yugoslavia sank into chaos and war signalled that Europe will not act to stop wars even among near neighbours. Western Europe was unable to make its own foreign and military policies when it was an organization of six or nine states living in fear of the Soviet Union. With less pressure and more members, it can hardly hope to do so now. Only when the United States decides on a policy are European countries able to follow it. As far ahead as the eye can see, western Europe will be a follower rather than a leader internationally.

The fate of European states continues to depend on decisions made in America. NATO's expansionist policy illustrates how the absence of external restraints on the United States affects its policy. The states of the European Union generally have shown no enthusiasm for expanding NATO eastward and have revealed little willingness to bear a share of the costs entailed. German officials, notably Volker Rühe, were among the few western Europeans to show enthusiasm. While the United States pressed ahead with expansion, the European Union, as expected, was content to stand by meekly and watch. In a statement that would be hard to credit were it not made by a European Union official, Hans van der Broek, commissioner for external relations with countries from central Europe to Russia, has said that the Union takes no position on NATO's expansionist policy because it has no 'competence' on NATO enlargement.[8]

In the old multipolar world, the core of an alliance consisted of a small number of states of comparable capability. Their contributions to one another's security were of crucial importance because they were of similar size. Because major allies were closely interdependent, the defection of one would have made its partners vulnerable to a competing alliance. The members of opposing alliances before the First World War were tightly knit because of their mutual dependence. In the new bipolar world, the word 'alliance' took on a different meaning. One country, the United States or the Soviet Union, provided most of the security for its bloc. The defection of France from NATO and of China from the Warsaw Treaty Organization (WTO) failed even to tilt the central balance. Early in the Cold War, Americans spoke with alarm about the threat of monolithic communism arising from the combined strength of the Soviet Union and China, yet the bloc's disintegration caused scarcely a ripple. American officials did not proclaim that with China's defection America's defence budget could safely be reduced by 20 or 10 per cent or even be reduced at all. Similarly, when France withdrew from NATO, American officials did not proclaim that defence spending had to be increased for that reason. Properly speaking, NATO and the WTO were more treaties of guarantee than military alliances old-style.[9] The end of the Cold War quickly changed the behaviour of allied countries. In early July 1990, NATO announced that the alliance would 'elaborate new force plans consistent with the revolutionary changes in Europe'.[10] By the end of July, without waiting for any such plans, the major European members of NATO unilaterally announced large reductions in their force levels. Even the pretence of continuing to act as an alliance in setting military policy disappeared.

I expected NATO to dwindle at the Cold War's end and ultimately to disappear as the four previous grand coalitions had done once their principal adversaries were defeated.[11] To some extent, the expectation has already been borne out. NATO is no longer even a treaty of guarantee since one cannot answer the question, guarantee against whom? Glenn Snyder has remarked that 'alliances have no meaning apart from the adversary threat to which they are a response'.[12] How then can one explain NATO's survival and growth? An obvious part of the explanation is found in what has long been known about organizations in general. Organizations, especially big ones with strong traditions, have long lives. The March of Dimes is an example sometimes cited. Having won the war against polio, its mission was accomplished. Nevertheless, it cast about for a new malady to cure or contain. Even though the most appealing ones – cancer, heart, lungs, multiple sclerosis, cystic fibrosis – were already taken, it did find a worthy cause to pursue, the amelioration of birth defects. One can fairly claim that the March of Dimes enjoys continuity as an organization, pursuing an end consonant with its original purpose. How can one make such a claim for NATO?

The question of purpose may, however, not be a very important one; create an organization and it will find something to do.[13] Once created, and the more so once it has become well established, an organization becomes hard to get rid of. A big organization is managed by large numbers of bureaucrats who develop a strong interest in its perpetuation. According to Gunther Hellmann and Reinhard Wolf, NATO headquarters was recently manned by 2,640 officials, most of whom presumably want to keep their jobs.[14] Twenty-five years ago, Bernard Brodie wondered whether NATO's useful life was over. Its founding fathers thought of it as a defensive alliance needed until Europe's recovery would enable it to provide its own defence. That time had surely come. Yet, as Brodie remarked, 'The inertias built into' NATO's international bureaucracy 'can only be imagined by those who have not experienced them'. He concluded by saying 'we are either blessed or burdened with this creation of a time that was very different from our own days'.[15] Clearly, Brodie thought that by 1973 the burden outweighed the blessing, and the burden continues to be borne disproportionately by the United States.

A second part of the explanation of NATO's longevity is more important than the first part. Liberal institutionalists take

NATO's seeming vigour as confirmation of the importance of international institutions and as evidence of their resilience. Realists, noticing that as an alliance NATO has lost its major function, see it simply as a means of maintaining and lengthening America's grip on the foreign and military policies of European states. The survival and expansion of NATO tell us much about American power and influence and little about institutions as multilateral entities. The ability of the United States to extend the life of a moribund institution nicely illustrates how international institutions are created and maintained by stronger states to serve their perceived or misperceived interests.

The Bush administration saw, and the Clinton administration continued to see, NATO as the instrument for maintaining America's domination of the foreign and military policies of European states. In 1991, Under-secretary of State Reginald Bartholomew's letter to the governments of European members of NATO warned against Europe's formulating independent positions on defence. France and Germany had thought that a European security and defence identity might be developed within the European Union and that the Western European Union (WEU), formed in 1954, could be revived as the instrument for its realization. The Bush administration quickly squelched these ideas. The day after the signing of the Maastricht Treaty in December 1991, President Bush could say with satisfaction that 'we are pleased that our Allies in the Western European Union ... decided to strengthen that institution as both NATO's European pillar and the defense component of the European Union'.[16]

The European pillar was to be contained within NATO, and its policies were to be made in Washington. Weaker states have trouble fashioning institutions to serve their own ends in their own ways, especially in the security realm. Think of the defeat of the European Defence Community in 1954 and the inability of the WEU in the more than four decades of its existence to find a significant role independent of the United States. Realism reveals what liberal institutionalist 'theory' obscures: namely, that international institutions serve primarily national rather than international interests.[17] Keohane and Martin, replying to Mearsheimer's criticism of liberal institutionalism, ask how we are 'to account for the willingness of major states to invest resources in expanding international institutions if such institutions are lacking in significance'.[18] If the answer were not already obvious, the expansion of NATO would answer it: to serve what powerful states believe to be their interests.

Domestic politics supply a third part of the explanation for America's championing NATO's expansion. With the administration's Bosnian policy in trouble, Clinton needed to show himself to be an effective leader in foreign policy. With the national heroes, Lech Walesa and Vaclav Havel, clamouring for their countries' inclusion, foreclosing NATO membership would have handed another issue to the Republican Party in the congressional elections of 1994. To tout NATO's eastward march, President Clinton gave major speeches in Milwaukee, Cleveland and Detroit, cities with significant numbers of eastern European voters.[19] Votes and dollars are the lifeblood of American politics. New members of NATO will be required to improve their military infrastructure and to buy modern weapons. The American arms industry, expecting to capture its usual large share of a new market, lobbied heavily in favour of NATO's expansion.[20]

The reasons for expanding NATO are weak. The reasons for opposing expansion are strong.[21] It draws new lines of division in Europe, alienates those left out, and can find no logical stopping place west of Russia. It weakens those Russians most inclined towards liberal democracy and a market economy. It strengthens Russians of opposite inclination. It reduces hope for further large reductions of nuclear weaponry. It pushes Russia towards China instead of drawing Russia towards Europe and America. NATO, led by America, scarcely considered the plight of its defeated adversary. Throughout modern history, Russia has been rebuffed by the West, isolated and at times surrounded. Many Russians believe that, by expanding, NATO brazenly broke promises it made in 1990 and 1991 that former WTO members would not be allowed to join NATO. With good reason, Russians fear that NATO will not only admit additional old members of the WTO but also former republics of the USSR. In 1997, NATO held naval exercises with Ukraine in the Black Sea, with more joint exercises to come, and announced plans to use a military testing ground in western Ukraine. In June 1998, Zbigniew Brzezinski went to Kiev with the message that Ukraine should prepare itself to join NATO by the year 2010.[22] The further NATO intrudes into the Soviet Union's old arena, the more Russia is forced to look to the south and east rather than to the west. This seems all the more ironic when one recalls that during the 1980s Russian military analysts began to believe that long-range threats to Russia would come from the south and east, not the west.[23]

Late in 1996, expecting a measure of indifference, I asked an official in the Indian Ministry of External Affairs whether India was concerned over the expansive NATO policy. He immediately replied that a policy seemingly designed to bring Russia and China together of course was of great concern to India. Despite much talk about the 'globalization' of international politics, American political leaders to a dismaying extent think of East *or* West rather than of their interaction. With a history of conflict along a 2,600-mile border, with ethnic minorities sprawling across it, with a mineral-rich and sparsely populated Siberia facing China's teeming millions, Russia and China will find it difficult to co-operate effectively, but we are doing our best to help them do so. Indeed, the United States provides the key to Russian–Chinese relations over the past half-century. Feeling American antagonism and fearing American power, China drew close to Russia after the Second World War and remained so until the United States seemed less, and the Soviet Union more, of a threat to China. The relatively harmonious relations the United States and China enjoyed during the 1970s began to turn sour in the late 1980s when Russian power visibly declined and American hegemony became imminent. To alienate Russia by expanding NATO, and to alienate China by pressing it to change its policies and lecturing its leaders on how to rule their country, are policies that only an overwhelmingly powerful country could afford, and only a foolish one be tempted, to follow.

Once some countries are brought in, how can others be kept out? Secretary Albright has said that no democratic country will be excluded from NATO because of its position on the map. A hurt and humiliated Russia can expect to suffer further pain. Secretary Albright thinks it ridiculous of Russia to fear NATO's inclusion of a distant Hungary, but the distance between additional members of the alliance and Russia would be shorter.[24] Anyway, it is not so much new members that Russia fears as it is America's might moving ever closer to its borders. Any country finds it difficult to understand how another country feels. Americans should, however, be able to imagine what their fears would be if they had lost the Cold War and Russia expanded the WTO into the Americas, all the while claiming that it was acting for the sake of stability in central America with no threat to the United States implied. Adept statesmen keep their countries' potential adversaries divided. The Clinton administration seemed to delight in bringing them together.

Even while American leaders were assuring Russia that NATO's expansion was not motivated by animosity towards Russia, American and NATO estimates of the costs entailed depended in large measure on speculations about when Russia would once again pose a military threat to Europe.[25] As Boris Yeltsin said in Moscow, with President Jiang Zemin at his side, 'someone is longing for a single-polar world'.[26] Pressure from the West helps to unite them in opposition to this condition. Both parties now speak of a 'constructive partnership aimed at strategic co-operation in the twenty-first century'.[27] The American rhetoric of globalization turns out to be globaloney: we fail to understand how our policy for one region affects another.

Winners of wars, facing few impediments to the exercise of their wills, have often acted in ways that created future enemies. Thus Germany, by taking Alsace and most of Lorraine from France in 1871, earned its lasting enmity; and the Allies' harsh treatment of Germany after the First World War produced a similar effect. In contrast, Bismarck persuaded the Kaiser not to march his armies along the road to Vienna after the great victory at Königgrätz in 1866. In the Treaty of Prague, Prussia took no Austrian territory. Thus Austria, having become Austria-Hungary, was available as an alliance partner for Germany in 1879. Rather than learning from history, the United States is repeating past errors by extending its influence over what used to be the province of the vanquished.[28]

Can one find any reason to be optimistic about the pointless policy of expansion? Perhaps this to start with: in a co-ordinated organization, more is less. The larger the number of members, the greater the number of interests to be served and the more varied the views that have to be accommodated. In the absence of a final arbiter, aligning interests becomes more difficult as their numbers increase. Just as a wider European Union means a shallower one, so a more inclusive NATO means a less coherent and focused alliance. Western Europeans think of NATO's expansion as being of low cost because with no foe to fear additional military expenditure would have little purpose. Thus French President Jacques Chirac said in effect not a centime for NATO's expansion, and British leaders said not a penny. Yet American leaders continued to claim that old and new European members would pay the major share of the costs. NATO argued enough about burden-sharing during the Cold War, and America by and large lost because it believed that fairly or not it had to do what Europe's and its own security required. A larger NATO will have more to argue about and, lacking the disciplining threat of a serious opponent, the arguments are likely to become more frequent and bitter than they used to be.

One can turn this the other way and say that differences will be muted precisely because the absence of a threat means it matters little whether they are resolved. The members of NATO, however, will still have the obligation to come to one another's defence. The American military will certainly take the obligation seriously, as it should. Moreover, because nuclear deterrence covers only a country's manifestly vital interests, it will not cover newly admitted members of the alliance. Deterrence is cheaper than defence. The increase in American commitments makes reliance on deterrence more desirable and less possible.

The expansion of NATO extends its military interests, enlarges its responsibilities and increases its burdens. Not only do new members require NATO's protection, they also heighten its concern over destabilizing events near their borders. Thus Balkan eruptions become a NATO and not just a European concern. In the absence of European initiative, Americans believe they must lead the way because the credibility of NATO is at stake. Balkan operations in the air and even more so on the ground exacerbate differences of interest among NATO members and strain the alliance. European members marvel at the surveillance and communications capabilities of the United States and stand in awe of the modern military forces at its command. Aware of their weaknesses, Europeans express determination to modernize their forces and to develop their ability to deploy them independently. Europe's reaction to America's Balkan operations duplicates its determination to remedy deficiencies revealed in 1991 during the Gulf War, a determination that produced few results.

Will it be different this time? Perhaps, yet if European states do achieve their goals of creating a 60,000 strong rapid reaction force and enlarging the role of the WEU, the tension between a NATO controlled by the United States and a NATO allowing for independent European action will again be bothersome. In any event, the prospect of militarily bogging down in the Balkans tests the alliance and may indefinitely delay its further expansion. Expansion buys trouble, and mounting troubles may bring expansion to a halt.

European conditions and Russian opposition work against the eastward extension of NATO. Pressing in the opposite direction is the momentum of American expansion. The momentum of expansion has often been hard to break, a thought borne out by the empires of Republican Rome, of Tsarist Russian, and of Liberal Britain.

One is often reminded that the United States is not just the dominant power in the world but that it is a *liberal* dominant power. True, the motivations of the artificers of expansion – President Clinton, national security adviser Anthony Lake, and others – were to nurture democracy in young, fragile, long-suffering countries. One may wonder, however, why this should be an American rather than a European task and why a military rather than a political–economic organization should be seen as the appropriate means for carrying it out. The task of building democracy is not a military one. The military security of new NATO members is not in jeopardy; their political development and economic well-being are. In 1997, Assistant Secretary of Defense Franklin D. Kramer told the Czech defence ministry that it was spending too little on defence.[29] Yet investing in defence slows economic growth. By common calculation, defence spending stimulates economic growth about half as much as direct investment in the economy. In eastern Europe, economic not military security is the problem and entering a military alliance compounds it.

Using the example of NATO to reflect on the relevance of realism after the Cold War leads to some important conclusions. The winner of the Cold War and the sole remaining great power has behaved as unchecked powers have usually done. In the absence of counterweights, a country's internal impulses prevail whether fuelled by liberal or by other urges. The error of realist predictions that the end of the Cold War would mean the end of NATO arose not from a failure of realist theory to comprehend international politics, but from an underestimation of America's folly.

Do liberal institutionalists provide better leverage for explaining NATO's survival and expansion? According to Keohane and Martin, realists insist 'that institutions have only marginal effects'.[30] On the contrary, realists have noticed that whether institutions have strong or weak effects depends on what states intend. Strong states use institutions, as they interpret laws, in ways that suit them. Thus, Susan Strange, in pondering the state's retreat, observes that 'international organization is above all a tool of national government, an instrument for the pursuit of national interest by other means'.[31]

Interestingly, Keohane and Martin, in their effort to refute Mearsheimer's trenchant criticism, in effect agree with him. Having claimed that his realism is 'not well specified', they note that 'institutional theory conceptualizes institutions both as independent and dependent variables'.[32] Dependent on what? – on 'the realities of power and interest'. Institutions, it turns out, 'make a significant difference in conjunction with power realities'.[33] Yes! Liberal institutionalism, as Mearsheimer says, 'is no longer a clear alternative to realism, but has, in fact, been swallowed up by it'.[34] Indeed, it never was an alternative to realism. Institutionalist theory, as Keohane has stressed, has as its core structural realism, which Keohane and Nye sought 'to broaden'.[35] The institutional approach starts with structural theory, applies it to the origins and operations of institutions, and unsurprisingly ends with realist conclusions.

Alliances illustrate the limitations of institutionalism with special clarity. Keohane has remarked that 'alliances are institutions, and both their durability and strength may depend in part on their institutional characteristics'.[36] In part, I suppose, but one must wonder on how large a part. The Triple Alliance and the Triple Entente were quite durable. They lasted not because of alliance institutions, there hardly being any, but because the core members of each alliance looked outwards and saw a pressing threat to their security. Previous alliances did not lack institutions because states had failed to figure out how to construct bureaucracies. Previous alliances lacked institutions because in the absence of a hegemonic leader, balancing continued within as well as across alliances. NATO lasted as a military alliance as long as the Soviet Union appeared to be a direct threat to its members. It survives and expands now not because of its institutions but mainly because the United States wants it to.

NATO's survival also exposes an interesting aspect of balance-of-power theory. Robert Art has argued forcefully that without NATO and without American troops in Europe, European states will lapse into a 'security competition' among themselves.[37] As he emphasizes, this is a realist expectation. In his view, preserving NATO, and maintaining America's leading role in it, are required in order to prevent a security competition that would promote conflict and impair the institutions of the European Union. The secondary task of an alliance, intra-alliance management, should continue to be performed by the United States even though the primary task, defence against an external enemy, has disappeared. The point is worth pondering, but I need to say here only that it further illustrates the dependence of international institutions on national decisions. Balancing among states is not inevitable. As in Europe, a hegemonic power may suppress it. As a high-level European diplomat put it, 'it is not acceptable that the lead nation be European. A European power broker is a hegemonic power. We can agree on US leadership, but not on one of our own'.[38] Accepting the leadership of a hegemonic power prevents a balance of power from emerging in Europe, and better the hegemonic power should be at a distance than next door.

Keohane believes that avoiding military conflict in Europe after the Cold War depends greatly on whether the next decade is characterized by a continuous pattern of institutionalized co-operation.[39] If one accepts the conclusion, the question that remains is what sustains the 'pattern of institutionalized cooperation'? Realists know the answer.

NOTES

1. I am indebted to Robert Rauchhaus for help on this paper from its conception to its completion. For insightful and constructive criticism, I owe thanks to Karen Adams, Robert Art, Richard Betts, Barbara Farnham, Anne Fox, Robert Jervis, Warner Schilling and Mark Sheetz. The paper derives in part from my 'Structural Realism after the Cold War', *International Security*, Vol.25, No.1 (Summer 2000).
2. Quoted by Ted Robert Gurr, 'Persistence and Change in Political Systems, 1800–1971', *American Political Science Review*, Vol.68, No.4 (Dec. 1974), p.1504. Cf. Paul Kennedy, *The Rise and Fall of Great Powers: Economic Change and Military Conflict from 1500 to 2000* (New York: Random House, 1987).
3. 'Cover Story: Communism's Collapse Poses a Challenge to America's Military', *U.S. News and World Report*, Vol.3, No.16 (14 Oct. 1991), p.28.
4. Michael Mastanduno, 'Preserving the Unipolar Moment: Realist Theories and U.S. Grand Strategy after the Cold War', *International Security*, Vol.21, No.4 (Spring 1997), p.488. And see Josef Joffe's interesting analysis of America's role, '"Britain or Bismarck"? Toward an American Grand Strategy after Bipolarity', *International Security*, Vol.19 (Spring 1995).

5. Kenneth N. Waltz, 'The Emerging Structure of International Politics', *International Security*, Vol.18, No.2 (Fall 1993), p.79.
6. Charles W. Kegley, Jr., 'The Neoidealist Moment in International Studies? Realist Myths and the New International Realities', *International Studies Quarterly*, Vol.37, No.2 (June 1993), p.149.
7. Jacques Delors, 'European Integration and Security', *Survival*, Vol.33, No.1 (March–April 1991), p.106.
8. *Europe: Magazine of the European Union*, June 1997, p.16.
9. See Kenneth N. Waltz, 'International Structure, National Force, and the Balance of World Power', *Journal of International Affairs*, Vol.21, No.2 (1967), p.219.
10. John Roper, 'Shaping Strategy without the Threat', Adelphi Paper No.257 (London: International Institute of Strategic Studies, Winter 1990/91), pp.80–1.
11. Waltz, 'The Emerging Structure of International Politics', pp.75–6.
12. Glenn H. Snyder, *Alliance Politics* (Ithaca: Cornell University Press, 1997), p.192.
13. Joseph A. Schumpter, writing of armies, put it this way: 'Created by wars that required it, the machine now created the wars it required'. 'The Sociology of Imperialism', in *Imperialism and Socialism* (New York: Meridian Books, 1955), p.25.
14. Gunther Hellmann and Reinhard Wolf, 'Neorealism, Neoliberal Institutionalism, and the Future of NATO', *Security Studies*, Vol.3, No.1 (Autumn 1993), p.20.
15. Bernard Brodie, *War and Politics* (New York: Macmillan, 1973), pp.338–9.
16. Mark S. Sheetz, 'Correspondence', *International Security*, Vol.22, No.3 (Winter 1997/98), p.170; Mike Winnerstig, 'Rethinking Alliance Dynamics' (paper given at the International Studies Association annual meeting, Washington, DC, 18–22 March 1997), p.23.
17. Robert O. Keohane and Lisa Martin, 'The Promise of Institutional Theory', *International Security*, Vol.20, No.1 (Summer 1995), p.40.
18. James M. Goldgeier, 'NATO Expansion: The Anatomy of a Decision', *Washington Quarterly*, Vol.21, No.1 (Winter 1998), pp.94–5; and see his *Not Whether But When: The U.S. Decision to Enlarge NATO* (Washington, DC: Brookings, 1999).
19. William D. Hartung, 'Welfare for Weapons Dealers 1998: The Hidden Costs of NATO Expansion' (New York: New School for Social Research, World Policy Institute, March 1998). Jeff Gerth and Tim Weiner, 'Arms Makers See Bonanza in Selling NATO Expansion', *New York Times*, 29 June 1997, pp.I, 8.
20. See Michael Brown, 'The Flawed Logic of Expansion', *Survival*, Vol.37, No.1 (Spring 1995), pp.34–52. Michael Mandelbaum, *The Dawn of Peace in Europe* (New York: Twentieth Century Fund Press, 1996). Phillip Zelikow, 'The Masque of Institutions', *Survival*, Vol.38, No.1 (Spring 1996).
21. J.L. Black, *Russia Faces NATO Expansion: Bearing Gifts or Bearing Arms?* (Lanham, MD: Rowman and Littlefield, 2000), pp.5–35, 175–201.
22. Ibid., pp.156–64.
23. Madeleine K. Albright, 'Stop Worrying about Russia', *New York Times*, 29 April 1998.
24. Steven Erlanger, 'A War of Numbers Emerges over Cost of Enlarging NATO', *New York Times*, 13 Oct. 1997, p.A1.
25. Michael R. Gordon, 'Russia–China Theme: Contain the West', *New York Times*, 24 April 1997, p.A3.
26. 'Yeltsin in China to Put an End to Border Issue', *New York Times*, 10 Nov. 1997, p.A8.
27. Tellingly, John Lewis Gaddis comments that he has never known a time when there was less support among historians for an announced policy. 'History, Grand Strategy and NATO Enlargement', *Survival*, Vol.40 (Spring 1998), p.147.
28. Black, *Russia Faces NATO Expansion*, p.72.
29. Keohane and Martin, 'The Promise of Institutional Theory', pp.42, 46.
30. Strange, *Retreat of the State* (Cambridge: Cambridge University Press, 1996), p.xiv; and see pp.192–3.
31. Keohane and Martin, 'The Promise of Institutional Theory', p.46.
32. Ibid., p.42.
33. Mearsheimer, 'A Realist Reply', *International Security*, Vol.10, No.1 (Summer 1995), p.85.
34. Robert O. Keohane and Joseph S. Nye, *Power and Interdependence*, 2nd ed. (New York: Harper

Collins, 1989), p.251; cf. Keohane, 'Theory of World Politics', in Keohane (ed.), *Neo Realism and Its Critics* (New York: Columbia University Press, 1986), p.193, where he describes his approach as a 'modified structural research program'.

35. Keohane, *International Institutions and State Power: Essays in International Relations Theory* (Boulder, Colorado: Westview, 1989), p.15
36. Robert J. Art, 'Why Western Europe Needs the United States and NATO', *Political Science Quarterly*, Vol.111, No.1 (Spring 1996).
37. Ibid., p.36.
38. Robert O. Keohane, 'The Diplomacy of Structural Change: Multilateral Institutions and State Strategies', in Helga Haftendorn and Christian Tuschoff (eds.), *America and Europe in an Era of Change* (Boulder: Westview, 1993), p.53.

The Bosnian Road to NATO Enlargement

BEVERLY CRAWFORD[1]

The end of the Cold War, the Soviet threat and the Soviet Union appeared to be the death knell of the North Atlantic Treaty Organization (NATO) alliance. Its security doctrine was obsolete; isolationist mutterings were heard in Washington; and there were numerous efforts to breathe life into competing institutions, like the Conference on Security and Co-operation in Europe (CSCE) – now the Organization for Security and Co-operation in Europe (OSCE), and the Western European Union (WEU). In the initial flush of post-Cold War uncertainty, pessimists predicted institutional chaos in Europe's security future that would set European nations against each other and draw the United States and Russia into European security conflicts.[2] Optimists, on the other hand, heralded the dawn of a new 'pluralism' in European security arrangements, suggesting a new 'division of labour' rather than a competitive struggle among institutions and between their member states.[3] They proclaimed that the European continent's peaceful evolution depended on transcending the Cold War requirement for military alliances. In 1992, President Clinton had placed a premium on relations with Russia, declaring a policy of 'strategic alliance' and a 'new democratic partnership' with the West's former enemy.[4] These initial events and trends did not bode well for NATO's future, much less its enlargement.

But by the decade's end, both optimists and pessimists were proved wrong; the United States was fully involved in European security, and with the US at the helm, NATO emerged again victorious as Europe's premier security institution, prepared to protect new democracies and expand its membership – pointedly excluding Russia. NATO had carried out the first air strikes in its history, against Bosnian Serbs, attacked Belgrade, sent ground troops to the Balkans, and 'won' the battle for Kosovo against Serbia. Other European security institutions, in which Russia participated, receded into their Cold War dormancy.

How was this victory possible for an organization whose mission was outmoded, whose members squabbled, and whose very existence had been challenged by its own members, and by competing institutions?

I argue here that the explanation for NATO's revitalization and decision to expand its membership is *path dependent*, and the path runs through Bosnia. The map revealing its destination was drawn in the Cold War and revived and modified in the war in the former Yugoslavia. Efforts on the part of institutions that included Russia – the United Nations (UN) and the OSCE – failed to resolve the conflict; each new failure deepened latent tensions between Russia and the West. Festering tension served to reinforce and modify ingrained Cold War beliefs in the 'Russian threat' – that Russia was either too strong or too weak to participate in European security arrangements. Perceptions of Russian weakness and obstructionism emerged in the Bosnian war,[5] leading Western decision-makers to fall back on old strategic guidelines for foreign policy behaviour and to conclude that NATO – an alliance that excluded Russia – was the only institution that could ensure security in Europe. The lesson of Bosnia was that institutions that included Russia were weak and could not provide security in Europe. This lesson was not lost on NATO: like any organization that achieves a 'monopoly', NATO prepared to expand both its membership and its functions – swallowing up the functions of competing organizations.

This argument supports the central claim of the realist theory of international relations: that power balances. Efforts to build a new 'security architecture' in Europe at the end of the Cold War were bound to fail, because, in their effort to advance a new definition of security, harking back to old visions of 'collective security', they ignored this central feature of the international system. The Bosnian war revealed a new kind of Russian 'threat' demanding a military response. And NATO was the only security institution in Europe that could exert military power. Because force is the bottom line of power, the wars in the former Yugoslavia reinforced a military definition of security, thought by many to be an outmoded concept in the post–Cold War world. In reinforcing a military definition of security, those wars gave NATO a premier position in Europe's security future. It was not pre-ordained that NATO be the institution that embodied this security concept; but rather NATO fought for and won that role in Bosnia and secured its position of pre-eminence in Kosovo. The wars in Bosnia and Kosovo were the path to NATO's renewed strength but not the cause. The cause can be found in the structure of the international system and the realities of power in the post-Cold War world.

In support of this argument I begin with an elaboration of the apparent puzzle of NATO's resilience and rebirth in the post-Cold War environment. I then trace the events that led to NATO's institutional victory in the Bosnian war and show how those events shaped the wider European security environment, leading to the consensual decision to expand NATO's membership. I conclude with a brief discussion of the reciprocal impact of European integration and NATO enlargement, suggesting long-term consolidation of NATO's institutional victory.

THE PUZZLE OF NATO EXPANSION

At the Cold War's end, most analysts predicted NATO's demise, or, at the very least, a fundamental restructuring and reorientation of the alliance. The dramatic change in Europe's political geography seemed to inspire new institutional preferences. In the United States, the Bush administration – while stressing a commitment to democracy in eastern Europe – was reluctant to discuss its security needs.[6] In Russia, the loss of the Warsaw Pact encouraged a preference for the OSCE as Europe's central security institution, both because Russia was an OSCE member and because the centrality of the OSCE would replace NATO's primacy. The Russian government declared that while NATO should offer security guarantees to 'emerging democracies', it would have to renounce unambiguously the extension of its military activities to the east, so as not to provide fuel for conservative forces in Russia and in the former Soviet military who might use the renewed Western threat to increase their domestic political power.

Indeed, the Clinton administration was initially responsive to the Russian position. In its first year, that administration had begun to seek stable partners who could assist in reducing America's overseas commitments and share the burden of world management. To this end, it had made its relationship with Russia a policy priority. It proclaimed that Russian stability and progress in reforms were vital to US interests. And Russia's continuing great power status, with far-reaching influence in Eurasia and Iran made it an important partner, a conclusion bolstered by Russia's co-operation with the US in the Gulf War of 1991. Indeed, Yeltsin was eager to establish Russia as a good world citizen. His foreign policy was strongly supportive of multilateralism in international diplomacy.

With the US taking this position, security organizations that included both Russia and the West began to gain credibility. In 1990 the CSCE's Paris Charter stated that the era of confrontation and divisions in Europe had ended, and it set the liberal constitutive norms around which a CSCE 'security community'[7] would be constructed: democracy, the rule of law, human rights, minority rights, political pluralism and respect for the environment. The CSCE was to be the protector and 'implementor' of those norms, and by 1995, its status was upgraded to that of an international organization.

In Bosnia, as I shall show in more detail below, the 'partnership' between the US, Russia and Europe, and broad-based multilateral organizations like the CSCE got off to a good start. Communism's collapse forged common goals between Russia and the West in that conflict: the West had 'won' the Cold War. Now the war of Yugoslav succession symbolized a blatant attack on Western values of peaceful conflict resolution, tolerance, equality and dignity of the individual. Defence of these values thus guided the initial Western response to the war and guided the Russian response as well, since Russian leaders desperately wanted to join the 'West'.

Thus, incentives were high for both Russia and the West to join together to encourage a diplomatic solution that would end the war and preserve Western values in the region. Russia was a full participant, giving its support to the deployment of the United Nations Protection Force (UNPROFOR) in Croatia, voting in favour of the UN economic sanctions against Serbia, co-operating in the proclamation of a 'no-fly zone' over Bosnia, and heartily agreeing to the establishment of a war crimes tribunal in the Hague. Russia was a member of the 'Contact Group' formed in 1994 to negotiate an end to hostilities between the warring parties.

With this full Russian participation in multilateral efforts, NATO was sidelined diplomatically; it had been reluctant to become involved at the outset, suggesting that the war would remain contained and would not endanger the alliance. Indeed, until 1994, NATO was plunged into an identity crisis; its members were reluctant to extend territorial guarantees eastward at the same time that they were thinning out their forces on the former front line. When Poland, Hungary and the Czech Republic first came knocking on NATO's door, the *most* its leaders could do was to create a new council, the North Atlantic Co-operation Council (NACC), enabling former Warsaw Pact countries and the Baltic states –

and later Russia – to consult with NATO.[8] Central Europeans then approached the WEU, hoping that association would bring them closer to European Union (EU) membership. But those hopes, too, seemed dimmed by the uncertainty of the WEU's function and the impact of German unification on European integration. Central European nations thus scrambled to conclude overlapping bilateral agreements with former Soviet republics, with one another, and with France, Britain and Germany.

But by the time the Dayton accords were signed, NATO emerged dominant over all other actors on the European security stage, upstaging Russia and gaining the institutional legitimacy to expand eastward. This dominance was demonstrated in Kosovo, and secured by NATO's military 'victory' there. As negotiations over NATO's future proceeded throughout the 1990s, it became clear that its future would be determined by its performance in Bosnia. When NATO was hamstrung in Bosnia by the 'great power' tensions behind institutional conflicts, negotiations on enlargement were stalled. Only when NATO emerged victorious in Bosnia could its enlargement be considered. The next section traces the events that led to this outcome.

NATO'S TRIUMPH IN BOSNIA

When the Yugoslav war began in 1991, it was hailed as the 'hour of Europe', an occasion for the then European Community (EC) to bolster and hone its 'common foreign and security policy', and act independently of the Atlantic alliance through European institutions to solve a regional conflict.[9] But when the war widened to Bosnia, drawing in Russia and an array of multilateral institutions (the UN, the OSCE and NATO), many analysts began to see the conflict as a test of 'the willingness of Europeans and Americans to adjust their Cold War political and security institutions to the changing geo-strategic circumstances in Europe'.[10] Most analysts and policy makers believed that the West should act jointly with Russia to end the first war on European soil since 1945.

The war began innocuously. On 25 June 1991 Croatia and Slovenia declared independence from Yugoslavia. The Yugoslav National Army (JNA) was called to prevent the secession of these two states; but both resisted, and fighting broke out.[11] EC foreign ministers quickly negotiated an agreement between Slovenia and Croatia to suspend their independence declarations if the JNA would withdraw its troops, and they sent an observer mission to Zagreb to monitor the agreement. Normally, the CSCE would provide monitors. But this unusual EC monitoring mission was at the request of the Soviet Union, who preferred that the CSCE take a back seat to the EC with regard to this crisis, fearing that CSCE involvement would serve as a precedent for interference in the Baltics.[12] Thus the CSCE was quickly sidelined, and EC foreign ministers took up the challenge.[13] The European Monitoring Mission (EMM), a 'first' in European political co-operation, was born, suggesting that the crisis was indeed helping to forge new levels of policy co-ordination in Europe, and that US and Russian involvement would be minimal. Furthermore, in order to compel the warring parties to accept binding mediation on the part of the EC, members agreed that they would jointly suspend arms sales and economic aid to Yugoslavia.[14] Later, the UN joined the arms embargo that would become an international bone of contention when the war spread to Bosnia one year later.

Despite these efforts, the war continued in Croatia. NATO was initially reluctant to become involved in the conflict. Its official policy statements paid lip service to Europe's geographic unity and interdependence, but expressed reservations about intervention in post-communist conflicts. The war in Yugoslavia was not expected to widen.[15] The EC thus asked the WEU to serve directly as its military arm, and requested that it develop options to strengthen the EC's ceasefire monitoring capability. But the WEU was stymied by internal disagreements, and failed to do so.[16] The absence of military power to enforce agreements suggested that those agreements would be meaningless in the eyes of the belligerents. By 1992, the war had ended in Croatia but had spread to Bosnia.

Until Bosnia was ravaged by war, the United States had taken no diplomatic initiatives, at the request of France and Britain, who had sought a 'European' solution to this regional crisis. But in late May 1992, US Secretary of State James Baker complained that the EC was doing nothing and simply waiting for the UN to act. His comments prodded the Europeans to impose sanctions against Yugoslavia without waiting for the UN. The UN had been stymied: supporting Serbia, Russia was hesitant to impose UN sanctions;[17] nonetheless EC pressure forced Russia's hand, and the Security Council voted for sanctions on 30 May.

The independent imposition of EC sanctions indicated growing tensions over the co-ordination of an institutional response to this first post-Cold War European crisis. British officials approved of a UN peacekeeping mission, but France opposed a UN-sponsored diplomatic effort, arguing that it would undermine EC initiatives. CSCE officials attempted to find a role for that institution in this crisis; they wished to be seen as a regional organization under UN auspices, with the power to co-ordinate peacekeeping operations.[18] As I will show below, however, the UN eclipsed the CSCE, and it again receded as an actor in this crisis. Indeed, in December 1994, when the CSCE met to discuss issues of European security and conflict resolution, Bosnia was not even discussed.[19] Still, however, no 'security institution' had emerged which was strong enough to enforce diplomatic agreements reached with the belligerents.

The Vance-Owen Plan: A Blow to Multilateral Co-operation

In October 1992, the Vance-Owen plan was unveiled, which proposed to divide Bosnia into ten geographic units within a single Bosnian state, granting the Serbs and Croats autonomy within Bosnia. By preventing Croats and Muslims from remilitarizing areas the Serbs would cede, the plan was a major concession to the Bosnian Serbs. The plan itself had no enforcement mechanism, although the UN had stepped in, and was prepared for peacekeeping. In April 1992, the UN Security Council had created UNPROFOR to protect humanitarian relief efforts and ensure the safety and security of the Sarajevo airport.[20] On 8 June, the Security Council had expanded the UNPROFOR mission to include the task of reopening the Sarajevo airport for relief supplies. On 13 August, the Security Council approved the use of 'all means necessary' to supply humanitarian aid to Bosnia, but cautioned that this not be interpreted as an attack on the Bosnian Serbs.[21] Under the Vance-Owen Plan, UNPROFOR would protect those areas that the Bosnian Serbs had been asked to give up. In this plan, NATO would be completely sidelined.

While the US opposed the plan because it called for the deployment of US ground troops for enforcement within UNPROFOR and because it had no role for NATO, Russia strongly supported it because it stressed the Russian contribution to the UN force. US officials did not want the Russians *in*, while the Clinton administration was pressured by domestic and European forces to stay *out*. Russian Foreign Minister Kozyrev had quickly called for a UN Security Council meeting to discuss the plan's implementation, putting the United States in the position of potentially having to use its veto power, a move that would strain the new 'strategic partnership'. Further exacerbating the tension, Russia was opposed to the air strikes against Bosnian Serb positions that the US supported, and Kozyrev's vocal opposition began to drive a wedge between the US and its allies, since the Europeans were opposed to air strikes as well.

Disagreements among NATO allies fuelled the debate over whether more 'European' security arrangements such as the OSCE or the WEU should be strengthened. Countering the US position, Russia also proposed a tightening of the arms embargo against Bosnia, and sanctions on Croatia if further attacks on Serb enclaves there ensued.[22] It appeared to some observers that Russia was helping to divide the West.

These disputes ensured the Vance-Owen plan's failure, and, knowing that the great powers were divided, both the Bosnian Muslims and the Bosnian Serbs soundly rejected it.[23] This failure created a diplomatic vacuum that led to even deeper contradictory domestic pressures in the West and Russia, threatening to unravel the multilateral decision-making process altogether. In the United States and Britain, public opinion called for Western intervention on behalf of the Bosnian Muslims, and the British Labour Party called for the bombing of Bosnian Serb positions. In the United States, public opinion overwhelmingly supported a lifting of the arms embargo against Bosnia, and Clinton's national security adviser, Tony Lake, called for intervention on behalf of the Bosnian Muslims. The German Foreign Minister called for Europe to break diplomatic relations with Yugoslavia.

But in Russia, domestic forces *opposed* a lifting of the embargo on Bosnia, and *supported* a lifting of the arms embargo on Serbia. Yeltsin feared that Russian acquiescence in a lifting of the arms embargo on Bosnia would alienate voters who might swing towards the hard-core nationalists.[24] He was also pressured by economic forces to lift the embargo on Serbia: *Moscow News* reported that Russian participation in sanctions against Yugoslavia and Iraq cost $30 billion per year in lost contracts.[25]

In the face the Vance-Owen plan's failure, these contradictory domestic pressures increased tensions among the great powers over future strategy. The US called for tougher sanctions against Serbia in an effort to pressure Milosevic to push the Bosnian Serbs to comply. Russia wanted to pursue the opposite strategy: to dangle the carrot of easing the sanctions in order to get Milosevic to put more pressure on the Bosnian Serbs.

Clinton recognized the danger to multilateralism of these increasing tensions, and he did not want to make any moves in Bosnia that might undermine stability in Russia.[26] He therefore did not push the demand for a lifting of the arms embargo, and promised not to pursue a second round of UN financial sanctions until after the April 1993 referendum on the new Russian constitution.

But within the American foreign policy establishment, there was growing criticism of Clinton's embrace of Russia. Many observers believed that Russian actions with regard to Bosnia were proof that Russia did not really intend to reintegrate itself into the international community, and was attempting to rebuild its old spheres of influence. In a report to the Senate Foreign Relations Committee in April 1993, Senator Joseph Biden called for a policy of Russian acquiescence rather than collaboration. He urged the Clinton administration to adopt a policy of 'working even more closely with Yeltsin to ensure Russian abstentions from Security Council resolutions that prove necessary'.[27] US officials began to perceive that Russia was not helping to achieve a settlement, and they stepped up pressure for the use of NATO to launch air strikes against the Bosnian Serbs, a move that would effectively exclude Russia in the enforcement effort.

Meanwhile, in the face of diplomatic failure in Bosnia, the fighting intensified, and the intensification required the West to formulate a new plan to moderate it. As a stopgap, France and Britain lobbied the US to support the creation of 'safe havens' for Bosnian civilians. By June 1993, the UN Security Council approved a joint action programme establishing six 'safe areas' at Sarajevo, Srebenica, Zepa, Tuzla, Goradze and Bihac. But the question of who would have the power to keep the havens 'safe' was still an issue of intense debate, and, for the first time, NATO was called in to help. But the UN resolution left it unclear whether NATO would use air strikes to retaliate against attacks on these areas or whether the UN troops would retaliate. As noted above, the US called for air strikes; Russia and the Europeans were opposed. Clarity on this issue and the prominence of NATO's role would be achieved only after the attack on the Sarajevo market in February 1994.

On 5 February 1994, an attack on an open market left over 60 civilians dead in Sarajevo. Assuming that the attack was launched by Bosnian Serbs, the 16 members of NATO issued an ultimatum demanding the withdrawal of Serbian artillery to at least 20 kilometres from the centre by 21 February. If the Bosnian Serbs did not withdraw, NATO threatened an attack on their military positions. The credibility of this threat was demonstrated when NATO jets shot down four light Bosnian Serb planes over Banja Luka for violating the flight ban.

The attack had galvanized the Europeans; neither the WEU, the CSCE nor the UN had been able to mitigate the bloodshed. NATO seemed to be the only hope. NATO's action had broad support among the Western powers. Although Russia opposed the idea of a NATO command in Bosnia, Russian credibility effectively to pressure the Bosnian Serbs had weakened, and it now had little choice but to accept the NATO alternative. Russian officials thus requested that the Serbs respect the NATO ultimatum. But Yeltsin also wanted to send Russian peacekeepers to Bosnia as part of the UN peacekeeping operation.[28]

First Inklings of NATO Expansion

The failure of the Vance-Owen plan and the failure of the US to support it may have been responsible for Russia's retreat from 'wholehearted international cooperation'.[29] Furthermore, the reformist leadership in Russia was growing disillusioned with the West for its lack of support for the reform process within Russia itself. The US decision not to embrace the Vance-Owen plan may have added insult to injury, representing to the Russians 'the loss of an opportunity to establish a co-operative mechanism for dealing with European security problems, including those faced by Russia in the former Soviet Union'.[30]

It was during this low point in the Bosnian war that plans for NATO's 'Partnership for Peace' (PFP) were launched, and it was after the attack on the Sarajevo market that the top policy elite in Washington decided openly to beef up NATO's role in Europe's still-debated security 'architecture'. The PFP would include Russia, and was intended to create working links between participants and NATO governments, a plan to adapt airfields to NATO standards, exercises in compatible command and control systems, and defence review planning. Through these means, the PFP would facilitate transparency in national defence planning and budgeting and develop co-operative military relations with NATO, developing forces better able to operate with those of the alliance. At the same time, the Partnership's goals of ensuring democratic control of defence forces; and maintaining the capability and readiness to contribute to operations under the authority of the United

Nations or the OSCE were goals that Russia could hardly refuse to endorse.[31]

Although it was not explicitly stated in NATO's official declarations, a few analysts put forth the counter-intuitive argument that the PFP would be the first step towards NATO expansion and the marginalization of Russia in the post-Cold War European security environment. In December 1994, Joseph Lepgold wrote that the PFP left open the possibility of NATO membership for the Visegrad group, the Baltic republics and perhaps Ukraine, and it assumed that either the Europeans could work towards mutual security with Russia or, if Russia were to resume expansion, the nations that would be threatened would have time to mobilize effectively.[32] NATO officials saw it as a valuable framework for evaluating the ability of each partner to assume the obligations and commitments of NATO membership – a testing ground for their capabilities.[33]

But the real testing ground for NATO capabilities was Bosnia. Partnership for Peace was in its embryo stage, and the idea of a treaty to enlarge NATO did not gain momentum. As the following section demonstrates, resolve to move ahead with a treaty to enlarge NATO was only forged on the battlefield in Bosnia.

The Contact Group Plan: Diplomatic Failure, NATO's Tied Hands

In March 1994, the United States had persuaded the Bosnian Muslims and Croats to form a Muslim–Croat federation with the signing of the Washington accords. To induce the Croats to sign the accords, the US promised that Tudjamn could regain parts of its territory, lost to the Croatian Serbs in the war. The US also helped Croatia build up its army by sending advisers and by permitting weaponry to flow into Croatia.[34] The accords halted the fighting between Bosnian Muslims and Bosnian Croats and provided for an eventual confederation with Croatia, thus undermining the legitimacy of a separate Bosnian state.

This new federation also opened the door for a new diplomatic effort. In May 1994, the foreign ministers of Greece, Belgium, Germany, the EU, France, Russia, the UK and the US met in Geneva. They created what was called the 'Contact Group' (composed of representatives from the US, France, Britain, Germany and Russia) to begin substantive negotiations again with the warring parties. The Contact Group proposed a plan that would turn Bosnia into two parts: a 49 per cent

Bosnian Serb and 51 per cent Muslim–Croat federation. This would require that the Bosnian Serbs surrender one-third of their territory and give up plans to create a union with Serbia. The plan's success depended heavily on Milosevic to pressure the Bosnian Serbs into acceptance by closing its border to Bosnia – thus halting the flow of arms and other supplies – and permitting UN monitors along border areas in exchange for the easing of sanctions. The Contact Group also urged Serbia to recognize Bosnia as an independent state and, over initial Russian objections, proposed that NATO troops enforce the ceasefire.

The key to successful pressure on the Serbs was Russia. Russia joined American diplomats to urge Karadzic to accept the plan and declared that it would take a stronger stand against the Serbs if they did not co-operate. Both Kinkel and Kozyrev agreed to use their joint influence with participants in the conflict to promote a ceasefire and accept the plan.[35] Kozyrev, however, still attempted to limit NATO's involvement: he opposed the US effort to transfer command over Bosnian operations from the UN to NATO.[36] With NATO's hands tied, the agreement could not be effectively enforced.

Russia's pressure on Serbia seemed at first to pay off: Milosevic ordered the border between Serbia and Bosnia closed on 5 August and, two months later, the UN eased sanctions against Yugoslavia. Nonetheless, the oil and trade embargo would remain in effect until Serbia recognized Bosnia as a unitary state.[37] Milosevic agreed to recognize Bosnia as a state but not a government in return for the lifting of all the sanctions. Russia suggested a 200-day suspension of the sanctions in exchange for recognition, but the four non-Russian Contact Group members feared that Russia would use its veto in the Security Council to ensure that the sanctions would not be reimposed and leverage over Milosevic would be lost.[38] They thus blocked the Russian initiative.

Furthermore, there was an intense institutional struggle over who would control the military enforcement of any agreement reached. A 'dual-key' arrangement required both UN officials and military commanders on the ground to approve NATO air strikes. Disagreement over the rules of engagement, however, made that arrangement ineffective. When Bosnian Serbs attacked Bihac in November 1994, NATO announced that it could not attack Bosnian Serb positions because the UN refused authorization to attack; for their part, UN officials believed that an attack would amount to a declaration of war.[39]

Each NATO air strike had provoked the Bosnian Serbs to take UN peacekeepers as hostages and increased pressure for the UN to pull back. On 7 May, a major shelling from Bosnian Serb positions into Sarajevo led Rupert Smith, UNPROFOR's commander, to order NATO air strikes. At first, his orders were countermanded by officials at UN headquarters in Zagreb, who argued that Croatian Serbs would retaliate with attacks in Croatia and those attacks would endanger UN troops; nonetheless, against UN orders, on 25 May, NATO conducted air strikes against Bosnian Serb positions near Sarajevo.[40] Confusion increased with the growing tension between the UN and NATO commands.

The problem was inherent in the UN mandate. As the Secretary-General reported:

> even though the use of force is authorized under Chapter VII of the Charter, the United Nations remains neutral and impartial between the warring parties, without a mandate to stop the aggressor (if one can be identified) or impose a cessation of hostilities. Nor is this peace-keeping as practiced hitherto, because the hostilities continue and there is often no agreement between the warring parties on which a peace-keeping mandate can be based.[41]

NATO, on the other hand, did not suffer under similar constraints and, with US backing, pushed to gain control over military decision-making with regard to air strikes. Russian disagreement and UN pressure, however, blocked this effort.

The West was thus unable to break the negotiating deadlock, and international negotiators could not enforce agreements already made. So, like the Vance-Owen plan, this agreement, too, broke down. Despite Russia's co-operation and signs that Serbia would pressure the Bosnian Serbs into acceptance, they resisted the plan. As long as the warring parties preferred the possibility of battlefield victory to the certainty of a compromise at the negotiating table, their incentive to reach a negotiated settlement would be low.

'Great power' leverage could have heightened that incentive, but the great powers disagreed about the military backing needed to exert it. In an effort to preserve multilateral co-operation, the US and Europe had reined in their impulse to unleash NATO, because of Russian objections. But those co-operative efforts were too weak. The Bosnian Serb army attacked UN positions, surrounded Sarajevo, blocked relief convoys and attacked Bihac, and the international community was unable to respond with concerted and co-ordinated military force. Clearly defeated, the Contact Group declared their plan a 'basis for negotiations' only. With festering differences between the US and Europe and with massive human rights violations in Europe's doorstep, questions about NATO's post-Cold War mission became more intense, and Europe's lofty new security agenda rapidly began to lose credibility.

Indeed, these stalemates had a profound impact on NATO's efforts to maintain its strength and enlarge its membership. In December 1994, NATO ministers initiated a comprehensive study of enlargement and agreed to try to complete that study by the end of 1995. But the Bosnian crisis had precipitated institutional conflicts between NATO and the UN. NATO's inability to act in Bosnia bogged down the enlargement process. Thus, plans for enlargement were simply postponed, due, in part, to a fear that Russia would react adversely and refuse further co-operation in Bosnia.[42] These frustrations may have contributed greatly to the decision taken in the spring of 1994 among a few top policy-makers in Washington to support enlargement as a way of strengthening NATO and keeping Russia out. And the US position was crucial to the initiation of the enlargement study, commissioned by NATO ministers in December. But squabbles among the allies, tensions with Russia and the West's need for Russian co-operation in Bosnia ensured that enlargement was not on the cards, at least for the time being. There was no more talk of identifying potential new members and setting timetables. Meanwhile, Russia formally signed on to the PFP, hoping that through PFP it could influence the decision on NATO enlargement. So the enlargement process was stalled through the first half of 1995. But events in the Bosnian war would soon move it forward.

NATO's Triumph and the Dayton Agreement

Back in Bosnia, with military options now greatly narrowed, the US thus stepped up pressure on Russia to agree to an enhanced role for NATO in countering Bosnian Serb strikes. Russian options to oppose the US were now narrowed, because of its own diplomatic failure to exert sufficient pressure on the Bosnian Serbs. Russian diplomatic credibility was therefore at a low point, and its protests against an enhanced role for NATO carried less weight. General diplomatic despair over rising institutional tensions and rivalry had opened the political space for a new solution, and when Russia finally agreed, NATO came to take the lead in military engagement. The turning point in official US policy and in NATO's future was the fall of Srebenica.

In July 1995, the 'safe havens' of Srebenica and Zepa fell to the Bosnian Serbs, and French and British forces were forced to withdraw. Clinton now felt that the US was in an impossible situation which, if left unaddressed, might well erode the international order that the US appeared determined to bolster and maintain. He thus took decisive action to push for NATO's pre-eminence in enforcement efforts.[43] NATO commanders were permitted to summon air strikes without UN approval, and they increased their own authority over military decisions. NATO's increasing autonomy was accompanied by task expansion: plans were launched for the creation of a 'rapid reaction force' of 4,000 troops to assist in a possible UN withdrawal.

With NATO's role enhanced, the United States initiated an alternative to the failing Contact Group plan in the summer of 1995. This alternative would prove to be the skeleton of the Dayton peace accord initialled the following November. The American plan built upon the Contact Group proposal in that it maintained the 49–51 per cent split between the Bosnian Serb and Muslim–Croat territories. But the Serbs would keep the Muslim enclaves of Zepa and Srebrenica, and they would get more territory around the Brcko corridor connecting the two parts of their territory. Muslims would gain territory around Sarajevo.

The plan stipulated that Croatia and Bosnia recognize each other's pre-war frontiers, and international sanctions on Serbia would be lifted when it recognized Bosnia as an independent state. Bosnia would remain a recognized state, but areas with a Serbian majority population would be free to confederate with Serbia. The Muslim–Croat federation would be permitted under the plan to confederate with Croatia. In practice, then, Bosnia would *de facto* cease to exist as an independent entity, even though it would continue to exist *de jure*.

To press for agreement, the United States used a series of carrots and sticks to prod each of the belligerents. To pressure the Bosnian Serbs, the US promised to support a lifting of the arms embargo on the Bosnian government and a withdrawal of UNPROFOR, but also promised NATO air strikes against the Bosnian Serb positions if they refused to accept the plan and continued their attacks. To pressure the Bosnian Muslims, who initially opposed the plan because it gave Zepa and Srebrenica to the Bosnian Serbs, US officials persuaded Croatia to limit its assistance to the Bosnian Muslims and squeeze them until they accepted the plan. US diplomats encouraged Tudjman and Izetbegovbic to agree on a joint military campaign against the Bosnian Serbs in territory adjacent to Croatia, but also encouraged Croatia to abandon plans to help the Muslims in central Bosnia.

All the major European actors and Russia seemed enthusiastic about the plan, although they disapproved of the threat of air strikes.[44] Attitudes changed, however, after a mortar attack in Sarajevo at the end of August 1995 killed 37 civilians. Assuming that the attack was launched by Bosnian Serbs, NATO began aerial bombardment of Bosnian Serb positions; this was NATO's biggest military assault in its entire history. At the same time, with encouragement from the United States, a joint Muslim–Croat offensive captured much of north-west Bosnia, and on 12 October, a ceasefire was reached. The belligerents went to the negotiating table in Dayton, Ohio on 1 November, and a peace accord was initialled by the presidents of Bosnia, Croatia and Serbia on 21 November.

A clear institutional hierarchy emerged in Dayton: the OSCE – long inactive in this crisis – was given the task of supervising the 1996 Bosnian elections, monitoring human rights activity, and promoting arms control. The EU was to provide a plan for the economic reconstruction of Bosnia Although the United Nations largely stepped into the background, the United Nations High Commission for Refugees (UNHCR) was given the task of leading humanitarian efforts. But the largest role was saved for NATO.

NATO was assigned the task of peacekeeping after the signing of the Dayton accords. An army of 60,000, called Joint Endeavor and deployed to enforce the accords, carved Bosnia into three zones, managed by the United States, France and Britain, all under the same NATO commander. To the rapid reaction force, NATO added IFOR, the joint implementation force. IFOR troops were instructed to employ standard NATO rules of engagement, meaning that they could pre-empt if they knew that an attack was imminent. The plan stipulated that IFOR could retaliate very heavily against the first sign of resistance. France now moved discreetly closer to NATO, allowing French troops to serve under NATO command. French officials also indicated that they were keen to maintain an American presence. Given NATO's performance, Russia had no choice but to agree.

In sum, the WEU's earlier failure to enforce ceasefires, the UN's failure to protect 'safe havens', UN–NATO co-ordination problems that further reduced the West's enforcement capability, NATO's successful show of force and the demonstration of its ability to co-ordinate military action when it was finally permitted to do so, France's participation in NATO's military activity, and finally, Russia's agreement – all combined to place NATO in a position of institutional prominence. By the time the agreement was initialled in Dayton, NATO had been strengthened beyond anyone's wildest hopes or fears. In Bosnia, the NATO alliance established itself as Europe's only meaningful security institution.

The Bosnian Road to NATO Enlargement

Although the Bush administration had advocated NATO's enlargement eastward shortly after the fall of communism, few had anticipated that NATO could actually expand its membership because its Cold War mission was now obsolete. Many argued that its military functions be taken over by other organizations and that the WEU be revived. France and Germany envisaged the WEU as a security arm of the EU and a bridge between the EU and NATO.

In this environment, NATO had scrambled to establish a new role in the post-Cold War environment, at first attempting to edge out the CSCE by usurping its tasks. As noted above, at the Rome NATO summit of November 1991, foreign ministers and representatives from all 16 NATO states created NACC, consisting of NATO members, eastern and central European states, and all Soviet successor states, including the Baltics as a forum for consultation on democratic practices. NACC would oversee military-to-military liaisons for co-operation on such issues as development of democratic institutions, civil–military relations, peacekeeping, conceptual approaches to arms control and disarmament, defence planning, scientific and environmental affairs, civil–military co-ordination of air traffic management, and the conversion of defence production to civilian purposes. Most of these tasks had been part of the CSCE mandate. But with NACC, NATO had attempted to take the initiative of community-building from the CSCE in a broader search for a new mission. Although many proponents of PFP and NACC saw them as alternatives to NATO, they actually served as incubators for NATO expansion.

In 1994, at a nadir in the Bosnian crisis, the final communiqué of the meeting of allied heads of state indicated that they expected and would welcome NATO enlargement, but they made no firm commitment, calling it 'evolutionary' and dependent upon political and security developments in Europe as a whole. By mid-1995, however, after NATO's successful performance in Bosnia, there was little doubt that it had been rescued as Europe's key security institution. It had become increasingly clear that under all the forms that the WEU could take, it would be almost entirely dependent on NATO resources and personnel.[45] In 1996 and 1997, the intense 'dialogues' with prospective new members began, and were concluded with the entrance of Poland, Hungary and the Czech Republic into the alliance in July 1998. These new members became quickly socialized and integrated into the alliance structure when NATO began the bombing of Kosovo in 1999.

CONCLUSION

The Bosnian war provided NATO with the renewed legitimacy that it needed to expand eastward. It left no doubt in the minds of both European and American leaders, that other institutions in which Russia participated would be too conflict-ridden and too weak to provide a common security umbrella for Europe. NATO enlargement was thus an unambiguous strategy to keep Russia out of the security institutions in Europe that really counted.

Recall that in the Bosnian crisis, after a brief struggle over whether the EC would continue to solve the crisis alone and what roles the EC, the OSCE and the UN would play, the principal actors chose the UN as the institution with the widest membership as the sponsor of negotiations. Tensions among the actors over appropriate strategy led to domestic pressures for alternative policies. Those pressures, combined with collective fears of chaos in post-Cold War Europe, led to the decision to revitalize NATO and minimize the role of the UN. A weakened Russia, anxious to be part of the 'West', had no choice but to support the choice for NATO's enhanced role in Bosnia. France, despite its preference for a European solution to the crisis, was not strong enough to push the process in a different direction. The United States, as the strongest power, exerted leadership in its effort to bolster NATO, and the strategy worked. Indeed, Bosnia provided an opportunity for NATO's first out-of-area action and set an important precedent, providing the legitimacy needed for enlargement and for its role in Kosovo.

These moves were consolidated in the Kosovo crisis and its aftermath. In September 1998, the UN Security Council approved

Resolution 1199 demanding a ceasefire in Kosovo, Serb withdrawal of military forces from Kosovo, the return of Albanian Kosovar refugees who had fled the intensified fighting that ensued after Dayton, and 'additional measures' if Serbia refused to comply. At first, compliance seemed assured: Milosevic permitted unarmed OSCE ceasefire monitors to enter Kosovo and, in an agreement reached with NATO Supreme Commander General Wesley Clark, agreed to a Serbian force reduction there. But reports of continued fighting led to the deployment of NATO troops in Macedonia. And the failure of the Rambouillet peace talks triggered NATO's successful air war against Serbia which began on 24 March 1999 and ended in June 1999. In the aftermath, Russia agreed to a Western presence in Kosovo to keep the peace, and agreed to a UN-headed effort to rebuild the country. By March 2000, however, the United States had made it known that it would prefer an OSCE-led administration of Kosovo, and had begun to thwart the UN-appointed post-war government of Bernard Kouchner.[46]

As reinforced in Kosovo, the institutional struggle and uncertainty ended with NATO dominance as Europe's premier security institution. NATO not only remained a strong military alliance, its mission expanded to include the consolidation of new democracies and the protection of human rights – tasks formerly given to the OSCE, the UN and the Council of Europe.[47] Its enlargement to include former Warsaw Pact countries is a clear indicator of that success, a success that was forged in Bosnia. In the absence of events in Bosnia, it is unlikely that those policy elites in the Clinton administration who supported enlargement would have gained the upper hand. Without the diplomatic blunders and institutional struggles in Bosnia, Russian opposition to expansion would have had more credibility. Under these conditions, NATO enlargement would surely continue to be stalled.

Finally, in his essay for this volume, Charles Kupchen makes a forceful argument for the inclusion of Russia in any future expansion of NATO's membership. If the analysis of this essay is correct, then the United States has paid lip service to the potential for Russian inclusion in NATO, but in fact made the decision to throw its weight behind enlargement in order to ensure that Russia would not be included in the post-Cold War European security alliance and that a NATO that excluded Russia would dominate all other European security institutions. Nonetheless, as in the Bosnian crisis, any future security crisis in Europe will most likely require Russian co-operation for its resolution; therefore, the OSCE and the Partnership for Peace will still continue to play the roles of providing for the inclusion of Russia in Europe's security future.

NOTES

1. I would like to thank James Goldgeier, Robert Rauchhaus, and two anonymous reviewers for their helpful comments.
2. John Mearsheimer, 'False Promises of International Institutions', *International Security*, Vol.19, No.3 (Winter 1994), pp.5–49; John Mearsheimer, 'Back to the Future: Instability in Europe after the Cold War', *International Security*, Vol.15, No.1 (Summer 1990).
3. They compared the present period to the shifting, *ad hoc* alliances and ineffective collective security arrangements that bred suspicion and fear in the interwar period. See Steven Weber, 'Does NATO Have a Future?', in Beverly Crawford (ed.), *The Future of European Security* (Berkeley: International and Area Studies Publication, 1992), pp.360–95.
4. On the policy of the first Clinton administration see Michael Cox, 'The Necessary Partnership?', *International Affairs*, Vol.70, No.4 (Oct. 1994), pp.635–58.
5. Peter Rodman argues that 'Russia's identity as a clumsy and troublesome factor in European politics is rooted in its history – and predates the arrival of the Bolsheviks and the advent of thermonuclear weapons'. See Peter W. Rodman, 'NATO's Role in a New European Security Order' (Working Paper 95, Old Dominion University Graduate Programs in International Studies, Norfolk, Virginia, 2 Oct. 1995), p.3.
6. Rodman, 'NATO's Role in a New European Security Order', p.5.
7. Emanuel Adler and Michael Barnett, 'Security Communities' (paper delivered at the 1994 annual meeting of the American Political Science Association, New York City, 1–4 Sept. 1994). See also Daniel N. Nelson 'America and Collective Security in Europe', *Journal of Strategic Studies*, Vol.17, No.4 (Dec. 1994), p.115. See also 'OSCE, The Charter of Paris for a New Europe', as reprinted in *NATO Review*, Vol.38 (Dec. 1990), pp.27–31.
8. Alan Cowell, 'Bush Challenges Partners in NATO over Role of U.S.', *New York Times*, 8 Nov. 1991, p.A4. The United States had argued for eastern European membership in NATO in order to enhance NATO's security role at the expense of competing arrangements which would exclude or downplay US participation. France, of course, in a transparent effort to reduce American influence in European security issues, blocked the idea, arguing that the expansion of NATO would duplicate the role of the CSCE.
9. See the statement of Jacques Poos, Foreign Minister of Luxembourg, as quoted in 'A Long Hour', *The Economist*, 22 July 1995, p.48.
10. Senator Richard Lugar, 'NATO: Out of Area or Out of Business' (address before the Overseas Writers Club, Washington, 24 June 1993). Not everyone agrees with Lugar's assessment, however. US Secretary of State Warren Christopher stated that 'the crisis about Bosnia is about Bosnia. It is not about NATO.' quoted in Elaine Sciolino, 'U.S. and NATO Say Dispute on Bosnia War Is Resolved', *New York Times*, 2 Dec. 1994, p.A4.
11. See Misha Glenny, *The Fall of Yugoslavia: The Third Balkan War* (London: Penguin Books, 1992).
12. '"Drei Tage lang am Telefon", Wie sich Hans-Dietrich Genscher bemuehte, die jugoslawische Krise zu loesen', (Three days on the telephone: How Hans-Dietrich Genscher tried to solve the Yugoslavian crisis) *Der Spiegel*, Vol.45 (8 July 1991), p.128.
13. EC Council of Ministers, *Declaration on Yugoslavia* (82nd EPC Ministerial Meeting, The Hague, 10 July 1991).
14. 'G-Aussenminister hoffen auf friedliche Loesung in Jugoslawien' [EC foreign ministers hope for a peaceful solution in Yugoslavia], *Frankfurter Allgemeine Zeitung*, 10 July 1991, p.5.
15. See NATO Press Service, press communiqués M-1 (91) 42, 6 June 1991; M-2 (91) 60, 21 Aug. 1991; S-1 (91) 86, and 8 Nov. 1991.
16. Trevor Salmon, 'Testing Times for European Political Co-operation: the Gulf and Yugoslavia, 1990–1992', *International Affairs*, Vol.68, No.2 (April 1992), pp.251–2.

17. 'The World against Serbia', *The Economist*, 30 May 1992, p.49.
18. Statements from CSCE Summit in Helsinki, 9 and 10 July 1994.
19. *This Week in Germany*, 9 Dec. 1994.
20. Resolution 749 (1992). Adopted by the Security Council at its 3066th meeting on 7 April 1992.
21. Resolution 771 (1992). Adopted by the Security Council at its 3106th meeting on 13 Aug. 1992.
22. Hannes Adomeit, 'Russia as a "Great Power": Images and Reality', *International Affairs*, Vol.71, No.1 (Jan. 1995), p.46.
23. The Muslims believed that the UN was too weak to protect Muslim and Croat civilians in Serb-dominated areas, and the US State Department undermined Muslim support for the plan by telling Bosnia's President Izetbegovic that the US would support him if he demanded changes. The Bosnian Serbs did not want to sustain the 'fiction' of Bosnia as an independent state and felt forced to give up too much of the wrong territory.
24. Jonathan Landay, 'Bosnian Serb Defiance Causes Deepening of the Contact Group, but Serbian President Consents to International Border Monitoring', *Christian Science Monitor*, 12 Sept. 1994, p.6.
25. 'A Storm at the United Nations: Why Kozyrev Needs It', *Moscow News*, 21 Oct. 1994, p.5.
26. 'Unhappy Anniversary', *The Economist*, 10 April 1993, p.57.
27. Joseph Biden, *To Stand Against Aggression: Milosevic, the Bosnian Republic, and the Conscience of the West* (Washington, DC: US Government Printing Office, 1993), p.14.
28. Laurie Laird, 'Shared History: Serbians Turn to Russia', *Europe: Magazine of the European Community* No.337 (June 1994), p.19. All political elites in Germany joined in a resolution to support the NATO air attack.
29. This argument is made by James Gow, *Triumph of the Lack of Will: International Diplomacy and the Yugoslav War* (New York: Columbia University Press, 1997), p.221.
30. Gow, *Triumph of the Lack of Will*, p.201.
31. On these goals see Gebhardt von Moltke, 'Building a Partnership for Peace', *NATO Review*, Vol.42, No.3 (June 1994), p.4.
32. Joseph Lepgold, 'The Next Step Toward a More Secure Europe', *Journal of Strategic Studies*, Vol.17, No.4 (Dec. 1994), p.8.
33. North Atlantic Assembly, International Secretariat, *Projecting Stability in an Undivided Europe: Partnership for Peace and a Pact on Stability in Europe*', draft Interim Report, 1995.
34. See John J. Mearsheimer and Stephen Van Evera, 'When Peace Means War', *New Republic*, 18 Dec. 1995, p.18.
35. *This Week in Germany*, 26 Nov. 1994, p.2.
36. Roger Cohen, 'Bosnia Peace Mat: Serbs and West at Loggerheads', *New York Times*, 29 July 1994, p.A3.
37. 'Bosnian Serbs: Feeling the Pinch', *The Economist*, 8 Oct. 1994, p.54.
38. 'Ex-Yugoslavia: To Go or To Stay?,' *The Economist*, 27 May 1995, p.43.
39. Roger Cohen, 'Serbs Closing in on Bosnian Town; UN and NATO Unable to Act', *New York Times*, 9 Nov. 1994, p.A1.
40. 'Ex-Yugoslavia: To Go or To Stay ?', *The Economist*, 27 May 1995, p.43.
41. UN Document A/50/608/1995/1. 3 Jan. 1995.
42. Rodman, 'NATO's Role in a New European Security Order', p.8
43. See Mark Danner, 'The US and the Yugoslav Catastrophe', *New York Review of Books*, 20 Nov. 1997, p.58.
44. 'Enter the Americans', *The Economist*, 19 Aug. 1995, pp.41–2.
45. The WEU does not include all EU members. Sweden and Finland have no plans to apply, while Turkey has an associate membership. Its staff has begun looking at the feasibility of the WEU acquiring its own satellite intelligence assets.
46. See Steven Erlanger, 'U.N.'s Kosovo Chief Warns that Mission Is "Barely Alive"', *New York Times*, 4 March 2000, p.4.
47. Robert E. Hunter, 'Enlargement: Part of a Strategy for Projecting Stability into Central Europe', *NATO Review*, Vol.43, No.3 (May 1995), p.3.

PART III: INSTITUTIONS AND CHOICE

Analysing NATO Expansion:
An Institutional Bargaining Approach

VINOD K. AGGARWAL[1]

Unlike most security issues, knowing where one stands on the expansion of the North Atlantic Treaty Organization (NATO) does not help us to distinguish easily between realist and reflectivist views or, for that matter, between hawks and doves. Indeed, when we consider the accession of Hungary, Poland and the Czech Republic in a limited 'first wave' expansion of NATO in March 1999, the contending sides become even more muddled. Put bluntly, the conventional theoretical approaches do not help us adequately to understand and predict the implications of NATO's enlargement. Rather than engage in policy advocacy, my purpose is to analyse the debate on NATO expansion and examine the likely implications of this expansion.

To examine the policy process that led to the decision to engage in limited expansion of NATO, I use an 'institutional bargaining game approach'.[2] First, I consider the issue of how existing institutions that currently address one or another facet of European security are currently arrayed, and then analyse the debate over possible widening and changing the scope of NATO. Second, I examine the original impetus for changes in NATO, and consider the factors that led to the initial bargaining game over NATO expansion. I then turn to strategies used by the US to make NATO expansion more palatable by altering this initial bargaining game. In concluding, I show why the Clinton administration decided to promote a limited widening of NATO, with no significant changes in mission or rearrangement of institutional functions. Despite the widespread concern about antagonizing Russia, and the lack of evidence for benefits from such widening, I argue that this change may not be as detrimental as predicted by many analysts.

THE THEORETICAL INDETERMINACY OF
EXISTING APPROACHES

The lack of correspondence between many of the leading theories and the debate over NATO expansion can best be seen through a consideration of some of the key issues related to US policy on NATO widening. First, will the admission of Hungary, Poland and the Czech Republic lead to a reduced or increased threat to them from Russia? Second, will this expansion stimulate aggressive Russian behaviour towards the US – possibly as a result of the rise of extreme nationalist groups? Third, will the geographical divide between Germany and Russia become a more or less stable area, and what might the implications of expansion be on Ukrainian security? And fourth, will NATO expansion serve as a means of stabilizing social and economic reforms in the transitional states of eastern Europe?

Using these four questions as a baseline, it is clear that there is no consensus among realists. For example, drawing on balance-of-power notions, one could argue that expansion *will* destabilize the American relationship with Russia, thereby creating a strong reaction that would lead to an increased threat to the Ukraine, Poland and Germany. Moreover, the costs of NATO expansion also might be higher than estimated, resulting in a drain of valuable resources that might otherwise be used to bolster NATO's existing military capabilities. But an equally plausible realist argument could be made that enhancing NATO's power projection could stabilize the region between Germany and Russia and keep Germany entrenched in NATO. Moreover, this effort may well signal to Russia that the US is serious about its new sphere of influence and could be seen as a logical strategy to pursue when one's adversary is weak. Thus one could argue that the contributions made by the military of the new entrants will far outweigh the economic costs.

At the other theoretical extreme, reflectivists find themselves equally divided. John Ruggie, for example, draws on the notion of security communities to suggest that NATO expansion is dangerous.[3] He claims that this action detracts from the central concern of having the European Union (EU) take on a larger role in security relations with respect to eastern Europe. Moreover, Ruggie argues that expansion needlessly provokes Russia, and suggests that this move will simply prevent the EU from tackling the problem of its own widening. But one could equally well make the plausible reflectivist argument that limited expansion is a logical step towards fulfilling the need to create a security community that is broadly encompassing in Europe. From this perspective, NATO's measured expansion, together with appropriate economic plans and assurances to the Russians, will help to stabilize the region as a whole.

Similar to the ambiguity of theoretical debates, the policy-oriented discussion between and among hawks and doves also lacks consensus. For example, hawks argued both for and against NATO expansion. On the one hand, some felt that 1999 was an appropriate time to move against the Russians and assert US power – given that Russia had been weakening. Others argued that President Clinton was too cautious, and that accepting only a few members sent the wrong signal. By moving forward slowly, he is sending the signal that the US is only peripherally concerned about non-members. From this perspective, more countries such as Romania, Slovenia and Bulgaria should have been accepted at the same time to maximize the return on the US display of resolve.

More dovish thinkers support the Russia–NATO agreements and formation of the NATO–Russia Council as a way of indicating the lack of US aggressive intentions in the region. They also believe that NATO will help stabilize the region by encouraging the formation of democracies. However, other doves are equally dismayed that the US should be engaging in actions to provoke the Russians when there is currently little perceived Russian threat to the eastern Europeans, or for that matter, the US.

In short, my reading of the discussion to date suggests that realist or reflectivist theories, as well as cruder ideological stances, do not provide us with a clear foundation from which to understand the implications of NATO expansion. Rather, analysts from these different schools appear simply to be using the veneer of theory to mask their own personal views in light of the underlying theoretical indeterminacy about the benefits and costs of this particular foreign policy action.

WHITHER NATO?

To examine the question of how NATO's expansion proceeded and might develop in the future, as well as shed light on the implications of different possible paths, it is helpful to make some analytical distinctions. One critical issue that NATO faces is how to change its mandate. While most analysts have focused on the question of the accession of new members, it is useful to consider the 'expansion' of

NATO in the context of two questions. First, should NATO continue to widen to encompass new members, and, if so, how many members should be added? Second, should this organization change its mission to include new tasks? Examples include the management of ethnic conflicts, peacekeeping, promotion of democracy, economic development, and the like. And finally, of course, the two other logical options are to maintain the *status quo* or both to widen and to change mission at the same time.

These questions raise the issue of how NATO might fit with other institutions involved in the region, in particular the EU. We can consider two approaches to reconciliation. First, institutions might be linked or structured in an organized and somewhat hierarchical fashion. I have termed this an example of 'nested institutions'.[4] Alternatively, they might be reconciled through a division of labour, or what I call parallel linkage. To illustrate these concepts, we can consider the development of the Asia–Pacific Economic Co-operation grouping (APEC) in 1989 and its relationship to the General Agreement on Tariffs and Trade (GATT). APEC's founding members were extremely worried about undermining the GATT, and sought to reconcile these two institutions by focusing on the notion of 'open regionalism'. APEC members saw this as a better alternative to using Article 24 of the GATT to justify this accord, a provision that permits the formation of free trade areas and customs unions. Although the interpretation of 'open regionalism' continues to be contested, the idea behind this concept was that while the members of APEC would seek to reduce barriers to goods and services among themselves, they would do so in a GATT-consistent manner.[5]

An alternative mode of reconciling institutions would be simply to create 'parallel' institutions that deal with separate but related activities – as exemplified by the GATT and Bretton Woods monetary system. In creating institutions for the post–Second World War era, policy-makers were concerned about a return to the 1930s era of competitive devaluations, marked by an inward turn among states and the use of protectionist measures. As a consequence, they focused on creating institutions that would help to encourage trade liberalization. By promoting fixed exchange rates through the International Monetary Fund (IMF) and liberalization of trade through the GATT (following the failure of the International Trade Organization (ITO)), policy-makers hoped that this parallel institutional division of labour would lead to freer trade. In the European context, one can see the development of the European Economic Coal and Steel Community and the Western European Union (WEU) as parallel organizations. The first was oriented towards strengthening European co-operation in economic matters (with, of course, important security implications), while the WEU sought to develop a co-ordinated European defence effort.

In the NATO context, what do these types of institutional reconciliation imply? A number of institutions, besides NATO, play a role in the European arena. These include the WEU, the Organization for Security and Co-operation in Europe (OSCE), the EU, and most recently, the United Nations High Commission for Refugees (UNHCR) in coping with refugee problems in Kosovo. In addition, in the Bosnian crisis, the UN was involved in security discussions in the region. Thus, parallel institutions would imply a division of labour and little overlap in the role of these organizations. By contrast, a nesting arrangement might lead to overlapping functions, but in the context of a clear ordering of institutional roles and mandates that did not divide simply along narrow functional lines.

To facilitate an exploration of the issues of expansion of NATO and institutional reconciliation, it is useful to array these dimensions as in Figure 1 and consider various options that NATO members might pursue as they make efforts to change NATO.

FIGURE 1

WHITHER NATO?

HOW TO CHANGE NATO?

	NO CHANGE	WIDEN	MISSION CHANGE	WIDEN AND CHANGE MISSION
PARALLEL *HOW TO RECONCILE INSTITUTIONS?*	Status Quo Ante (Division of labour among NATO, EU, OSCE, WEU) **(A)**	Incorporate new members without task expansion (How many members to add and when?) **(C)**	Develop new tasks (Intervene in regional conflicts, manage ethnic conflicts) **(E)**	Incorporate new members with task expansion (Stabilize new members in addition to other tasks?) **(G)**
NESTED	Restructure relationships among institutions (What ordering among institutions?) **(B)**	New members and reorder relationships among institutions **(D)**	Develop new tasks and agreement on institutional ordering **(F)**	Incorporate new members with task expansion and reorder institutions **(H)**

THE PUZZLES:
(1) Why change policy?
(2) Which cell should one move to?

The combination of these two ideas gives us a first cut into where NATO stood before the decision to widen. Cell A shows the *status quo ante*, before the decision to widen was made, and points to a division of labour among several institutions with mandates in Europe. Cell B indicates the possibility of restructuring relationships among institutions (say OSCE and NATO, for example) without being accompanied by any widening or change in tasks. The next two cells, C and D, consider the prospects for widening, with D also indicating that institutions would be restructured. Turning next to E and F, the first case reflects an agreement among NATO members for the organization to pursue a range of new tasks, not previously central to the institutional mission. If such a change took place, as in cell F, we would see such task changes and/or expansion accompanied by new institutional ordering. Finally, cells G and H point to a very significant transformation of NATO with new members and task expansion in the first case, and an additional reordering of institutions in the latter.

We can now consider two questions. First, what impetus was there to change policy, that is, to move away from the *status quo* as indicated in cell A? Second, what cell was this policy likely to move to? For a better understanding of the actual outcomes, it is of course essential to consider why other possible outcomes were not chosen. Each of the cells that are depicted in Figure 1 can actually be seen as the result of several different bargaining games, even though they are combined in this figure. Thus, the question of NATO widening can be seen as a game primarily between the US and Russia, with key input from existing NATO allies and pressure from eastern European countries to join. The issue of NATO task expansion primarily involves the NATO members. And the question of restructuring institutions, while primarily a NATO issue, also crucially concerned the Russians and the OSCE. Finally, the interaction of the different games is also something that influences the outcome of any single game.

Given the complexity of the multiple players and games involved in the question of NATO expansion, it is not a simple matter to depict the bargaining process in each game. However, to shed light on some of these processes, it is useful to consider the notion of institutional bargaining games as a schematic to derive insight into the bargaining process. It is to these tasks that we now turn.

INSTITUTIONAL BARGAINING GAMES FOR NATO EXPANSION

To understand how NATO might be transformed, we can use the theoretical arguments that I have developed in *Institutional Designs for a Complex World.*[6] We can first consider the nature of an impetus that challenges the *status quo*. The result is to set in motion one or more bargaining games constituted by elements consisting of goods and externalities, actors' individual situations, and institutions. Together, these factors can be combined to yield bargaining games with pay-offs for different actors. Figure 2 depicts the elements of the initial NATO bargaining games set in motion by the initial impetus of the end of the Cold War.

FIGURE 2

NATO INSTITUTIONAL BARGAINING GAMES

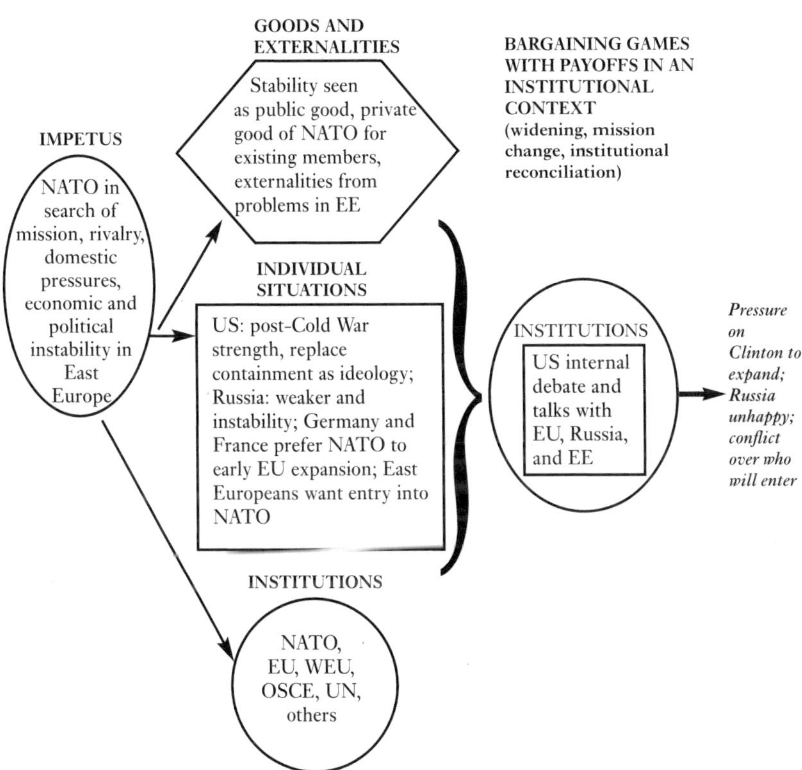

In general, an initial impetus significantly alters the pre-existing bargaining context. Examples include the oil shock of 1973, the breakdown of the Bretton Woods system in 1971, and as, noted, the end of the Cold War following the collapse of the Soviet Union. In the NATO case, the end of the Cold War led to several significant changes for NATO. First, and most obviously, NATO found itself in search of a new mission. As the former Soviet Union began to weaken, NATO's *raison d'être* came to be questioned. What mission should the institution pursue – if not containment of the former Soviet Union successor states? Second, as eastern Europe began to undergo a dramatic transformation, the question of what countries and what institutions would take the lead in bearing the cost of stabilizing these newly changing states came to be an issue that was hotly contested by NATO and the EU. Much debate occurred over whether the EU should rapidly expand eastward, tying these countries economically into the union, or whether NATO should take the lead. Third, ethnic pressures to widen NATO emanated from groups in the United States with ties to their former homelands, thus enmeshing an electoral logic with the future of NATO.

The result of these pressures affected three elements, leading to bargaining games over the future of NATO. The first of these factors, goods and externalities, strongly influenced the bargaining games. Different types of goods were involved in this case. Stability in eastern Europe and the region more generally can be seen as a public good from which all could benefit. At the same time, NATO itself could be seen as a private good that benefited its members, allowing for exclusion and little jointness. Put differently, extending NATO to include other states could diminish the good of security for its members. And finally, both economic and political problems in eastern Europe can be seen as leading to externalities such as economic disruption, immigration flows, and other effects that would potentially damage NATO member states – and possibly the EU member states and the stability of the EU itself.

For a better understanding of the implications of this basic characterization of the 'type of goods' involved in an issue area, we also need to consider the effects of actors' individual situations and the institutional context within which interaction takes place. In other words, knowing the types of goods gives us only a first cut into understanding the nature of problems that actors face and their incentives. Knowledge of the types of goods involved in the bargaining does not by itself allow us adequately to determine specific pay-offs of games because the position of national actors or the institutional setting may alter the bargaining problem. In NATO's case, different countries had varying interests stemming from their individual situations as defined by their (1) international position (both issue specific and overall capabilities); (2) domestic coalitional stability; and (3) elite beliefs and ideologies. While the logic of the choice of these factors is discussed elsewhere,[7] here we can focus on a rough description of the positions of some key actors, namely the US, Russia, Germany and France.

The US emerged as the clearly dominant power in the region and internationally with the collapse of its arch rival, the Soviet Union. Thus, at the overall level, and specifically in the region, the US assumed an unchallenged position in the system. Domestically, as noted above, considerable dispute over whether to expand NATO or not ensued as a result of differing perceptions of strategic interests and the electoral concerns faced by the Clinton administration. And at the ideological level, the question of what type of global strategy would come to replace containment has become an issue of significant dispute. Russia emerged as the key successor state to the Soviet Union in dramatically weakened shape, both economically and militarily. In addition, domestic instability continued to plague Russia, with the rise of a host of competing political interests and extremist groups. Germany and France were eager to see NATO take on the role of stabilizing eastern Europe, rather than placing this burden on the European Community (EC). As the EC struggled to move forward with its own deepening, a result of the Maastricht Treaty (1992), these states saw NATO expansion as a ready substitute in the short run for EC (and now EU) widening. Finally, eastern European countries were for the most part eager to join NATO – both as a security guarantee and as possibly facilitating their integration into the EU.

THE INSTITUTIONAL CONTEXT

As states attempt to secure their preferred outcomes, they will interact strategically, possibly in the context of one or more institutions. Institutions will influence how actors interact, and may either provide focal point solutions for co-ordination games or help states to overcome collective action problems.[8] Institutions are also likely to have important distributive consequences, and may influence actors' bargaining behaviour by tying the hands of both other international and domestic actors.[9] In the case of NATO expansion, several institutions can be considered as possibly influencing the nature of the bargaining. For example, the EU, as already discussed, could potentially serve to stabilize eastern Europe and promote democracy in the region. Indeed, several US analysts and senators have argued that the EU should take the lead on expansion, rather than NATO. Similarly, the OSCE, which already involves 55 states including Russia, could possibly work to enhance security in the region. The OSCE has concerned itself with democratic institutions, minority rights, and various types of confidence-building measures that might allow it to play some of the roles sought for NATO through its widening. At the same time, the lack of military recourses and the participation of such a large number of members had hindered the institution's effectiveness in accomplishing some of the goals sought through NATO expansion. The WEU, the presumptive defence arm of the European Union, provides another institutional structure within which some of the goals of stabilizing security in eastern Europe might take place. With the notion of Combined Joint Task Forces (CJTFs) that would involve NATO and the WEU, the possibility of some division of labour with NATO has also been raised. Finally, the United Nations has some potential impact on security in the region, although its performance in the Bosnian crisis did not suggest that this institution could displace NATO.

NATO BARGAINING GAMES

We can now attempt to combine the three elements of goods, individual situations, and institutions to gain insight into different types of institutional bargaining games. Understanding how such games are constituted will also give us insight into the strategies that actors might subsequently pursue in an attempt to change the games in which they find themselves. It is worth noting that an exact *a priori* specification of the effect of the three elements on game pay-offs is a difficult if not impossible task. Thus, we can only indicate the general contours of the resulting games and likely outcomes. As suggested in Figure 2, the resulting bargaining games over NATO expansion consist of several key national actors (the US, Russia, Germany, France and eastern European states) as well as pressures from institutions.

Let us begin with the game of widening, referring to Figure 1 on the possible choices. In this game, we can consider three possible outcomes:

continuing with the *status quo*, limited widening, and significant widening. In the strategic interaction between the US and Russia, as well as the other players, a key issue would be the extent of opposition to widening by Russia and the demand for widening in the US. Russia did not readily perceive that NATO and its further expansion would provide a public good from which it and other states would benefit. Instead, the good was quite clearly seen as a private one, with benefits accruing only to members. Turning to the individual situations of countries, in view of domestic pressure in the US to widen, and the strong post-Cold War position of the US, the pay-offs from limited widening could be relatively high for the Clinton administration. In the initial stages of the US domestic bargaining game (not analysed here)[10] the debate centred around possible use of informal co-operation between NATO and the militaries of eastern European states: the Partnership for Peace (PFP) as a mode of conciliating pressures for widening. This *status quo* position was acceptable to most in Washington, DC in the initial stages. But as domestic pressures grew and Clinton himself became more committed to widening, PFP began to recede as an option and limited widening became the US policy objective. The key issue affecting the US pay-off from such widening was of course the extent to which the Russians would oppose this action, as well as the contribution that the Europeans would make both financially and in terms of permitting early EU accession by east European states. For the Russians, no NATO expansion would be best, with the gradual erosion of NATO itself being optimal (see the discussion below on changing tasks and rearranging institutions). But in view of Russia's relatively weak position, any concessions in other arenas as well as the most circumscribed expansion would be a fall-back position. For France and Germany, expansion of NATO without financial commitment or a promise of EU aid or expansion would provide an optimal outcome.

Turning to NATO's mission scope, there was considerable agreement by all parties that the creation of many new roles for NATO was not an option. Indeed for the Russians, a 'shallowing' of NATO and displacement to other tasks would diminish the perceived threat that Russia faced. But again, given Russia's relatively weak position, this was hard for the Russians to promote. For the US and others, changing NATO's mandate or expanding it would not suit any major internal coalition's interest and thus proved to be ruled out.

Finally, with respect to institutional restructuring, the US could possibly allow some other institution to take on a key security role. Given the problems in the UN, the leading contenders could be a restructuring and nesting of NATO within OSCE or NATO–WEU operations under joint US–EU arrangements. But for the US military, and many other interests backing this view, such a change would be anathema, as it would place US soldiers under joint leadership or simply lead to a cumbersome decision-making process as in the OSCE. This was even recognized clearly by others. In NATO's mission in Kosovo, for example, the French Ministry of Defence complained that General Wesley K. Clark was 'responsible not only to the North Atlantic Council but also to his national hierarchy, at the highest level'.[11] For the Russians, a shift of security considerations to the OSCE would be optimal, as it would then have a more significant voice and undercut US dominance through the NATO process. For France and Germany, a greater voice in NATO and use of NATO troops by the WEU would suit their interests. In short, the very low pay-offs for the US in view of its individual situation would rule out significant institutional restructuring.

In view of the outcomes of these individual games, such polar combinations as simultaneous widening, task changes, and institutional restructuring were beyond the pale, particularly for the US. For Russia, ideal changes could involve dominance by the OSCE with institutional shallowing and little widening. And for France and Germany, in view of their inability to secure significant control over NATO through an EU–WEU process, the outcome of widening looked appealing.

In light of these strategic considerations and constraints, the pay-offs in the key widening game would be highest for the Clinton administration with limited widening, no change in mission, and some possible co-ordination with the WEU to transfer some of the possible military burden to the EU (possibility 'C' in Figure 1). But given that Russian opposition would reduce the US pay-off significantly, the next question was: how might the widening game be managed to ensure high pay-offs for the US? It is to this question that we now turn.

ALTERING THE NATO EXPANSION GAME

When will actors make efforts to promote game change? Logically, they consider their existing pay-offs in the current bargaining game and compare these with their projected pay-offs from instituting some form of game change. To make this calculation, states evaluate their ability to secure more favourable outcomes by assessing their own power resources in light of their own individual situation and that of their opponent(s). The relevant power resources that they might use include material capabilities, either issue specific or overall, an appeal to like-minded allies, and institutions as a power resource.[12]

Figure 3 identifies the choices that actors might make in the NATO bargaining game in an effort to improve their pay-offs.

FIGURE 3

THE NATO EXPANSION GAME

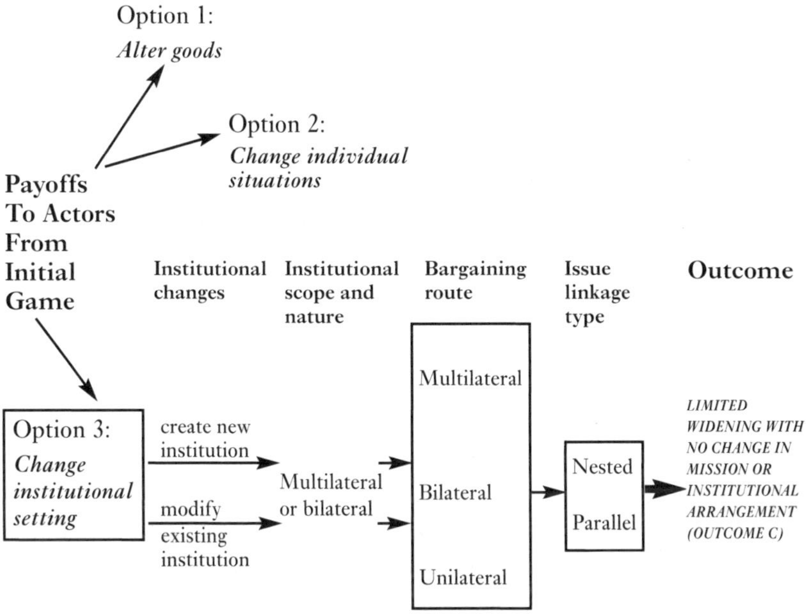

As this figure illustrates, actors have three options. First, they can attempt directly to *manipulate the types of goods* involved in negotiations. An example of this would be the formation of an alliance that excludes other actors. Second, they can *alter either their own or their opponent(s')* *individual situations*. These could include such efforts as overthrowing governments, building up one's own capabilities in specific issue areas, or attempting to change the views of decision-makers in other countries. Third, they can *change the institutional context* within which actors are operating. If actors choose to pursue an institutional strategy to alter games and influence bargaining outcomes, actors seeking to make game changes must make several additional decisions. Specifically, they must: (1) decide if they would be better off by creating a new institution or modifying the existing one(s); (2) choose the characteristics of the institution that they want (and specifically, for our interests, the institutional scope); (3) select the bargaining route they want to follow; and (4) decide whether to engage in issue linkages, and, if so, the type and nature of these connections.

Altering Goods

In the case of the NATO expansion game, the US pursued a multi-pronged strategy to ensure that it would receive high pay-offs by reducing Russian opposition to NATO expansion. Turning first to the nature of good, the US attempted to give the Russians some access to the private good of the NATO alliance while also emphasizing the public good aspects of the alliance. By brokering a bilateral US–Russia arrangement under the US Partnership for Peace programme (June 1994), the US allowed the Russians to save face by avoiding direct Russian subordination to the NATO alliance. Under the terms of this agreement, the Russian military voluntarily participates in expensive, multinational war games and other high-level strategic response teams. Although Russian participation in the PFP has fluctuated dramatically – even freezing its commitment in January 1995, it has generally agreed to the terms of this agreement albeit in protest to further NATO expansion. The later NATO–Russia agreement reflects the coexistence of the US–PFP agreement with the US explicitly stating that the primary purpose of NATO expansion is for it to become the basis for a more comprehensive security co-operation programme for all.

Changing Individual Situations

In order to make a NATO–Russia agreement more palatable to both domestic audiences and other NATO members, US policy efforts were directed at bolstering eastern European transitional democracies. In addition, the Clinton administration intended to build upon the warm, personal relationship established with President Boris Yeltsin by not pursuing NATO expansion ratification until after domestic elections.[13] In this connection, the Joint NATO–Russia Council formation at the end of May 1997 was designed to recognize Russia's special status in the region. In Brzezinski's words, the council is an 'acknowledgement of Russia's role as a regional power; and that it is entitled to be NATO's partner – though not a member – regarding common security issues'.[14]

In an effort to decrease Russian opposition domestically to NATO widening as well as diminish US opposition by signalling a co-operative relationship with Russia, the US helped pave the way for Russian inclusion in other Western-dominated international political institutions. In this connection, President Clinton and other G-7 members offered to facilitate Russia's entrance into this exclusive group at the Helsinki summit in March 1997. As a result, the G-8 held in Denver in June 1997 was generally interpreted as G-7 concern at softening the diplomatic impact of the recent accord over NATO expansion. Despite its continuing territorial dispute over the Kurile Islands, even Japan abandoned its lone position of Russian G-7 exclusion. Similarly, the US continued discussions with Yeltsin to shore up continued support for economic development while simultaneously securing the inclusion of Russia into the APEC grouping. Following the US lead, Japan has also agreed to intensified economic co-operation in six fields while actively supporting Russia's entry into both the APEC and World Trade Organization (WTO) processes. As a result, Russia became one of the newest members in 1998 (following a 1997 decision to admit it). Because of the special role that the US played in getting Russia into APEC, some analysts from smaller members have criticized the potential 'all-powerful politburo' that Washington is creating in consolidating Moscow's position in all global political structures.[15]

Changing Institutional Settings

In attempting to decrease Russian opposition to NATO widening, in addition to efforts of altering goods and individual situations, the US also promoted the development of a new 'institution' and the modification of NATO itself. We turn first to an examination of NATO–Russian relations.

Creating a New Institution?: The Founding Act on Relations between NATO and Russia of May 1997 can be seen as the creation of a new institution with connections to NATO expansion. This bilateral agreement between NATO and Russia followed intense bilateral and multilateral bargaining. A key question remains as to what the relationship between a newly widened NATO and this new arrangement will be, an issue that we will examine below.

Modifying Existing Institutions: Turning now to modification of existing institutions in the context of changing the institutional setting, a key question concerned the scope of NATO expansion and the nature. With respect to scope, NATO could have chosen to modify membership in a broader fashion and responded to European pressure to include Romania and Slovenia. Although Romanian foreign policy has dramatically changed since 1996, its efforts at rapprochement with Hungary and the treaty with Ukraine in June 1997 were not enough to persuade the US to include it in the first round of expansion. Citing a February 1997 Pentagon report, a disappointed Senator Roth, who chairs the North Atlantic Assembly (the alliance's parliamentary arm), stated that 'cost is the biggest factor in Congressman's minds ... three is easier to do than five because smaller is cheaper'.[16] Certainly, estimates of enlargement costs have ranged from the NATO Secretariat's $5 billion to the Pentagon's $35 billion in 2009 to the US Congressional Budget Office's $125 billion. Despite French, Italian and German support, the uncertainty over the costs has not helped win the support of Washington. Especially since both France and Britain are on record as saying that the additional cost of enlargement should be zero, Clinton has made it clear that the new NATO members would have to assume most of the costs themselves.[17]

With respect to NATO's nature, there was little consensus on a new mission for NATO. Indeed, the Clinton administration's promotion of widening as supporting democracy and peacekeeping was strongly opposed by such senators as Jesse Helms, who viewed this task expansion as likely to undermine NATO's traditional central mission to defend the territorial integrity of its members. Thus, while such widening could be sold domestically as a positive development in NATO, particularly to liberals, it simultaneously raised the danger of opposition from conservatives. Moreover, new missions could also entail new costs. In the end, then, with little cognitive consensus or political agreement on new roles for NATO, task expansion was kept off the agenda.

The bargaining route to NATO widening involved both multilateral discussions with allies as well as bilateral bargaining with individual European states and Russia. Although the US could resist excessive expansion of NATO (from its perspective), participation by allies on this issue was obviously essential.

Linkages Among Institutions: The question of institutional linkages is particularly significant. Could institutions such as the EU, WEU, OSCE, UN, and others somehow be arranged in nested fashion? In the end, it was quite clear, given the concerns about changing missions for NATO, that nesting would not be feasible politically, either domestically or internationally. For example, the Combined Joint Task Forces idea that would entail co-operation between the WEU and NATO raised significant questions about how the US would react to involvement of NATO troops in missions that were not endorsed by NATO itself. And the notion of NATO somehow being incorporated into OSCE activities raised concerns once again of undermining NATO's traditional mission of territorial defence.

With respect to the NATO–Russia agreement, some NATO expansionists fear that this arrangement could give Russia an unprecedented role in diverting internal decision-making processes of the central North Atlantic Council (NAC). If Russia were skilfully to use the consultation mechanisms, it could supplant the NAC, giving Russia a voice within the alliance without meeting the demanding obligations of membership. But it is more likely that such heavy-handed Russian efforts will be met with fierce resistance and Russian attempts to subvert NATO ratification decisions to expand will result in loss of Joint Council political influence. On the other hand, Russia's co-operative presence with the stabilization force (SFOR) in Bosnia under NATO command has already established the precedent of Russia as a *de facto* associate with greater formal access to NATO decision-making processes. The outcomes are likely to be dependent on how substantive or tactical the particular leaders choose to interpret the link behind the creation of the council.[18] Either way, the council creates a new institutional framework within which decisions will be made.

Furthermore, it is the tactical aspects of the link which are much more explicit. In exchange for Russian recognition of an enlarged Euro-Atlantic alliance and US presence, the US and the West agree that Russia must have some special status and recognition in such regional decision-making in their own backyard. The NATO–Russia Founding Act states explicitly that NATO has and will continue to expand its political functions. In the agreed text, there are explicit references to 'new members' and the enlargement of Euro-Atlantic security 'space'. For Russia, this represents a significant break with the post-1945 policy of eliminating the US presence in Europe. For the West, this represents a significant policy shift from the original NATO purpose of keeping the Russians out, the Americans in and the Germans down.

At the same time, the agreement provides that further NATO expansion will be based on the principle of the inherent right of all states to choose the means to ensure their own security, while recognizing Russia's past status as a regional power with special interests in central Europe. Finally, diplomats have stressed the fact that this agreement is not a legally binding treaty that requires formal ratification. Thus, although the council expands the co-operative security agenda to increase consultations regarding conflict prevention, military doctrine, arms control, nuclear safety, counter-proliferation and even theatre missile defences, it has no real teeth.

CONCLUSION

This paper has sought to present an institutional bargaining game approach to analyse NATO expansion. I suggested that the decision to expand NATO must be understood in a broader context that includes the issue of task changes for NATO as well as possible rearrangement and restructuring of relationships among institutions. The key analytical question addressed here is why a movement from the *status quo* to limited widening proved to be the outcome – rather than the several other options that could have been pursued.

To analyse the questions of policy change and the particular choice, I drew upon work on institutional bargaining games. I showed how the initial impetus of the end of the Cold War set in motion a search for a new mission for NATO and how concerns about eastern European stability led to a bargaining game over NATO expansion. In considering the elements that define the basis of the bargaining game, I focused on the types of goods and externalities involved as a result of this initial impetus, as well as the individual situations of key actors in the game and the institutional context within which the game evolved. The pay-offs for the US of the resulting game of widening depended greatly on how Russia would react to this action. As a result, we considered the strategy pursued by the Clinton administration to alter the goods involved, change Russia's individual situation, and modify institutions – all with the objective of increasing its pay-offs by decreasing Russian opposition and securing domestic US support. In the end, limited NATO widening, without changes in NATO's basic mission or relationship to other international institutions, proved to be the most plausible outcome.

The outcome we have seen of NATO widening, the NATO–Russia Joint Council and the parallel linkages of Russia's inclusion in APEC and other international institutions are better understood together than apart. As the results of the institutional bargaining game analysis indicated, the *status quo* was better than expansion. Yet given entrenched interests, the availability of parallel institutional linkages, and the efforts to alter the nature of the game with the existence of multiple stable substantive and tactical institutional outcomes, limited expansion should not prove to be a disaster.

While this outcome appears stable in the short run, limited widening is not without its costs. Such an action has simply postponed the broader question of the expanded political role of NATO, the relationship of NATO to other organizations, and other crucial questions in post-Cold War Europe. How NATO will evolve in the future is thus an ongoing question – rather than one that has been settled.

NOTES

1. I would like to thank Trevor Nakagawa for his research assistance. Discussions with Beverly Crawford, Elizabeth Kier and Daniel Verdier were invaluable. Comments from two anonymous referees were very helpful in revising the paper.
2. For a discussion of this approach, see Vinod K. Aggarwal (ed.), *Institutional Designs for a Complex World: Bargaining, Linkages and Nesting* (Ithaca: Cornell University Press, 1998).
3. John Gerard Ruggie, 'Consolidating the European Pillar: The Key to NATO's Future', *Washington Quarterly*, Vol.20, No.1 (Winter 1997), pp.109–25.
4. Aggarwal, *Institutional Designs for a Complex World*, pp.5–7.
5. For a discussion of APEC's fit with GATT, see Vinod K. Aggarwal, 'Analyzing Institutional Transformation in the Asia–Pacific', in Vinod K. Aggarwal and Charles Morrison (eds.), *Asia–Pacific Crossroads: Regime Creation and the Future of APEC* (New York: St Martin's Press, 1998), pp.23–64.
6. Aggarwal, *Institutional Designs for a Complex World*, Chapter 1.
7. Aggarwal, *Institutional Designs for a Complex World*, Chapter 1.
8. See Art Stein, 'Coordination and Collaboration: Regimes in an Anarchic World', in Stephen Krasner (ed.), *International Regimes* (Ithaca: Cornell University Press, 1983), pp.115–40; Duncan Snidal, 'Coordination versus Prisoners' Dilemma: Implications for International Cooperation and Regimes', *American Political Science Review*, Vol.79, No.4 (Dec. 1985), pp.923–42; Robert Axelrod and Robert Keohane, 'Achieving Cooperation under Anarchy: Strategies and Institutions', *World Politics*, Vol.38, No.1 (Oct. 1985), pp.226–54; and Lisa Martin, 'Interest, Power, and Multilateralism', *International Organization*, Vol.46, No.4 (Autumn 1992), pp.765–92, among others.
9. See Vinod K. Aggarwal, *Liberal Protectionism: The International Politics of Organized Textile*

Trade (Berkeley and London: University of California Press, 1985); and see below on the use of institutions to control other actors. For additional discussions, see Stephen Krasner, 'Global Communications and National Power: Life on the Pareto Frontier', *World Politics*, Vol.43, No.3 (April 1991), pp.336–66; and Jack Knight, *Institutions and Social Conflict* (Cambridge: Cambridge University Press, 1992).

10. See James M. Goldgeier, 'US Security Policy toward the New Europe: How the Decision to Expand NATO Was Made' (paper presented to the American Political Science Association, Washington, DC, Aug. 1998), for an excellent discussion of how the US decided to shift from promotion of the PFP to actual widening of NATO.

11. *New York Times*, 11 Nov. 1999, Section A, p.6.

12. For a discussion of use of these power resources in different bargaining situations, see Vinod K. Aggarwal and Pierre Allan, 'Evolution in Bargaining Theories: Toward an Integrated Approach to Explain Strategies of the Weak' (paper presented to the American Political Science Association, Chicago, Sept. 1983), and Vinod K. Aggarwal, *Debt Games: Strategic Interaction in International Debt Rescheduling* (New York: Cambridge University Press, 1996). From a neorealist perspective, Kenneth N. Waltz, *Theory of International Politics* (Reading, MA: Addison-Wesley, 1979) discusses the options of self-help and appeals to alliances as options for states.

13. See Goldgeier (1998), p.18.

14. *Financial Times*, 27 May 1997, p.20.

15. *Russian Press Digest*, 27 Nov. 1997, Document 17.

16. *Financial Times*, 28 May 1997, p.2.

17. *New York Times*, 10 July 1997, Section A, p.14.

18. See Ernst Haas, 'Why Collaborate? Issue-linkage and International Regimes', *World Politics*, Vol.32, No.3 (April 1980), pp.357–405 for a discussion of tactical and substantive linkages in this context, and Aggarwal, *Institutional Designs for a Complex World*.

Organization Theory: Remedy for Europe's Organizational Cacophony?

ERNST B. HAAS

SOME ORGANIZATION THEORIES APPLIED TO INTERNATIONAL ORGANIZATIONS

The eastward expansion of the North Atlantic Treaty Organization (NATO), apart from unloosening a spirited debate about the American national interest in Europe's future, also gives organization theorists an opportunity to show off their wares. I was asked to pick some themes pioneered by Berkeley theorists to illuminate the display.

I begin with a warning. Organization theories that apply to public international organizations like NATO, the European Union (EU), or the Organization for Security and Co-operation in Europe (OSCE) are different from the organization theories taught in schools of management. They deal with entities that have no bottom line, no private clients, no customers, and no employees lacking security of employment. They are entities formed by governments to serve the sets of purposes jointly (but not necessarily evenly) entertained by the founders. They are able to evolve beyond the objectives of their founders, to acquire new (or fewer) tasks, more (or less) authority, and gain (or lose) legitimacy in the eyes of their member states. In the case of NATO we might wish to think about whether the eastward expansion implies gains or losses for the organization, and for other organizations in Europe with which it competes.

Three theses derived from different theories tend to predict that all European organizations concerned directly or indirectly with security will gain in both authority and legitimacy. Redundancy theory predicts that efficiency in the attainment of some common objective (for example, more regional security) is best attained by having several organizations attempt to achieve the same outcome. If one fails, the others will take up the slack. Having more than one organization dedicated to doing the same job is a kind of insurance policy. So what if NATO and the OSCE have identical objectives and overlapping memberships, asks the redundancy theorist.[1]

The theory of hierarchical nesting holds that effective goal-attainment is maximized if several organizations with related and overlapping mandates are arranged in a hierarchical, or pyramidal, order. All will work towards the same or similar and closely linked objectives. They will not undo each other's work because all of them serve the same norms. The 'top' organization incorporates and interprets the norms. Instead of having a set of competing organizations, this theory sees them as parts of a single harmonious regime. This would be the case in Europe if the OSCE, as the broadest of the existing organizations, defined the regime's norms and 'deputizes' NATO, the EU, the Western European Union (WEU) or the Council of Europe (CE) to carry out specific tasks that flow from the norms.

Cognitive nesting theory proposes a different principle of order. It suggests that commonly perceived problems are more likely to be solved to everyone's satisfaction, at least for a while, if the actors succeed in 'nesting' their beliefs about causality in a consensual hierarchy of ideas. Solving the problem of security, for instance, might take the form of a theory of mutual deterrence that finds a common denominator for the separate national security interests of the participating states, that sees a cause of insecurity not in the 'other's' presumed *animus belligerendi*, but in mutual suspicion; and thus the members define regional security as everybody reassuring everybody else by means of confidence-building measures, not military preparations. Cognitive nesting is facilitated by the existence of transnational groups of experts who help political leaders arrive at a consensus.

The critical reader may immediately suspect several large rats. Do these theories really explain or justify the eastward expansion of NATO? There certainly is a lot of redundancy now between the tasks of the OSCE, NATO, the EU, the CE, and the WEU, but that redundancy does not explain its own perpetuation. Other words for redundancy are confusion, overlap and competition. Who needs them? Hierarchical nesting can work only if there is a strong interstate consensus on the need for, and the actual existence of, a 'security regime' in which all organizations have a discrete part to play and where the norms are crisp and clear. Bosnians and Kosovo Albanians are witnesses to the elusiveness of the consensual norms.

Cognitive nesting, in turn, depends on the existence of an epistemic community of security experts whose claims to knowledge carry the warrant of a science and who have enormous influence over political leaders. There is no such community. These organization theories do not explain why NATO has expanded and might expand further. They certainly do not justify expansion. What does?

WHY HAS NATO EXPANDED EASTWARD?

The public explanation for Poland, Hungary and the Czech Republic joining NATO is that membership will create democratic and free market stability in eastern Europe, though it is far from clear why this should be so. A less publicly avowed reason is the continuing fear of Russia entertained by these new members, no matter how irrational. A final reason often heard is that these three want to be 'a part of Europe' after languishing for 45 years in someone else's embrace. They really want to join the EU, but as they do not now qualify they chose NATO as the club with fewer conditions for membership. And whatever the reason, the three had a powerful ally in the US Congress.

Even if all of these reasons correctly explain the desire of the three new member states, that does not tell us why the alliance, and especially its leader, acquiesced so enthusiastically. Germany clearly had an interest in pushing Europe's military border as far east as possible. The US had a real interest in shoring up democracy in the east and in creating a favourable setting for free-market capitalism. Some members of Congress and other 'triumphalists' no doubt saw in an expanded NATO a confirmation of the West's victory over communism and a cementing of its gains.

I suspect, however, that most if not all of these objectives could be achieved by relying on a strengthened OSCE, which would have the additional advantage of not alienating a Russia that is also seeking to democratize and convert to capitalism (particularly if the next batch of countries seeking to 'join Europe' are the Baltics and Ukraine).

I suspect that the main reason for the choice of NATO as the redundant guarantor has to do with America's self-perception as the global hegemon. Statement after statement from Washington suggests that American leaders, whether declared triumphalists or not, see the US as the anointed agent of global progress, the leader who will ensure peace, prosperity and democracy for all. Washington seems to believe in an historical role for this country which justifies diplomacy, sermons and sanctions designed to persuade, cajole and, if necessary, compel others to see matters as Washington does. The hegemon's role is that of moral exemplar and practical enforcer of the American recipe for progress and happiness. America, for all its faults, is still seen as that city on a hill dear to the rhetoric of eighteenth-century New England divines.

NATO is America's instrument for asserting military hegemony in Europe as long as Europeans seem happy to have the US assume the burden of defending them. With the end of the Cold War, NATO was in imminent danger of losing its reason for being. Giving it the new mandate of ensuring democratic stability in eastern Europe, through 'out-of-area' operations and expanded membership, provides a new lease of life for NATO – and for America's continued hegemonic role in Europe. Conversely, American willingness to enlarge NATO's mandate continues to limit the Europeans' incentives to provide for their own defence and for the protection of their newly democratic neighbours.

DOUBTS ABOUT THE EVOLUTION OF A HARMONIOUS SECURITY REGIME

Even if the three theoretical postulates I mentioned do not explain or justify NATO expansion, there are other insights derivable from organization theory which suggest that NATO's new mandate will not improve regional security in Europe. In fact, it may worsen it because of the continued cacophony of organizational missions and commitments.[2]

The consensus on NATO's new mission is shaky. So far the only 'out-of-area' missions are the Bosnian operation mandated by the Dayton agreement and the air war against Serbia, followed by the occupation of Kosovo. Their earlier consensus on the use of NATO forces against Iraq is eroding. Despite an apparent willingness to act as the agent of the United Nations in Kosovo (consistent with hierarchical nesting), episode-by-episode approval is necessary and the unanimity rule governs decision-making in the NATO Council.

The Bosnian operation, compared to previous UN peacekeeping efforts and UN-authorized NATO bombing missions, is certainly a big success. Nevertheless, it is hazardous to project this success into the future. Norms governing such operations have not been generalized. They are still being negotiated as the operation proceeds from disarming combatants to arresting war criminals, promoting the return of refugees to their former properties, and supporting one set of politicians over another. Similar uncertainties dog the Kosovo occupation. It is not to be expected that member states will readily agree on general norms, especially if their enforcement entails casualties.

In any event, these success stories do not validate our three theories of organization. The redundancy principle is not validated. NATO took over from the UN and the WEU, not because these organizations failed, but because the US changed its policy towards Bosnia from disengagement to active commitment and wanted to implement that commitment via NATO. There was no hierarchical nesting. Authority was established by an *ad hoc* concert of the states most interested in a settlement, acting outside any previously established organizational context. Cognitive nesting was fragmented at best. The main intervening states, by the time of Dayton, seemingly subscribed to a consensual scheme of causality for re-establishing and consolidating peace. However, the main local forces never accepted that scheme as theirs and have tried to circumvent it as best they could in Bosnia and Kosovo.

MY PREFERRED ORGANIZATIONAL SOLUTION, UNJUSTIFIED BY THEORY

I would like to persuade America to stop playing a global hegemonic role, to act instead as one powerful and influential country among many. The difference between global moral hegemony and arrogance is sometimes hard to detect. Today's daily paper (13 May 1998) features the headline 'Clinton Decides to Punish India' for the nuclear weapons tests announced the day before.

Even though India is not a party to any of the nuclear non-proliferation and underground test ban agreements, she is being 'punished' for not adhering to the policy preferred by Washington. Many countries do not follow these policies; many are often being 'punished', however ineffectively. Is it really the business of the US to 'punish' countries that follow their own national interests?

Multilateral institutions and processes have been created to cope with conflicts among national interests, to resolve such differences by negotiation, by incentives to comply with consensual rules, and − if warranted − by sanctions to enforce them. Insisting on unilateral hegemony, even if camouflaged by means of an alliance agreement or 'partnerships', risks treading the path of hubris. It is my objective to contribute to the socialization of the US into the practices of multilateralism, and eventual American enmeshment in authoritative multilateral institutions. The extension of NATO serves the opposite objective: to perpetuate unilateral hegemony. America must get used to the idea that it is not the sole saviour of humankind, that its national institutions are not the only legitimate ones.

There is also an analytic basis for the institutional formula to ensure European security which I prefer. The cacophony of European institutions is not a harmless indulgence in exuberance for multilateralism any more than it is a response to the design imperatives favouring redundancy. The multiplicity of overlapping organs responds to various national interests that lack full co-ordination: different member states favour different organizations as the preferred vehicles for their multilateralized policies, depending on the momentary perception of interests. For instance, France usually pushes the WEU for missions which otherwise would appear to be overly US-dominated; western Europeans usually prefer a role for the Council of Europe for human rights investigations, whereas eastern Europeans seem to feel more comfortable with the OSCE. In many instances, the toleration of institutional cacophony disguises an unwillingness to do much of anything collectively because it facilitates shuffling the issue among organizations without charging any of them with anything concrete.

How to do better? Who would do what in a truly efficient multilateral security architecture for Europe? The prescription – and preferred outcome – I now present is based upon one core presumption: that the process towards the evolution of a supranationally organized Europe is irreversible. The nation-state as we have historically experienced it in western and central Europe is a thing of the past even though we cannot predict the exact membership of the unified Europe of the future, nor specifically all the competencies and governance structures it will feature. However, we may take for granted that the EU will acquire stronger defence and foreign policy mandates, no matter how much power remains in the hands of member states, no matter how many new mandates are found for regions and transterritorial networks.

NATO will become fully obsolete if and when Europe unites and acquires its own foreign and defence policy. At that point the continued presence of the US in the European security realm becomes a core issue. Until then it can be fudged.

We ought to tolerate the slow disintegration of NATO; let the alliance atrophy from disuse, from lack of an enemy. What about out-of-area operations? Such operations in Europe ought to continue as long as no practical alternatives exist. However, once the capability of the UN for simple peacekeeping tasks – as opposed to the more complex peace-building missions – is re-established, NATO need not concern itself any longer with them.

The natural substitute for NATO in a Europe no longer divided, fearing interstate aggression, is the OSCE. As currently constituted, the organization is too unwieldy; its unanimity-based decision-making rule guarantees a slow response because of the large membership. But its mandate is precisely geared to the core political problems facing Europe: separating mutually incompatible ethnic groups or persuading them to bury their mutual animosities by means of respected and powerful collective conflict resolution institutions that will obviate future Bosnias, Chechnyas and Kosovos. It is the natural entity for a continental collective security task. Probably, a reform would have to result in something like the UN Security Council as the agency to implement collective security, with permanent membership for the largest states. Its powers for peace-building and peaceful conflict resolution ought to be built up, and its nascent ability to deal with conflicts involving national minorities ought to be developed with special care.

The Council of Europe has an admirable record in the multilateral protection of human rights in Europe, by means of fact-finding, conciliation and binding judicial settlement. Its experience ought to be relied upon for the further regionalization of the human rights regime.

That leaves the EU as the core of a larger and more tightly integrated supranational Europe. As presently constituted, the EU has little to contribute to continental security, notwithstanding its current limited peace-building role in Bosnia and Kosovo. A more important role awaits the fuller development of supranational policy-making in the fields of foreign and defence policy. Currently, the European Council and the political secretariat of the EU Council of (Foreign) Ministers function as no more than a permanent conference of member states tied together by a network of lower-level officials in permanent contact. The weakness of institutions is one reason for the lack of a sustained consensual European response to the Balkan crises, though perhaps not the main one.

If and when the logic of Maastricht works itself out in the direction of a single European foreign and defence policy, the EU will become the core of the OSCE, the hegemonic member for every task and purpose of the organization. There will no longer be any need for NATO, no matter how far east it expands. And the US will no longer have a core role to play in European security. The sooner that happens the happier the American public ought to be.

NOTES

1. The classic piece on organizational redundancy is Martin Landau, 'Redundancy, Rationality, and the Problem of Duplication and Overlap', *Public Administration Review* (July–Aug. 1969).
2. Constructivists have demonstrated their ability to apply their ways of thinking to security issues, not just to issues of co-operation. See Peter J. Katzenstein (ed.), *The Culture of National Security* (New York: Columbia University Press, 1996) and Emanuel Adler and Michael Barnett (eds.), *Security Communities* (Cambridge: Cambridge University Press, 1998).

A Modest Proposal for NATO Expansion

STEVEN WEBER

For 40 years, the North Atlantic Treaty Organization (NATO) was the principal answer to almost any question about security in Europe, no matter which side of the Atlantic posed it. The end of the Cold War changed the character of at least some of the questions. It also opened up a set of discussions about new possible answers. Academics, political commentators and others rushed into the fray to promote the idea of reorganizing the institutional architecture of European security. It was a broad debate that raged across the merits and demerits of organizations like the Western European Union (WEU), the Conference on Security and Co-operation in Europe (CSCE) now renamed the Organization on Security and Co-operation in Europe (OSCE), the European Union (EU) and others.

But the debate didn't last very long. Certainly there have been small changes in the competencies of many of these organizations, and the EU is in the process of discussing seriously a step forward towards creating a 'security identity' more meaningful in a practical sense than the WEU. While what happens at the EU in particular is worthy of attention, it is a longer-term proposition. For the first decade after the end of the Cold War and probably for most of the second decade as well, the only question of real practical significance on the political–security agenda will be whether NATO should expand.

There are lessons embedded in that experience. One lesson, at least for many academics, should be modesty about theoretical understandings of security, institutions and the nexus between them. Probably the most logically compelling argument about the future of NATO at the end of the Cold War was made by realists. The argument was simple: states ally against potential threats.[1] When the threat collapses, the alliance goes with it. But this argument is clearly wrong. NATO is healthy. A highly bureaucratized organization has adapted to a new environment by changing some of its missions, reforming force structures, and now taking in new members. And this has not happened in opposition to the interests of the major states who constitute NATO's decision-making power. It has happened because powerful states wanted it to happen.

Why? The answer I propose is simply because the most important determinants of European security in the future remain highly uncertain. If mainstream security theories are still viable, then the future of Russian reform is the most important driving force in European security, and that future is impossible to predict. It may be even harder to predict if Europe in the early twenty-first century will be a continent transformed by monetary integration of at least 11 countries, the Internet, and structural unemployment of around ten per cent of the working population. In that case the uncertainties could be more profound as older theoretical logics dissolve while new driving forces on state behaviour emerge. And those are just some of the obvious things that we are reasonably sure will happen in Europe over the next five years. We can also be reasonably sure that there will be surprises.

Analysts should be quite cautious about using historical analogies or trusting in highly abstract theoretical arguments in this kind of situation. Still, there is very little more than that to rely on when policy decisions need to be made. My plea is simply to reduce the level of confidence in our understanding of the situation, which would have the effect of diminishing the hyperbole and exaggeration that has surrounded NATO expansion. Given what we know, I will argue that this decision, albeit important, is not a decision of historic proportions and is not likely to be a decisive turning point in post-Cold War politics. When historians look back at the last decade of the twentieth century they are unlikely to see NATO expansion as a major watershed.

Much of the political rhetoric is overblown. This unfortunately creates a cycle of self-fulfilling prophecies where a decision comes to be, in a political sense, more important than it is in a purely strategic sense. That is surely a reality that decision-makers must confront. But one of the ways to confront it is to challenge the premise. My alternative premise is that NATO expansion will probably make a modest contribution to things in Europe that the US cares about – security, stability, successful transitions in at least some parts of eastern Europe, and continued cohesion among the Western allies. And it will do that at a moderate cost – to national budgets and more importantly to the Russians. Russia has very little to fear from NATO expansion and might, under certain circumstances, stand to gain a few modest benefits from the process.

OLD PROBLEMS AND NEW PROBLEMS

Institutions exist in part to solve problems that states find difficult to solve on their own. If there were no longer real-world problems that NATO could make a contribution towards managing, the arguments in favour of retaining it would be much weaker. That is not the case, by almost anyone's reckoning. In fact, the 'old' security problems of post-Second World War Europe are not gone. It used to be said that NATO's job was to keep the Russians out, the Americans in, and the Germans down. These issues are surely diminished but they are not solved.

The arguments on this point are straightforward and almost banal. Russia's transition to a peaceful modern state without expansionist ambitions in Europe is not assured. Almost everyone in the West would like to see that transition succeed, but history and common sense tell us that we just don't know the outcome and probably can't put a very precise probability estimate on it. In this context, NATO has been portrayed as an insurance policy. Like all insurance policies, the question then becomes how much does it cost to insure a valued asset, measured against both the magnitude of the possible damage and the likelihood that it might indeed come to pass.

In my view, only two of those three variables are knowable within a decent range of uncertainty. Predicting Russia's future is probably less of a good bet than predicting a major earthquake in San Francisco. What we do know is that both have the potential for catastrophic outcomes. But there is a significant difference between insuring additional houses against earthquake damage, and adding a few small states to a functioning military alliance. There are very few (if any) economies of scale in extending earthquake insurance to additional houses. But extending the promise of security to a few small states has much lower marginal costs, since most of the capabilities necessary to provide that promise are already in place and are essentially surplus in the current environment. NATO is less like earthquake insurance and more like a health insurance plan, where the marginal cost of adding one more subscriber to a well-functioning plan is not that large.

Keeping America involved in European security issues may sound capricious but it is not. Clearly, the historical, economic and cultural ties that bound America to Europe more strongly than to Asia or Latin America in the twentieth century will be weaker in the twenty-first. If interests drive foreign policy commitments, American foreign policy will almost surely continue its gradual tilt towards other parts of the world. A period of transition always involves extended discussion of how much of the past to retain. Ethical arguments can be strong drivers in this context. It makes sense to many Americans to reward aspiring democracies in what used to be 'eastern Europe'. Countries that happened to end up on the wrong side of the Iron Curtain in 1945 should not now be punished for that unfortunate luck, but should instead be welcomed into the 'Western' alliance with all its rights and privileges. After all, Americans generally don't like the idea of exclusive clubs. They prefer the idea that anyone can graduate to membership if they fulfil the requirements. Some of the eastern European states have done just that, and many Americans will find a policy designed to keep them out just too cynical to support.

For Germany, NATO is still part of the integrative logic of international institutions that legitimate its expanding political, economic and security roles. Germany is a great power, but not a traditional one. Predictions that the end of the Cold War and reunification would change that status have so far proved to be wrong. The major channel though which Germany pursues its long-term vision has been the European Union, and European integration has entered a new phase with economic and monetary union. NATO may be a secondary part of this story, but it is still an important part for Germany at least until the EU is ready to take on a more substantial security role. Neither Germany's allies nor Germany itself perceive benefits in leaving eastern Europe outside of the major Western institutions. EU membership may ultimately be the more important, although it will take a longer time to resolve because of the internal politics of distributing costs within the EU. That is no argument, however, to delay what can be done more easily (because of overwhelming US power), and probably less expensively, to integrate eastern Europe into NATO.

NATO also has new problems to deal with. The most immediate and visible of these has been to shut down a war on the European continent. There are many different ways to read what has happened in the former Yugoslavia. What is clear is that NATO forces were the decisive intervention that shut down the war and prevented it from expanding – in more than one instance. NATO is probably the only international institution in the world right now that can reliably stop a war. This role might be surprising given the predilections of many states, including the US, to keep their forces and the NATO alliance itself outside of the very messy situation in the Balkans. But when other attempts failed NATO succeeded. This experience resonates in eastern Europe, where ethnic friction and border issues remain real possibilities for violent conflict.

Stabilizing the so-called transition states is a second 'new' problem for NATO. Poland, Hungary and the Czech Republic are actually the easy cases. Political and economic reform has come at different rates in these three states, but all are probably now past the point of substantial risk. These three countries will succeed in their transitions and make it into the modern political–economic world, in my view with or without NATO membership. The added security they gain from membership may accelerate things a bit, for example by making these countries slightly more attractive to foreign direct investment. It is harder to gauge the political effects of NATO membership within these states, although the explicit vote of confidence from the West could be an important factor should current growth in European economies slow in ways that complicate the eastern economies' recovery path. A defence guarantee is a strong sign that the West, and the US in particular, is committed to the idea that transitions succeed and do so peacefully.

NATO is also now being seen as an institutional framework within which Europeans can contribute more effectively to 'global' security issues. There is a peculiar tension here since the US has generally taken the lead, and has wanted to do so, in this realm. The US will try to enhance this aspect of NATO's evolution over the next decade, particularly to the extent that it can be configured in a way that would increase the contribution of allies without sacrificing substantial decision-making power. That may sound like a bad deal from the perspective of the larger western European states. But it is not necessarily so bad for the eastern European states, who may value the opportunity to contribute to peacekeeping and other related security tasks through a NATO framework.

THE DEMAND FOR NATO

In the 1950s the rationale for NATO was much simpler than it is today. The West needed a military alliance to deter and defend itself against Soviet aggression. NATO came into being for that reason. Like all institutions, NATO took on bits and pieces of other functions over time but there remained a clear hierarchy among them such that defence against the Soviet Union always took priority. In 2000, there is no single overwhelming reason for NATO to exist. The several problems that I discussed above, plus or minus one or two, may be additive but the package does not have the same dominant feel to it.

NATO is unlikely to be the answer to all of these problems. But nobody says it has to be, since a division of labour among security and other institutions in Europe is evolving and will continue to evolve over time. The question is whether NATO is sufficiently useful to retain and expand the organization. Certainly the states that are members of NATO think it sufficiently useful to them. They continue to invest money, credibility and political resources in NATO in an ongoing attempt to reform the institution and now to expand it.

What states actually choose to do should be taken seriously by observers seeking explanations. In 1989 it was common to hear among American academics that NATO was out of business. A decade later, it is most of the serious alternatives to NATO that are out of business, or still waiting to get into it.

The timing of this story is remarkably similar to that of International Business Machines (IBM), which just as many pundits thought was headed for disaster at the end of the 1980s. The analogy is apt because neither NATO nor IBM is particularly nimble as an organization. Both faced radically changed environments. And both surprised the analysts, particularly by the extent to which they were able to rethink their respective missions and bring new ideas into practice. It is also apt because IBM is still in many respects the 'big blue' of old, just as NATO retains many of the organizational and decision-making structures that were characteristic of it during the Cold War. Yet for both organizations, the 'customers' are buying a new set of products. There were choices. For several years after 1989 the CSCE (now the OSCE), the WEU, and other organizations were vying for a serious commitment from states for a security role in Europe. Political scientists might call this 'revealed preferences' but essentially what happened is that Western states voted with their feet, and they voted for NATO. How surprising is it, then, to see the eastern Europeans wanting to make the same choice.

Is this just mass confusion or, worse, stupidity? One role of theory is to suggest what it is that actors should want, or should do, in order best to achieve their goals (which are often assumed). Theories of security institutions assume that states want to maximize their security at minimum cost and with the minimum necessary price to autonomy. Assume for the sake of argument that the several problems I discussed above cover some of the main issues that states in Europe wish to see managed more effectively over the next decade. Could we design an optimal institutional structure to make this happen, at minimum cost to budgets and autonomy? And if we could design it, would it be feasible to create it?

INSTITUTIONS FOR SECURITY

To design an optimal set of institutions for almost any real-world problem is almost never a trivial task. Consider the confounding variables in European security: 20 or perhaps 30 relevant states (not to mention other influential actors), different attitudes towards risk, substantial uncertainty about the future, complicated legacies of political, cultural and ethnic discord, military organizations in the process of reform, and more. Any institutional design for European security is, at best, a very messy experiment. No one should be too courageous or confident. I think it is clear that there is simply no sufficiently robust theory to make sense of what is optimal in this situation.

Two consequences follow. The first is a better awareness of humility given the context in which these decisions must be made. Some critics of NATO and of expansion will say, 'if NATO did not now exist we would not create it'. That is probably true, but it is just as true of almost all organizations that exist in the real world. It is not a helpful argument, unless it can be extrapolated to the obvious next question: what would you create?

The second consequence is the need to choose an angle from which to view the problem. One fundamental angle on security institutions follows from the basic politics of state-to-state interaction in an anarchic international system. Assume a set of states shares to a considerable extent assessments of the nature of threats in the international system. They wish to form an alliance to increase their security against perceived threats. This decision to ally does not, however, erase anarchy. An alliance is quite like a set of contracts between autonomous and independent firms, which remain autonomous and independent. Constructing an alliance can then be seen as a kind of contracting problem. And the central question becomes, *ex post*, will an actor fulfil the terms of the contract that is signed, *ex ante*?

This taps into a mainstream perspective in international relations theory. The basic insight is that in an anarchic environment, contracts are both incomplete and difficult to enforce. Following this, states have a hard time making reliable promises to each other and thus are constrained from investing in co-operative relationships. This is 'suboptimal' since there clearly exist certain situations where states want to make credible promises to each other and would benefit from being able to do so. If states are dissatisfied with these 'market failure' type outcomes, they may try to design mechanisms that would improve and enhance the credibility of certain promises that they would like to make to each other.

Groups of states face two kinds of threats, to which promises might apply. The first is usually the main reason they join together in the first place – an external threat from a potential aggressor who is not part of the group. The second is more insidious but often just as dangerous. It is an internal threat from a member of the group itself, which at some point in the future might choose to betray its alliance partners and use force against them to gain an advantage.[2] A group of states can create an institutional structure that is designed to lessen one or the other threat. *But it is very hard to design an institutional structure that lessens both at the same time.*

Figure 1 below illustrates the logic of this dilemma. The key point is the particular kind of promise that states want to make to one another. I use this lever to differentiate between two ideal types of security institution, the alliance and the security community. Political scientists use both of these terms frequently but often imprecisely. The obvious advantage of viewing both through the context of promises and contracting is to create a unified theoretical perspective that can highlight the logical differences between them.

In an ideal-type alliance, states join together to defend against a common external enemy. This requires that states make promises to each other that an attack on one is an attack on all. Each individual state must promise that it will use force to defend its allies even when its own security is not immediately threatened. This is a difficult promise to make credible *ex ante*, since *ex post* the incentives to defect would frequently be high. History is full of cases where the alliance promise was not very credible and was not in fact adhered to when push came to shove. What is less easy to see in the historical record is the non-appearance of alliances that might have come to be if this promise could

FIGURE 1

	Alliance	Security Community
Purpose	States join to defend against a common external enemy.	States join to increase common welfare by enhancing interdependence.
What kind of promise?	An attack on one is an attack on all: 'I will use force to defend my allies even when my own security is not threatened.'	Disputes between states are settled peaceably: 'I will not use force against any member of the security community.'
What kinds of institution add credibility to the promise?	Authoritative or hierarchical decision structure. Unified military command. Maximum integration of armed forces	Egalitarian decision structure. Peaceful dispute settlement procedures. Other means for enhancing transparency such as sharing information, confidence building measures.

have been made in a credible way. The consequence is that even states which have no overt intention to defect or free-ride on alliance commitments must take steps to enhance the credibility of their promise, to bind themselves in ways that would discourage defection, and to reassure their allies that they are in fact so bound.

There are many different ways partially to enhance the credibility of an alliance promise.[3] The US came up with several tricks during the Cold War to try to make its promise credible to the European allies. Forward basing of American soldiers and nuclear weapons – the so-called 'tripwire' – was the most obvious. Institutional arrangements can contribute as well. An alliance is most credible if states can agree to an authoritative or at least a hierarchical decision-making structure. A unified military command, with as much co-ordination among national armed forces as is practicable, would also contribute. States might agree to joint training, exercises and procurement. The aim of these measures would be to maximize integration of command, deployment and operation of armed forces so that when an external threat challenged the alliance, individual states would find it prohibitively difficult to do anything other than proceed with the plans of the alliance and fight in defence of the group.

The goals of a security community are different and actually somewhat broader. States in a security community engage each other in high levels of economic, social and political interdependence. Their willingness to do so rests on a promise that they will not use force among themselves and that disputes will be settled peaceably. States that cannot credibly make such a promise will be constrained from accepting the vulnerabilities that accompany the kind of interdependence that yields the joint benefits of a security community.

While it is probably easier for states that share democratic values, norms and a common history of successful co-operation to promise credibly that they will not use force against each other in the future, those things by themselves are not likely to be sufficient. Institutions can play a reinforcing role here, as they do in alliance systems. But the ideal-type institutions of a security community would look very different from those of an alliance. Authority and coercion go against the notion of formally equal states that recognize each other's legitimate sovereignty. Thus, instead of stressing hierarchy, the institutions of a security community will stress equivalence. Decisions will be taken by consensus and implemented voluntarily. The primary function of institutions will be to enhance transparency and to facilitate the sharing of information among states that have every reason to want to share information with each other. Confidence-building measures and legal–technical procedures for the peaceful settlement of disputes will be more important than the efficient decision-making and implementation structures more suited to an alliance.

This kind of analysis could be developed further with additional arguments from organization theory, or elaborated into formal models. But even in this simple state, it yields an important insight. There are clear contradictions between the kinds of institution that make sense for an alliance, and those that make sense for a security community. The lack of a 'perfect' institutional structure for European security going forward into the twenty-first century is not just a matter of politicians' inability to think clearly or solve problems rationally. And it is not only a matter of uncertainty about the contours of the future environment, although that is certainly a complicating factor. It is, fundamentally, a matter of a logical contradiction that cannot be solved in its current form. Europe almost certainly needs both an alliance and a security community going forward, but it cannot have either without some cost to the other.

NATO is a peculiar mix of an alliance and a security community.[4] I have written in detail elsewhere about the quirky story of how it got to be that way, but for the current debate on enlargement the story of NATO's origins is less important. Over time, NATO's principal alliance goal – to defend western Europe against external aggression from the Soviet Union – was balanced against a security community goal: to prevent the use of force among NATO member states and particularly to solve the Franco-German security problem. NATO's institutional structure, predictably, reflects a compromise between the logical demands of these goals. Like all compromises it is awkward. It includes unprecedented elements of supra-sovereign authority over the armed forces of states. At the same time, it constrains that authority in ways that severely complicate the task of mounting an efficient and effective defence.

NATO's institutional structure was at once a source of frustration for military planners and a source of comfort for political analysts. The military planners wanted a more effective alliance. The political analysts assumed away the challenge of deterrence and proclaimed that NATO was first and foremost a 'political alliance' – by which they meant something approximating to a security community. In fact, NATO was and is both. It promotes both objectives, in ways that are certainly non-optimal, often clumsy, and sometimes expensive.

When the Cold War ended, NATO's peculiar institutional structure attracted new criticism. It was portrayed as an historical anachronism, an inefficient jumble of incentives, a poorly organized and unwieldy organization that could not recast itself and should be junked. This criticism missed the important point that states later recognized when they chose NATO as the preferred institutional framework within which to go forward. Quirky historical processes sometimes generate structures that are reasonably well adapted to an unexpected change in their environment. Under conditions of great uncertainty, to be 'adapted' often means to remain *adaptable*. Hedging your bets is not a good way to create efficiency in the pursuit of any single particular goal, but it can be a very attractive approach when the environment is changing in ways that make the goal or goals that will be desired more uncertain.

RUSSIA'S ROLE

The obvious objection to this argument is that there exists a major uncertainty that NATO cannot effectively hedge: Russia's response to NATO expansion. This is a substantial concern, for security and symbolic reasons. National pride is a real thing. No state would look on favourably as its former colonies (of less than a decade ago) joined up in an alliance, even a defensive one, with the former adversary. But pride is not a worthy basis for making intelligent, self-interested medium- and long-term policy decisions. Both sides benefit from trying to move the discussion out of and beyond the realm of pride, towards concrete security issues and a more level-headed assessment of what is sensible and good for Russia.

There is a pattern in Russian responses to NATO after the end of the Cold War. In 1989, Mikhail Gorbachev's government seemed genuinely opposed to NATO and especially to reunified Germany's membership of it. In a January 1990 discussion at Berkeley, Alexei Arbatov threatened that Russia would go to war before it would permit German reunification within NATO. This did not make sense and was very soon disowned as the Soviet government step by step removed any substantial conditions for the 2 + 4 accord on German reunification. In return, the Russians received commitments for substantial economic support for their reform programme as well as a vague promise on the part of the West that it would work to reorganize a security system for Europe.

Vehement opposition was moderately useful as a bargaining ploy, as it often is for bargainers that are in a weak position of power. But in the end this approach was self-limiting. Both sides recognized that NATO membership for Germany probably served Russia's interests more effectively than the possibility of having as its major security interlocutor in Europe an independent Germany left to seek security on its own, or a German-dominated European coalition without the US.

The Russian discussion about Hungary, Poland and the Czech Republic has had similar dynamics. At first there were the warnings of angry nationalists decrying NATO expansion as evidence of America's aggressive intentions. The Yeltsin government was content to use these dramatic voices as a backdrop for its bargaining strategy, seeking to get as many as possible in return for 'allowing' these three countries to join NATO. In fact it seems as if Western opponents of NATO expansion took the hysteria of Russian nationalists far more seriously than did most Russians. But since bargaining power lies in the eyes of the beholder, the West made a number of concessions in the Founding Pact to soothe the sting and make some of what irritates Russia about NATO less irritating.

The new consultative mechanisms between NATO and Russia may prove useful over time (even though they did not contribute much to reducing tensions around the Kosovo campaign). But if Russian interests were truly threatened in a definitive way by the expansion of

NATO, nothing in the Founding Pact would change that situation. Russia accepted the deal simply because Russian interests are not profoundly threatened. Surely, viewed from the perspective of a very stark *realpolitick*, it is not good for Russia that countries closer to its geographic borders are going to be NATO members even if they do not accept the forward basing of other countries' troops and weapons. But from a more balanced perspective it is just as clear that this does not alter the balance of power in Europe in any substantial way. That is why Russia's response to NATO expansion, now that the deal has essentially been done, has the characteristics of a deafening silence.

The more serious risk to American interests in this setting comes from another source, and that is the magnitude of American power itself. Susan Strange wrote that power resides in those who control not only systems that provide or detract from the security of others. Power is a function also of control over production techniques, finance, and access to knowledge and ideas. At the start of the twenty-first century the United States enjoys a very strong position on each of these four parameters. A predominance of power is a potential threat to other states, regardless of NATO's expansion. And so it is not surprising (although it is unfortunate) that some Russians judged American policy in Kosovo as a cynical use of NATO to extend American domination over Europe, just as the Chinese believed that the bombing of their Belgrade embassy was an intentional act of humiliation rather than a stupid bureaucratic mistake.

Certainly it will be an important element of Washington's foreign policy to moderate these worries as best it can. Obviously, attitudes and words do something; actions do more; and costly actions are more effective than cost-free ones. The question becomes, did NATO expansion change in a significant way the Russian (or Chinese) interpretation of American and NATO policy in Kosovo? Since decisions about NATO so far have been low-cost for the West, the impact should have been small. Russia objected to certain aspects of NATO policy in the Balkans, but the expansion of the alliance to include Hungary, the Czech Republic and Poland didn't change that calculus for Moscow in any substantial way.

In the medium term NATO expansion, and the Western commitment it represents, could very well be good for Russia. Assume that Russia wishes and is able to move closer to the 'modern' world, by continuing its complicated transition to democracy and a globally integrated market economy. Surely that move will be facilitated by having stable, peaceful and secure democracies in the immediate neighbourhood of eastern Europe? Regional stability and successful transitions are a positive sum outcome. A prosperous and secure eastern Europe is good for everyone – this will serve Russia's interests in particular – and it threatens no one, at least in terms of the security of states. NATO makes a modest contribution to the likelihood that this positive sum outcome will obtain.

One objection is that NATO expansion complicates the West's ability to cultivate a co-operative relationship with Russia and will provoke the Russian government to oppose Western interests elsewhere. The logic of this argument has never been clear to me. Why should Russia move closer to Iraq or Libya as a result of NATO expansion? What would Russia gain by doing this, and how would that compensate for what it might imagine itself to have lost in eastern Europe? Or consider the prospect of a future Sino-Soviet axis hostile to the West. To think that adding the Czech Republic, Poland and Hungary to NATO alters the balance of power in the world so fundamentally, that it would push Russia and China closer together to compensate in ways that oppose the US, strains credulity. It certainly doesn't make sense in the context of balance-of-power theory. If such an alignment were to be provoked by Western action, surely it would have been the reunification of Germany that served as the driving force. Proponents of this argument have one more issue they need to confront. Why does the impending expansion of the European Union not set off the same balancing dynamic? In the case of the EU, there is a Baltic state at play as well. And the level of co-operation and integration within the EU far exceeds what is on offer in NATO membership. It takes a very narrow definition of the stakes in international politics at the beginning of the twenty-first century to justify fear of NATO enlargement combined with sanguinity about the EU.

There is a practical element to this discussion that depends on the balance of power not in the international system but in Russia's domestic polity. Could NATO expansion provoke in Russia exactly the negative turn towards retrograde nationalism that the West wishes to avoid? This argument was made by Western opponents of NATO expansion, repeatedly in late 1997 and early 1998. It does not seem to have been borne out. Apparently, as I suggested earlier, NATO expansion does not constitute a big enough change in Russia's geopolitical scenarios to drive substantial shifts in what Russia is or wants to do in the world.

If Russia does in the near future undergo a substantial turn for the worse, some Western commentators will likely claim that it was NATO expansion that tipped the balance. But will they actually know that to be true? I am sceptical in advance, for the following reason. If the domestic political balance in Russia is so tenuous, so finely poised on the brink of chaos, that any action the West takes in opposition to Russian interests might tip it over, then it might as well be NATO expansion as something else, because something else would surely happen. I find it peculiar, and ultimately unsustainable, to argue that the US and its Western allies should be deeply constrained in pursuit of national interests by the threat of Russian nationalists. This is a normative argument, but it is also ultimately a practical one. The argument 'this will infuriate and embolden Russian nationalists' can be used to oppose anything the US wishes to do, that Russian nationalists do not wish us to do.

In sum, abstract arguments from international politics are indeterminate and sometimes contradictory about the consequences of NATO enlargement. Caution should be the name of the game as we intervene in a complex system whose interactions and causal links we don't understand well. We should also be cautious in assuming, or creating the impression by appearing to assume, that a particular decision is momentously important and could change the course of history in significant ways. George Kennan has called NATO expansion the single greatest foreign policy blunder of the twentieth century. But he has not convincingly said why that should be so.

The stakes should not be exaggerated. NATO expansion is not the equivalent of the Treaty of Versailles. Russia is not the Weimar Republic. In many ways, the treatment of Russia at the end of the Cold War is more reminiscent of the treatment of Germany post Second World War than Germany post First World War. While there has been no Marshall Plan equivalent, Russia has received enormous aid from Western states and international institutions. It has been invited to join major world forums, including what is now with Russia the G-8. Western firms and investors are simply waiting, hopefully, for Russia's dual transition to succeed in sufficient measure. Ten years from now, Russia can surely be a member of the club of democratically governed, economically integrated market economies. It faces no more of a barrier to that club than did Korea in the 1980s. It may face less of a barrier than China will. The end of the Cold War is not a vindictive peace. It is up to Russia to take the next steps. Holding back on NATO expansion, which Western members and eastern European applicants have judged to be in their interests, because Russia has failed so far to take those steps is not sensible.

NOTES

1. Kenneth N. Waltz, *Theory of International Politics* (Reading, MA: Addison-Wesley, 1979); Stephen Walt, *The Origins of Alliance* (Ithaca: Cornell, 1987).
2. Waltz, *Theory of International Politics*; Walt, *The Origins of Alliance.*
3. See my discussion of various strategies in 'The United States, the Soviet Union, and Regional Conflicts after the Cold War', in George W. Breslauer, Harry Kreisler, and Benjamin Ward (eds.), *Beyond the Cold War: Conflict and Cooperation in the Third World* (Berkeley: International and Area Studies, 1991).
4. I discuss the evolution of NATO as an institution in *Multilateralism in NATO: Shaping the Postwar Balance of Power 1949–1961* (Berkeley: International and Area Studies, 1991).

NATO Enlargement:
A Step in the Process of Alliance Reform

GALE A. MATTOX[1]

The enlargement of NATO was a correct decision both for the alliance objective of stability and security in Europe and for the candidate countries. The decision was taken only after a long process of debate and discussion: first, by the member country policy-makers; second, within the Atlantic alliance; and finally, albeit less intensively in most countries, within the member countries during the ratification process.[2] While there was a wide range of reasons for supporting enlargement – reasons spanning the political spectrum left to right – it was not a decision taken lightly by any country. Contrary to the assertions of its opponents, the enlargement of NATO fell within the context of very explicit objectives for the alliance – democratic governance, free-market reforms and rule of law, as well as civilian control of the military. Furthermore, the countries aspiring to membership were required to have resolved any border or other problems, not an insignificant hurdle and one with direct implications for the overall stability of Europe. There are justifiable arguments for other approaches to ensuring security for the continent – having enlargement of the European Union (EU) precede NATO enlargement, for instance – but no other approach was realistic during the time in which the decisions were made from 1994 to 1997. NATO enlargement to include Poland, Hungary and the Czech Republic was the right decision at the right time.

But NATO enlargement is also only justifiable in the context of broader reform of the alliance and of the European security structure more generally. The task of reform is not impossible, but it is a tall order and will require innovative thinkers and a significant dose of political will on the part of the United States as well as our European and Canadian allies. For those schooled in the Cold War, it will require major readjustments of the traditional perceptions of European security which many experts claim to have made, but which a realistic assessment of the current approaches to security often contradict. There is a range of reforms which will be necessary for the enlargement process itself or 'getting it right', from internal reforms of NATO to external relations with states from relations with non-members to relations with the broader international community, to, finally, new relationships with other institutions and a redefinition of the respective responsibilities for continental security. While the New Strategic Concept adopted at the 1999 Washington 50th anniversary summit incorporates on paper many of the necessary reforms, their translation into action requires a further commitment.[3]

NATO ENLARGEMENT: A CORRECT DECISION

After the revolutions of 1989 and the evolution of democratic reforms and free markets within the countries which overthrew the governing communist regimes, there was an expectation that the West would open its doors to the newly emerging democratic states. This basically did not occur, with one exception. In the case of the German Democratic Republic, the West German government began to invest heavily in the newly 'free' German state. In less than a year, the two states had unified and the investment became a German domestic investment. Other former East Bloc states were not as blessed and the windfall in assistance that many had expected failed to occur. There were many reasons why there was no 'Marshall Plan for the 1990s'. First, there was uncertainty about the direction many of the former communist states would take. Would they remain on a democratic course? This problem was compounded as many of the old faces from the 'former' communist regimes reappeared.

Second, many of the 'Western' European countries were preoccupied with the consolidation of the EU which involved both implementing the provisions of the Single European Act and admitting three new members – Sweden, Finland and Austria – who proved to be net financial contributors to the EU. Finally, the words of welcome to the newly free-market states became empty echoes as the eastern states began to attract companies and investment which otherwise might have settled in the West. The enthusiasm for open borders faded quickly after 1989–90 and the open arms/open doors policies became more tentative. This prompted massive disappointment for the central European countries as well as the states of the former Soviet Union after the disintegration of the Soviet empire in December 1991.

The reasons for eastern European interest in membership of the EU and NATO were clear – their leaders hoped for economic assistance to introduce the standards of living enjoyed by the West, and for security assurances to reinforce the independence they had achieved from the Soviet Union and to integrate them westward rather than eastward. For the central Europeans, the Visegrad Pact was to have provided initial security needs as the countries prepared themselves for EU membership. The EU would be a connection to the West, as Czech statesman Vaclav Havel maintained in a speech to the European Parliament in 1994 about the EU tradition of Christian values, civil society and the rule of law.[4] The early inclination was to focus on EU membership, particularly given the reduced threat perceived in Europe from what became the former Soviet Union. Furthermore, the establishment in Brussels of the North Atlantic Co-operation Council (NACC) had brought these countries into NATO at least in a consultative forum. But as it became evident that the EU was not prepared to make a commitment to enlargement, the interest by the central Europeans and others by 1993 had clearly turned to securing membership of NATO. Put quite simply, NATO membership became the ticket into the Atlantic community – it would tie any new members to the community of democratic nations which the long-time opposition groups in the communist societies had so long desired. If membership of the EU was out of reach, perhaps NATO membership would not be. The point was that membership of either the EU or NATO would make it much more difficult to turn back the clocks to communism.

But does enlargement that makes sense for the central Europeans necessarily make sense for NATO or has it been a misguided decision for the alliance as critics maintain? If the objective of NATO is security and stability in Europe and this is necessary as the alliance theorists in this volume and elsewhere maintain, then the decision to enlarge was indeed correct and even necessary. The arguments in favour are relatively straightforward and clear.

First, security in central Europe means security for all of Europe and, as the United States has identified its security with that of Europe, at least since 1949, it also means US security.

Second, enlargement will reinforce the democratic forces newly emerging in each of the new member states. The ties between these states and the present NATO members will bring the governments and public under close scrutiny with respect to adherence to the expectations of democratic regimes. Deputy Secretary of State Strobe Talbott has noted that 'it would be the height of injustice and irony – the ultimate in double jeopardy – if these countries were, in effect, punished for the next 50 years because they had been, against the will of their people, part of the Warsaw Pact for the past 50'.[5]

Third, as a requirement of membership, civilian rule over the military has been established and will be difficult to roll back. The process of enlargement has introduced re-education of the military and adoption of the appropriate modes of behaviour by these new members. This is not to deny varying degrees of success, but the complementarity of militaries today within the current member states is astonishingly high and the same phenomena may be expected in the new states admitted to membership. While critics have attacked the potential costs involved in developing the new members' militaries, it is not clear that the costs are substantially higher (than for a 'partner' country) or that modernization would not have occurred in any case.[6]

Fourth, enlargement sets out a marker for those states not slated to become members at this time. Partnership for Peace (PFP) will continue to encourage the development of similar standards for its membership and its exercises will bring about greater interoperability of militaries with a resultant increase in transparency and co-operation between former enemy forces. The inclusive nature of PFP as well as the Euro-Atlantic Partnership Council (EAPC) will mean a melting of barriers between armies. The outreach to Russia and Ukraine, in the form of the Founding Act and Ukraine Charter, was an attempt to reassure those countries who are not likely to become members in the near future that the enlargement was not designed to reconstruct walls/new dividing lines in Europe, but, rather, to include all Europeans in a security agenda for the next decade.

Fifth, for those who argue that enlargement will increase US hegemony and push Russia to undertake countermeasures, there is no indication of this occurring. The signing of the START agreement was dead in the water before enlargement and will only be ratified when the Russian Duma deems it advantageous for reasons which transcend and are separate from enlargement. A stable Europe is as much in Russian interests as in the interests of NATO members. The various steps to encourage close NATO–Russian co-operation are substantial and leave NATO a quite different organization than was true in the days of the Cold War. The argument that enlargement reinforces US hegemony in

Europe, furthermore, ignores the reforms now underway by NATO and the significant changes that PFP and other initiatives such as the Founding Act between NATO and Russia (and the consequent Permanent Joint Council) have introduced into the alliance.[7]

Finally, should enlargement be extended to countries beyond the initial three? There clearly has been an expectation of additional members in the future.[8] The US Senate debate which included a resolution calling for a 'pause' in new memberships dampened the American enthusiasm, but does this mean 19 members and no more? It should not, but it also should not be taken for granted that there will be a future enlargement. No state should be considered without meeting the prerequisites laid out in the NATO Enlargement Study and in the Membership Action Plan introduced in April 1999 during the Washington 50th anniversary summit in the New Strategic Concept.[9] Furthermore, without substantial reform of the present structure as laid out below and, in part, contained in the NATO new strategic concept, a second or even third or fourth enlargement should not occur.

Under what circumstances, then, might a wider enlargement be reasonably considered? Should there be a future enlargement, it would preferably not include states on the Russian border or states formerly part of the Soviet Union. More likely and far more acceptable would be an enlargement to territory not contiguous to Russia, namely to Austria, Romania and Slovenia, thus joining Hungary to the rest of NATO and including Austria which is viewed within the fold now of the EU in any case. While Austria has for the moment delayed a decision on NATO membership, Romania and Slovenia as well as Bulgaria have expressed interest and have their supporters.[10] Other countries could understandably precipitate far greater opposition from Russia, even to the point of creating greater instability than stability and thus contradictory to the goals of alliance. The Baltics have perhaps been the most vocal in expressing their desire for admission and Lithuania declared enlargement a major foreign policy goal, thereby, many assert, taking itself out of the running for the EU.[11] Despite the enthusiasm of the Baltics and the support of the Baltic communities in the United States and elsewhere, an enlargement to include Latvia, Lithuania and Estonia would be foolhardy in the near future given the proximity to the heavily militarized Kola Peninsula and Kaliningrad. However, the current plans to offer EU membership to Estonia in the first enlargement and to Latvia and Lithuania possibly in the second may prove the best preparation for NATO membership – or, more likely in the near future, a less threatening alternative to NATO, particularly if included in the process of Common Foreign and Security Policy (CFSP). More broadly, a scenario for enlargement could only be imagined in the face of very substantial alliance reforms, considerably beyond what is now projected together with substantially broader Russian–NATO co-operation.

The inevitable question over membership is that of Russia. While the theoretical possibility of Russian membership – also Ukrainian and other former republics – should be maintained, more likely and even more fruitful is actually a close Russian–NATO relationship in which there is active consultation, co-operation and even broad military co-ordination in crisis regions. This assumes a more stable domestic situation in Russia as well as a European security architecture in which the Russians play a far greater role than is today the case. It is unlikely that such a scenario would be possible without a continued role for the United States in Europe, albeit that presumably could be reduced in the face of a more cohesive EU and development of a true European CFSP.

The Atlantic alliance has a moral and historical obligation to support the development of democracies and free market reforms in the states of the former Eastern Bloc. Enlargement of NATO as well as enlargement of the EU are necessary steps in fulfilment of that obligation as candidate states meet the requirements of membership of those organizations. For the issue at hand, NATO enlargement, simply a change in the membership of the organization, will not suffice – it must be accompanied by fundamental reform also of the institution and with it the outdated strategy and doctrines.

EUROPEAN SECURITY FOR THE FUTURE

While NATO enlargement is and should be a reinforcement of democratic and economic reforms as well as human rights in the three countries offered membership in Madrid in July 1997, it would be a mistake to see the act of enlargement as the end of the process of change for NATO. Rather, enlargement must be instead a process important for the three countries and a precedent for any other countries included in future enlargement. An integral part of the process is a series of reforms which are also essential to NATO as it enters its second 50 years of existence, including both internal structural reform and external NATO relations with other countries. In addition, the broader outlines of the European security architecture more generally need to be reconciled with the revolutionary and evolutionary changes throughout the continent since 1989.

These nascent and evolving reforms fall into four general categories. First and foremost, the Atlantic alliance must get the enlargement process 'right'. That is, the requirements for the process of enlargement itself must remain clear and perceived as transparent, or their viability as a precedent for future members (or even those countries not likely to become members but linked via the PFP and other ties) will be greatly reduced. Second, NATO has already mapped out a series of internal reforms and the successful completion of those reforms will be important in moving the alliance from its Cold Warrior image to one adapted to the post-Cold War era. Third, NATO's relations externally both with non-member European countries as well as states contiguous to Europe and with the international community, including the United Nations, have been under close scrutiny and deservedly so. A clearer definition of the relationship of NATO to other states in its external affairs and a more defined role as an actor in the international community has become increasingly necessary.

Fourth, and importantly, the context of European security continent-wide with respect to other institutions is critical. While NATO is currently carrying the heavier load and has taken the lead on a number of crises, it is not an appropriate structure for many of the tasks and responsibilities even now confronting Europe and certainly posing challenge in the future. This broader context of European security includes the Organization for Security and Co-operation in Europe (OSCE), the Western European Union (WEU) or its successor and a plethora of other organizations such as the Baltbat, the Eurocorps, and the Polish–German–Danish corps to name only a few. Each of these areas of reform is important to the context within which enlargement is carried out.

'Getting It Right'

What does 'getting it right' mean for the enlargement process? Most importantly, it means that admittance to the alliance be only the first step in a process which needs also to include fulfilment of the requirements of democratic governance, free-market economies, protection of human rights, development of civil–military relations and the maintenance of peaceful relations with neighbours and other members. The signing of agreements between states with outstanding conflicts over borders, ethnic issues or other issues was noteworthy and essential to the process of admitting new members, but the final signatures on a treaty in Missouri on 12 March 1999 should not have transmitted any illusions that those states will never be tempted to fall back to earlier conflicts and tensions. There should be clear expectations of adherence to the accepted criteria for admittance and no reluctance on the part of the current members to move quickly to rectify contradictory trends.

'Getting it right' means also that the broader measures taken to ensure a less tense relationship with Russia and Ukraine not be abandoned now that enlargement has occurred. This is not to say that the process will be without its own inconsistencies and problems. Designing a NATO–Ukranian charter which will satisfy one of the largest countries geographically next to Russia in Europe and with a population the approximate size of France and one of the most likely to confront severe internal turmoil in the next ten years was not an easy task.[12] Although Ukraine has indicated its interest in membership of NATO and the EU, it is clear that it is realistic about its prospects. However, there are expectations, particularly among the elite, that Ukraine's agreement to sign the Nuclear Non-Proliferation Treaty and dismantle its capabilities incurred a commitment from the West to take its security and other concerns seriously, and to treat such concerns in equally serious fashion as it treats those of Russia. The agreement on a charter shortly after the time the Founding Act with Russia was signed was an important signal of Ukraine's role in Europe. But just as the signing in July 1997 has heightened anticipation over a significant NATO–Ukraine relationship, a stalemate and/or lack of progress would be a corresponding let-down. The alliance must remain sensitive to this relationship. Ultimately, it is in Europe's interests that the democratic forces within Ukraine are reinforced, an increasingly difficult process currently.

Even more contentious but essential will be the development of the provisions of the NATO–Russian Founding Act.[13] Off to a slow beginning, the framework for the relationship within the parameters of the Act is taking shape. It is admittedly a difficult transition from Cold War enemy to a presence in Brussels NATO headquarters, but nothing is more central to long-term peace in Europe than the direction Russia takes. While there has been criticism over the decision to assure the

Russians that NATO enlargement was not directed towards them with the establishment of a Permanent Joint Council (PJC), it is critical that the alliance and Russia work to 'get it right'.[14] There is no question that the task is substantial – on the one hand, Russia must be satisfied that NATO actions are co-ordinated and transparent; on the other hand, the PJC cannot give the Russians a virtual veto over NATO actions or the perception that the Russian voice carries more weight than members'. As the charges by the Russians of lack of consultation on Kosovo demonstrate, the task will at times be fraught with frustrations. But the achievement of a productive relationship could mean not less than the stability of Europe. Again, those who view these new arrangements as one-sided are deluding themselves about the need for a balanced and nuanced relationship with both Russia and Ukraine which permits fruitful dialogue and co-operative ventures and, in the long run, reduces the level of tension in Europe.

Finally, 'getting it right' means that the process of enlargement by the new members will need to be consistent and closely monitored. Not only will it be important to continue the path of reform begun by the three candidate countries in first requesting membership and submitting their application, but the progress of those countries in continuing to adhere to the guidelines and requirements laid out in the enlargement study as well as the individual country agreements will lay the groundwork for any potential extension of NATO membership. Foremost, a backsliding by the new members, particularly a refusal to commit the resources promised for reform of their forces and other civil reforms, will provide fodder for minority but vocal domestic critics. In the case of the United States, one need only look at the budget quagmire produced by critics of the United Nations in the past few years to realize that Congress can be unforgiving if it perceives a significant inequality of burdens. In addition to domestic critics or hesitant members, the impact of an uncertain and disorganized process of integrating the new members could be perceived as a weakening of the alliance structure more generally. Rather than creating stability in Europe, this could have a destabilizing impact. Finally, the forces in the non-member countries using the new members as models for the road their countries should take, not necessarily even for membership but for acceptance in the transatlantic community, could be undermined.

Attention to the process whereby new members are integrated does not mean that active duty forces need to be introduced into the countries, much less nuclear forces, nor does it mean that there is a need for a remilitarization of Europe.[15] Indeed, the December 1996 statement that NATO did not intend to station nuclear forces in Europe will reduce the need for both permanent bases and any foreign forces. It will not eliminate the possible need for prepositioned supplies and readiness exercises to underpin the Article 5 guarantee.[16] To the contrary, this is a situation to be avoided. It does mean that Poland, the Czech Republic and Hungary need to continue with modernization of their forces to reach interoperability with the rest of NATO.[17] It will necessitate continued manoeuvres with NATO *and* non-NATO members. And it will mean persistence in the task of introducing more balanced civil–military relations in the candidate countries.

Finally, it will mean vigilance on the issue of human rights and freedoms. This is a natural task for older democracies, but a more difficult road for newer democratic regimes used to falling back on authoritarian measures under threatening circumstances. This latter task carries heavy responsibilities for the current members. All these aspects of 'getting it right' will mean that discussions of reductions in member NATO budgets or the candidate states at this point would be counter-productive to the objective of a successful integration of the new members.

Addressing Internal Reform

This latter point also is important for the second category of essential reforms – addressing the necessary internal structural changes to the alliance. Unfortunately, closure on all the changes to the command structure was difficult and the topic led to highly contentious exchanges, particularly between the US and France. It is to be hoped that the alliance will move beyond these issues to the job of fulfilling the new concept agreed on in Washington at the 50th anniversary celebrations building on the work done at the London summit of 1990 and the Rome summit of 1991.[18] Whether the 1999 Washington New Strategic Concept moves the alliance away from the foundations of the Cold War and into a new relationship adequate to the demands of the future is yet to be determined. Many of the necessary elements are present, but lack adoption and, at this point, member agreement.[19]

Possibly one of the most significant is the concept of Combined Joint Task Forces (CJTF) agreed in a June 1996 communiqué at the Berlin meeting of ministers but still not implemented.[20] Under the CJTF not only will the current members of the alliance be able to pursue interests which may or may not be perceived as essential by other members, but PFP members will also be able to participate in multilateral actions by the Atlantic alliance. There is additionally a third provision for such forces to include countries which are neither NATO nor even PFP members. The details of the implementation of this concept continue to plague its introduction. It would appear to be exactly the type of new direction necessary for the alliance and it is past time to adopt it into alliance doctrine and operations.[21]

A final major issue for this internal restructuring that must provide the basis for NATO to move into the twenty-first century is the direction to be taken by the alliance in working with the associated members. There are two areas in which substantial reforms have been introduced – in the PFP programme and the EAPC. The PFP programme was initially introduced in January 1994 as a mechanism through which to develop a minimal interoperability within and among the former Warsaw Pact nations and NATO. It was seen by its advocates as an early step on what was to be a long road to a yet undefined but closer relationship with NATO, potentially membership albeit not necessarily. While the enlargement decision was taken more quickly than PFP advocates may have desired, the PFP nevertheless has proved highly successful and popular.

For the now-candidate member states, the PFP permitted an opportunity to demonstrate their commitment to NATO militarily through joint exercises and a range of co-operative programmes. For those states which may later or even never become members, it has been an avenue to closer relations with NATO as they attempted to balance or replace their former ties to the now-defunct 'East'. In 1996 NATO named a Senior Level Group under which the alliance then adopted a series of enhancements for the PFP which have expanded the military scope of the co-operation with more exercises, including crises and civil emergency management, direct interaction at headquarters between NATO and PFP officers, and a more parallel budgeting process as well as greater armaments co-operation and others. The Washington summit in 1999 also included even further PFP enhancement. One manifestation of these enhanced efforts has been the stabalization force (SFOR) operations in Bosnia and the Kosovo force (KFOR) in Kosovo. The overall PFP balance sheet is quite positive with a very robust programme of exchanges and co-ordination. It is limited by budgetary constraints in many of the newly emerging democracies struggling to stretch their resources and NATO members attempting to realize a peace dividend and direct more attention to domestic issues while reducing military expenditure. The impact on NATO operations with PFP nations has, however, been largely very positive with the almost painful recognition that co-operation in many respects between militaries now outpaces political co-operation.

NATO designed the EAPC to address political co-operation, but this has not yet become nearly as active as the PFP.[22] Its political nature complicates the role it could or should play. Its predecessor, the NACC, was the earliest attempt by NATO to draw in the former Warsaw Pact members and preceded the PFP by several years, but its size and mandate made for difficulties. Renamed at the Sintra meeting in 1997, the EAPC was charged with providing an expanded political dimension to the relationship between NATO members and non-members. The Council is charged with drawing up its own work plan and the PFP has been subordinated in theory to it.[23] Also the EAPC members are to develop greater access and influence in political decision-making. Finally, its area of consultation with NATO has expanded to include arms control, peace operations, regional matters, and others. But while all these responsibilities are impressive on paper, actual implementation has not matched the expectations of the non-NATO members.

The alliance addressed many of the above deficiencies in the New Strategic Concept but it remains unclear if the political will to fulfil its broad reforms will truly emerge. The Defence Capabilities Initiative (DCI), for instance, is behind schedule and the domestic budgetary situation in the European member states does not reveal any change; in fact, the contrary is more likely. The reasons are twofold – first, most of Europe is focused on extremely high unemployment and the need for substantial structural reform of their economies at the same time that the EU and its member states are consumed with the politics and operation of the European Monetary Union (EMU) and the Euro. Second, NATO itself is now also overwhelmed with the challenge of Kosovo as well as Bosnia. However, it is exactly these latter issues which reflect starkly the new era in Europe and expose the difficulties for the alliance in addressing them with Cold War mechanisms. The process of change is admittedly slow and sometimes painful. But it also underscores the importance of the effort to formulate a new concept for the alliance, not to mention the heightened expectations of the non-member states for more input and co-ordination on a wide range of issues.

Expanding the Concept of Security

A third area important to the adaptation of the Atlantic community to the post-Cold War era lies in institutions outside the NATO structure.[24] These include the OSCE, the United Nations, the WEU/EU, the Council of Europe and a range of multilateral corps and units with specific tasks contributing to the overall security of the continent. But while the need to include these institutions in the broader definition of security is clear, more essential will be the evolution of strategic thinking to incorporate the institutions into the concept of security in the future. Security during the deep freeze of the US–Soviet relationship was clearly defined in terms of armaments and firepower – the side with the greatest kill capacity would deter the other and peace would prevail. For those without nuclear, or sufficient, armaments, the most prudent course was alliance with a superpower. The two security systems which emerged had significant ideological ramifications and the East–West divide was deep. Conscious of the attendant risks of nuclear war, the superpowers avoided situations in which direct confrontation might evolve.

The potential for superpower confrontation on a global scale, much less in Europe, today is markedly diminished. Unfortunately, the barriers to conflict have correspondingly dropped, even if that confrontation may not have global implications. The focus of efforts at containing conflict must be redirected from the armaments races of the past 50 years to the prevention and containment of very different types of tensions, from border skirmishes to intra-state conflicts which were less likely in the Cold War. If the Atlantic community takes away no other lesson from the various conflicts within the territory of the former Yugoslavia, it is important that it recognize the failure of the Cold War approach in assuming, first, an easy solution to the conflict, and second, when that failed, a quick resolution. The likelihood today of containing tensions and even open conflict based on the possibility of an East–West nuclear confrontation is absent. The probability of conflict has become consequently greater even if on a smaller scale, but the likelihood of impact on neighbouring countries either from becoming part of the conflict itself as in Yugoslavia or in being put at risk with an influx of refugees as in Macedonia or disruption of trade and other aspects of life as in Bulgaria, Hungary and other states is high.

The longer-term issue lies in – at times tedious or unglamorous – conflict prevention through institutions such as the OSCE with stringent arms control restrictions and election monitoring, as well as human rights oversight underpinned by the efforts and agreements of the Council of Europe. These efforts in the OSCE are undertaken by the rather weighty but necessary membership of 53–54 states which may include as well parties to the potential conflict or allies on both sides of the contentious issues. Once a conflict threatens or is underway, an OSCE or other observer mission may be appropriate when a NATO presence would only aggravate the problems. A United Nations force may also in confrontations provide a less threatening peacekeeping presence than NATO, particularly in the grey area of non-Article 5 conflicts. In many instances of conflict, this has in fact been the case. The rethinking of European security must embrace this broader concept of security which requires a co-ordination of policy multilaterally and across several institutions.

Another innovation in European security since the revolutions of 1989 has been the establishment of a number of co-ordinated efforts, in most cases across national borders. The French–German Brigade, one of the oldest, became a Eurocorps of four member states with the goal of providing for enhanced co-operation against any threat or potential conflict. The Baltbat involves the Baltic states backed by the United States and other NATO members to increase security around the Baltic Sea. The Medforce is an effort to organize states which border on the Mediterranean and hope to reinforce mutual security interests in the region. Other groupings have also proliferated, such as the Polish–German–Danish unit based in Stettin, Poland. All of these and others are attempts to pursue security from a regional basis while, quite practically, pooling diminishing resources and efforts. These efforts should be approached as enhancements and not rivals to European security. While NATO enlargement should only proceed gradually and carefully within strict requirements for future members and within the clear comfort level of current members, European security arrangements on a continent of evolving democracies should reflect and encourage a continent-wide approach to security. A fall-back to an East–West divide or the construction of discouraging lines between countries struggling to join the community of democratic nations would be irresponsible and highly ill-advised.

The most potentially revolutionary of the European attempts to conceptualize continental security in the post-Cold War period paradoxically came in reaction to the military success of the Kosovo air war operation. That success in the air was clearly a US operation with European assistance but there is no doubt that it would not have been possible without the United States in spring 1999. The European Union used both the Cologne (May 1999) and Helsinki (December 1999) summits to give meat to the bones of the declaration for a Common Foreign and Security Policy contained in Maastricht over five years previously. The speed with which the EU moved to restructure the directorates and appoint former (actually still in office at the time) Secretary-General of NATO Javier Solana to the post of 'Mr Pesch' or Mr CFSP was impressive and demonstrates the importance of political will.

In December the EU Heads of State announced the intention to stand up a rapid reaction force (RRF) of 60,000 by 2003 at their summit in Helsinki, Finland and Headline goals were established within two to three months. This force is to permit the EU to have the resources to fulfil the Petersburg tasks of peacekeeping, peacemaking, humanitarian relief, and a range of other tasks articulated eight years previously but never before having the real support of the EU. While there is a distinct lack of clarity on the issues of double-hatting (will the new RRF compete with NATO?), membership (will non-NATO members be involved in operations using NATO assets?) and, perhaps most importantly, decision-making (what if the Europeans undertake a task on which the US disagrees? Will NATO assets be used and could the action pull the alliance into conflict?). Finally, given limited resources and the drop in European defence budgets on average below two per cent nationally, will the new force be the impetus for enhanced European spending or simply draw the already low resources even lower?

The US reaction has varied from little or no concern to fairly substantial warnings of the end of the close US–European relationship. While there is a potential that a European Union CFSP/Common Defence and Security Policy (CDSP) (there is now a distinction between CFSP and CDSP as well as security and military commissions looking at both aspects) could drive a wedge in the Atlantic alliance, careful diplomacy should be able to work a solution that strengthens rather than weakens the US–European relationship. The effort will not be possible without increased European defence spending if the RRF is not, as promised, simply accomplished with shifting forces, like the magician's balls under three cups! Such a result could reinforce the overall security and provide an alternative to a massive full-scale air war when less force could accomplish the same ends.[25] In other words, there are legitimate issues and a range of yet-unanswered questions with respect to the proposed EU–WEU RRF, but there is no reason why the European efforts should be the cause for undue concern – to the contrary.

In sum, within a broad definition of continental security, the issue of a separate European defence force should not be as problematic as its detractors suggest. First, the CJTF concept in NATO, which posits that interested nations without the active participation of others may band together to resolve a conflict logically, should also permit other institutions to have the latitude to address issues which NATO may not be prepared to address or even feels is outside its appropriate purview. While such actions by EU members may be easier to co-ordinate within the framework of NATO and conceptually as a 'European pillar' of NATO, that should not then preclude necessarily the development of a distinct European defence entity which is complementary to and operates in co-ordination with NATO. The WEU and NATO have met to work on co-operative planning processes, but the task is difficult and not always supported by members who fear one or the other of the organizations will be disadvantaged.[26] Unfortunately, neither Europe nor the US to date have yet found the appropriate balance in the EU–WEU–NATO relationship. It is an area that deserves closer attention on both sides of the Atlantic before the next crisis or set of crises.

The road to restructuring the European security framework will not be without detours and difficulties. Above all, it requires a high degree of co-ordination which is not yet present. While the proliferation of multilateral efforts on a regional level has distinct benefits, most of the current undertakings are nascent and not yet developed. The clue in all these efforts is a distinct policy approach from NATO in particular, but also by all the European organizations. There is a need for a concept of collective effort and multilateral approaches at a level above that at which NATO, the OSCE or the EU now operate. While NATO enlargement was a positive step both for the newly emerging democracies and the Atlantic alliance itself, it was one of many steps along the road to reform which NATO itself must take and has begun with the New Strategic Concept. But the real and necessary transformation of the European security architecture requires a broader framework to include the OSCE, UN, EU/WEU and the many other bilateral and multilateral institutions on the continent. Until all the states in Europe are in some manner a part of the structure and stability has been achieved, the US and Europeans will not truly have constructed a European security framework for the next millennium.

NOTES

1. The views expressed here are solely those of the author and do not represent the views of the US government or any organization or agency with which the author is affiliated.
2. In the case of the United States, there was a robust debate between foreign and defence decision-makers decided finally by a presidential decision in 1994. Of all the countries, the US Senate ratification was perhaps the most contentious despite a favourable vote by 80 senators. Note that this latter stage ignited a debate within the intellectual/academic community, particularly among scholars of Russia and the former Soviet Union, which impacted substantially on the debate in the Senate. This 'public' debate which began in 1996/early 1997 in earnest focused initially on the implications for the US–Russian relationship, abated somewhat after the NATO–Russia Founding Act 1997 and then shifted to issues of cost and timing as well as the potential impact on the future direction of NATO.
3. North Atlantic Council, Heads of State and Government, *An Alliance for the 21st Century*, Washington Summit Communiqué and Accompanying Documents (Washington, DC: NATO Press Office, 24 April 1999).
4. Comments were made by Vaclav Havel in address to the European Parliament, 8 March 1994, Strasbourg, France.
5. Strobe Talbott, 'Russia Has Nothing to Fear', *New York Times*, 18 Feb. 1997, p.A25. As early as 1994 the administration stated that 'the aim of NATO's future expansion, however, will not be to draw a new line in Europe further east, but to expand stability, democracy, prosperity and security cooperation to an ever-broader Europe'. *A National Security Strategy of Engagement and Enlargement* (July 1994), p.22.
6. For an overview of the cost debate and the various estimates, see Richard L. Kugler, 'Costs of NATO Enlargement: Moderate and Affordable', *Strategic Forum* (National Defense University, Institute for National Strategic Studies), No.128 (Oct. 1997).
7. The Permanent Joint Council (PJC) established under the Founding Act to provide ongoing dialogue between Russia and the NATO members was suspended by the Russians during the tensions over Kosovo in spring 1999, but the suspension lasted less than a year, an indication of the importance both sides attach to the consultative process in NATO even between former 'foes'.
8. In Senate testimony, Secretary of State Madeleine Albright commented that 'we gain nothing by ruling out a country as a future ally if it is important to our security, and if it proves that it is willing and able to contribute to our security. Let me say very clearly that we have made no decisions about who the next members of NATO should be or when they might join. But we should also have some humility before the future'. Statement before the Senate Foreign Relations Committee on NATO Enlargement, 24 Feb. 1998, p.7.
9. NATO Information Service, *Enlargement Study and Guidelines* (Brussels, Sept. 1995).
10. Before the Madrid summit 1997, the French expressed strong support for Romania and the Germans for Slovenia, both of whom were overridden, according to press accounts, by the Americans who worried about Senate ratification. While the US has insisted that further enlargements not be discussed until after the admission of the current candidates, President Clinton has also voiced his determination that the 1999 enlargement not necessarily be the last one.
11. In contrast, Estonia gave priority to EU membership and has been named as a candidate member whereas Lithuania and Latvia have not been accorded such a status. Needless to say, this has led to domestic debate and disconcertion within Lithuania. For a discussion of the Baltics, see R. Asmus and R. Nurick, 'NATO Enlargement and the Baltic States', *Survival* (Summer 1996), pp.121–42.

12. NATO, *Charter on a Distinctive Partnership between the North Atlantic Treaty Organization and Ukraine* (Madrid, Spain, 9 July 1997): *NATO Review – Documentation*, Vol.45, No.4 (July–Aug. 1997) pp.5–6.

13. NATO, *Founding Act on Mutual Relations, Co-operation and Security Between NATO and the Russian Federation* (Paris, France, 27 May 1997): *NATO Review – Documentation*, Vol.45, No.4 (July–Aug. 1997), pp.7–10.

14. Having proposed an arrangement with the Russians outside of NATO, former Secretary of State Henry Kissinger has been critical of the decision to bring the Russians into NATO via the PJC. In remarks to a conference in Warsaw, Poland on 4 Dec. 1997, he cautioned that – now that the Founding Act was signed – the alliance needed to circumscribe the issues addressed with the Russians in the PJC to avoid any appearance that they were dictating terms to NATO on issues.

15. NATO announced in Dec. 1996 that it currently and in the foreseeable future had 'no plan, no need and no intention' to station nuclear weapons in the new member countries, nor did it 'contemplate permanently stationing substantial combat forces'. Albright, Statement before the Senate Foreign Relations Committee on NATO Enlargement, p.8.

16. Under Article 5 of the North Atlantic Treaty, states agree that 'an armed attack against one or more of them in Europe or North America shall be considered an attack against them all' NATO, *NATO Handbook* (Brussels, 1997) p.14.

17. The new members recognized the need to demonstrate their willingness to share the burden in both Bosnia and Kosovo with varying, but important, contributions.

18. See NATO Information Service, *London Declaration on a Transformed North Atlantic Alliance* (Brussels, 5–6 July 1990) and *Rome Declaration on Peace and Co-operation* (Brussels, 8 Nov. 1991).

19. For instance, the Defence Capabilities Initiative (DCI) agreed on in April 1999 at the Washington Summit has over 50 necessary reforms, many quite expensive and requiring substantial changes, and action may be expected to be slow.

20. NATO Information Service, *NATO Summit Declaration* (Brussels, June 1996).

21. Although CJTF has not yet been officially adopted, it is clear that the NATO deployments which have included Russians, Ukrainians and others in Bosnia have mirrored the CJTF concept quite successfully.

22. NATO, *Basic Document of the Euro-Atlantic Partnership Council* (Sintra, Portugal, 30 May 1997): *NATO Review* – Documentation (July–Aug. 1997) pp.11–12. (Also English Document: NACC/PFP(C)D(97)5.)

23. Despite these changes, the PFP efforts have been more substantial and almost embarrassingly outstripped the EAPC in breadth and activity.

24. The use of the term 'post-Cold War era' is awkward eight or at least seven years after the end of the Cold War and, yet, the mere use of the term aptly describes the failure to date to adapt to the dramatic turn world history took in 1989–91. Perhaps the advent of the twenty-first century will resolve this dilemma by its arrival and simply lend its name. Let us hope that the politics will have evolved to justify the new title 'twenty-first century'.

25. Alternatively, the Europeans may not be able to expend the resources and the US critics' concerns will be for naught! Greater European burden-sharing and participation in its own continental defence has always been a stated US objective; it would seem contradictory now to become alarmed when Europeans finally move in that direction.

26. For instance, the first co-ordinated exercise between staffs is not projected until the year 2000.

PART 1V: DOMESTIC POLITICS AND NATIONAL INTERESTS

The Origins and Future of
NATO Enlargement

CHARLES A. KUPCHAN

On 30 April 1998, the US Senate approved by a vote of 80 to 19 the inclusion of Poland, Hungary and the Czech Republic in the North Atlantic Treaty Organization (NATO). In ratifying NATO enlargement, the institution charged by the founding fathers to provide prudential oversight of US foreign relations gave its blessing to what many of America's pre-eminent strategists consider an act of folly. George Kennan voiced a sentiment widespread among analysts of international relations when he called enlargement the most fateful error of American policy in the entire post-Cold War era.[1]

I will consider two questions in this essay. First, what went wrong? Democracies are supposedly more peaceful than other states because they pursue moderate, centrist policies. Bad ideas, when they emerge, are to be shot down by the public deliberation that comes with representative government. But the Clinton administration doggedly pursued for four years a course of action that jeopardizes Russia's rapprochement with the West and saddles Americans and western Europeans with new and unnecessary defence commitments. The US Senate, America's repository of political wisdom and restraint, then gave its blessing by an overwhelming margin. Why?

Second, what course of action should NATO pursue now that its formal enlargement is proceeding? Should the eastward spread of NATO stop with the admission of Poland, Hungary and the Czech Republic? Or should it continue? If so, how, when and where should successive waves of enlargement take place? As NATO evolves, what should be the relationship between Europe's own process of integration and the development of the Atlantic security order? Advocates and opponents of NATO enlargement now need to join forces to forge a vision of where the Atlantic security order is headed and how it can be managed to contribute most effectively to European stability.

My main argument as to the sources of enlargement is that a small, but powerful, group of enthusiasts within the Clinton administration orchestrated the expansion of NATO and overcame widespread opposition within the bureaucracy and the broader foreign policy community. A select few at the top – including President Clinton and his national security adviser, Anthony Lake – drove policy and manoeuvred NATO enlargement around the many obstacles that stood in its way. The Senate approved the policy after little debate mainly because most senators simply did not care about the issue. To the limited extent that electoral politics mattered, supporting enlargement offered at least some political pay-offs, while opposing it offered none.

As far as the future of enlargement is concerned, I argue that opponents of enlargement should now become its greatest champions. By proceeding with its expansion, the Western democracies are making NATO the centrepiece of a new Atlantic security order. If NATO enlargement is to be a vehicle for uniting, rather than redividing Europe, the West has only one viable option: opening NATO to Russia itself. As long as Russia recovers from its current economic downturn and continues down the path of democratic reform, its ultimate inclusion in the alliance is now a logical necessity and a strategic imperative. At the same time, the pacification of Russia and its inclusion in the West will reduce the need for a dominant US role in managing European security. I therefore argue for the devolution of security responsibilities to the European Union (EU) and a transatlantic security compact that becomes less Atlantic and more European.

WHAT WENT WRONG?

The Case against Enlargement

The case against NATO enlargement is quite straightforward and compelling: the costs far outweigh the benefits.[2] Yes, Poles, Hungarians and Czechs will feel more secure knowing that NATO members are bound by treaty to defend them. But these countries face no external threat today. Indeed, the main hurdles before them are primarily economic ones. And by forcing new members to spend scarce resources on weapons and aircraft which they do not need, NATO only worsens their economic plight.

But even if NATO enlargement were important to the stability of central Europe, the benefits would still fall well below the main cost:

jeopardizing the West's relations with Russia. Having had a bigger NATO forced upon them by the United States and its allies, the Russians have had no choice except to live with a first wave of enlargement. But the costs are already evident. The Duma put off forward movement on nuclear arms control. Russia has been seeking closer relations with China, with both parties explicitly opposing NATO enlargement and looking to each other to help foster a more egalitarian and multipolar landscape. And even if Russia's relations with the West ultimately withstand the expansion of NATO, taking the risk of alienating and isolating Moscow makes no sense in light of the potential costs. Central Europe could always be brought into NATO down the road, if and when Russia were again to pose a military threat. But to hedge today against a non-existent threat, and in doing so threaten the redivision of Europe, makes no strategic sense.

Historical lessons back up the logical case against enlargement and reinforce the importance of embracing defeated adversaries. The successful peace settlements of the past 200 years entailed reaching out to defeated adversaries, not humiliating them. The Concert of Europe that emerged after the defeat of Napoleon preserved peace for decades precisely because it included a vanquished France in its great power councils. Germany and Japan are today stable and wealthy democracies because the United States and its allies had the good sense to integrate them into the West at the close of the Second World War. In contrast, the Versailles Treaty was imposed on a defeated Germany and exacted onerous reparations. The resentment it engendered among Germans contributed to its rapid demise. Winning the peace today similarly entails integrating a struggling Russia into the West, not treading upon the Russians when they are down.

Some advocates of rapid NATO enlargement into central Europe respond that a new dividing line will in fact benefit Russia's relationship with the West by dampening the instability and filling the security vacuum in central Europe that earlier this century drew Russia and Germany into competitive clashes in the region. Stabilizing central Europe by attaching it to the West, they contend, is the best way to ensure cordial great power relations.[3]

This is but a misreading of history. Central Europe has been the site of so much bloodshed this century not because it is a security vacuum or inherently unstable, but because it has been the stamping ground of the continent's major powers. Stability in central Europe will be determined by relations between Russia and the West, not vice versa. If Russia's relationship with the West is good, central Europe will not have a security problem. If Russia's relations with the West are conflictual, central Europe will be a very dangerous neighbourhood – whether or not it is formally a part of NATO.

Enlargement also breeds a host of strategic and political dilemmas. The Baltics, Slovakia, Slovenia, Bulgaria, Romania and Macedonia are now getting in line for membership, hoping to be in the next wave of NATO enlargement. But are Americans prepared to keep pledging their lives to defend countries they could not find on a map? Did not the conduct of NATO's battle for Kosovo reveal the profound reluctance of the US leadership to sustain American casualties in meeting the new challenges to European security? Is Russia supposed to stand by idly as every country on its western flank joins an opposing military bloc? To what endpoint is the process of enlargement headed? These are only some of the very difficult questions that must be answered as NATO embarks down the path of formal enlargement.

The Origins and Politics of a Bad Idea

If NATO enlargement is such a bad idea, how did it come about? A small group of backers brought NATO enlargement to life during the first Clinton administration.[4] Anthony Lake, the national security adviser during the first term, was the key player; he ensured that President Clinton was on board and drove the policy. With the help of a few other supporters – Deputy Secretary of State Strobe Talbott and then Assistant Secretary of State Richard Holbrooke among them – Lake deftly out-manoeuvred the strong opposition to enlargement that existed within the Pentagon and State Department.

When the Clinton administration first studied during the second half of 1993 how to draw Europe's new democracies into the West's security structures, it decided against formal enlargement and instead opted for a programme of military co-operation known as the Partnership for Peace (PFP). At the NATO summit in January 1994, NATO members presented the PFP as the alliance's main vehicle for outreach to the east. Formal NATO membership for central European countries was by no means precluded, but it was pushed off into the future.[5]

Exactly when and why the Clinton administration decided to expedite formal enlargement rather than continue with the more informal process of integration envisaged in the PFP remains unclear. The key decisions were taken in the spring of 1994, only a few months after the NATO summit. Two main considerations appear to have been at play.

First, Lake from the outset had been a strong proponent of formal enlargement. One of his key objectives was to promote and lock in the spread of democracy. He saw NATO enlargement as a way of attaining these objectives in central Europe. By all accounts, he orchestrated during the spring of 1994 the internal policy review that led to the decision to make formal NATO enlargement, not the PFP, the centrepiece of US policy. The urgency of the policy review stemmed in part from the fact that President Clinton was to visit Poland and Germany in May. With both countries strong proponents of enlargement, this trip offered a prime opportunity for Clinton to announce the new turn in American policy.

Second, the administration found that its initial support for the PFP exposed its political flanks to critics on the right. Henry Kissinger, Zbigniew Brzezinski and other influential voices argued that the PFP was a half-way measure and that the United States should move quickly to ensure that central Europe never again falls under Russian domination.[6] Prominent central Europeans, including Polish President Lech Walesa and Czech President Vaclav Havel, made similar critiques.[7] Their ethnic constituencies in the United States picked up on these arguments and gave them electoral significance. With the Republican Party supporting enlargement and voters of central European extraction concentrated in important swing states such as Michigan, Ohio and Pennsylvania, Clinton faced potent political incentives to get behind NATO expansion.[8]

This outside pressure for NATO expansion had strong Russophobic strains. In contrast, support for enlargement from within the administration was based primarily on liberal arguments about locking in democracy. Lake and his allies on the inside benefited from conservative pressure to expand NATO, but the two pro-enlargement groups made strange ideological bedfellows.

The odd alliance between conservatives and liberals did succeed in securing broad-based political support for enlargement. But it also produced a public justification for NATO expansion that was riddled with logical inconsistencies. A single policy initiative had to keep happy two groups that were behind enlargement for very different reasons. The conservative wing of the coalition viewed enlargement as a strategy for dividing Europe and keeping the Russians permanently out. The liberal wing saw enlargement as a means of creating, in President Clinton's own words, a 'Europe that is undivided, democratic, and at peace for the first time since nation states appeared'.[9] These differing objectives led to deeply troubling inconsistencies on four fronts.

First, Clinton kept insisting that enlargement would 'erase' Europe's dividing lines.[10] But, in reality, it is simply moving those lines eastward. Indeed, shifting NATO's frontier to the east and taking the military steps needed to defend it gives much more salience to the existence of an exclusive strategic bloc than if NATO's old boundaries were left to be forgotten as the Cold War recedes into the past. By erecting a new dividing line while claiming just the opposite, the Clinton administration preserved the unholy alliance of right and left. But its rhetoric bore little resemblance to reality.

The second line of argument that obscured the strategic rationale for enlargement emerged from the administration's insistence that NATO expansion was not directed against Russia. In Secretary Madeleine Albright's words, 'NATO is a defensive alliance that ... does not regard any state as its adversary, certainly not a democratic and reforming Russia that is intent on integrating with the West'.[11] But an alliance is by definition a coalition of states that bands together against an external adversary. Moreover, it is quite obvious that hedging against a reassertion of Russian ambition has been one of the main motivations – if not *the* main motivation – behind NATO enlargement. The central Europeans want NATO membership primarily because of fear of Russia. That NATO is amassing capability against Russia is the main reason that Moscow opposes enlargement. And despite its rhetoric, the Clinton administration's actions make it clear that it recognizes that enlargement is in part directed against Russia. Otherwise, the administration would not have expended so much effort to negotiate the NATO–Russia Founding Act and to find other ways to compensate Moscow for enlargement, such as repeatedly inviting President Yeltsin to meetings of the G-7.

That enlargement 'will make NATO stronger and more cohesive' is the third argument that might have helped build support for the policy, but that was based on dubious logic.[12] NATO is not the cohesive alliance that it once was. The problem is less the addition of new members than the absence of a transcendent threat and the sense of common interest that it engendered. The years of haggling and paralysis that preceded NATO's eventual deployment in Bosnia made clear just how difficult it now is to forge a consensus within the alliance and co-ordinate effective military action. As new members enter NATO, the alliance will grow only looser and more unwieldy. NATO did demonstrate remarkable cohesion during the conflict over Kosovo, but sustaining support for the operation among the three new members was no easy task. Again, these inconsistencies were tolerated – and perhaps even encouraged – in order to please those expanding NATO to guard against a Russian threat while simultaneously keeping happy those seeking to transform NATO into a much more flexible instrument for a broad range of missions.

The fourth claim that crumbles quickly under scrutiny has to do with costs, both to the new members and to taxpayers in the United States and western Europe. The Clinton administration asserted that NATO enlargement would help central Europe's new democracies keep down their levels of defence spending. 'Feeling more secure', Deputy Secretary of State Strobe Talbott explained, NATO's new members 'will feel less incentive to build up their armaments to deal with real or perceived insecurities'.[13] But enlargement is having precisely the opposite effect. In the absence of external threats, central European countries initially slashed their defence budgets during the 1990s, justifiably devoting scarce resources to their still fragile economies. No longer. Meeting NATO standards requires major increases in spending on the military. Indeed, the defence budgets of new and prospective members are rising sharply as they modernize their armed forces and prepare for participation in NATO's integrated military structure.[14] Not surprisingly, America's defence industry, eyeing a new market, has been a major supporter of enlargement. It is no coincidence that an executive from Lockheed Martin served as the head of the US Committee to Expand NATO – an influential group that helped garner political support for enlargement.

The administration's assessments of the costs of enlargement to current NATO members were equally suspect. The Congressional Budget Office put this cost at $61–125 billion over 15 years. As America's European allies and Congress voiced opposition to such expenditure, the Clinton administration successively came in with lower estimates, eventually arriving at a figure of $1.5 billion over ten years. In light of the infrastructure needed to upgrade defence systems in central Europe, most analysts agreed that this figure was way too low and was primarily the product of efforts to make enlargement more palatable to the Europeans and to the American taxpayer.

The Senate

If the strategic rationale for NATO enlargement is so weak, and the main arguments marshalled in its favour so flawed, why did its ratification sail through the Senate? That NATO expansion made it through the executive branch is not that remarkable. Key people at the top of the decision-making apparatus backed it, and the bureaucracy then had to follow orders. Sometimes bad ideas win out. But one of the key purposes of the legislative branch is to check and second-guess the executive. The US Constitution requires the Senate to pass treaties by a two-thirds majority precisely because of the weightiness of the issues at stake. And most other major decisions about the nature of America's obligations abroad have appropriately received the scrutiny they deserve.[15] So what went wrong? Why did more than two-thirds of the Senate approve a very bad idea, almost without blinking?

To begin, narrow electoral concerns triumphed over the national interest. Voting for enlargement kept happy Americans of central European extraction, the defence industry, and conservative Russophobes. In contrast, voting against enlargement may have been the right thing to do, but it had no political pay-offs. Indeed, because the Democratic and Republican leaderships were both pro-enlargement, party discipline discouraged senators from straying from the fold.

But electoral pressures leave unanswered why the Senate settled for a truncated debate. Most of the Senate hearings on enlargement were pep rallies, not opportunities for thoughtful deliberation. Even the more probing debate that finally took place the week of the vote did not dig as deep as it should have. Most senators simply played along with the numerous inconsistencies plaguing the administration's case for enlargement.

So why the wilful ignorance? Lack of interest certainly played a role. Without the Soviet Union around, foreign policy no longer draws a captive audience. The American public shares some of the blame. To its credit, the Clinton administration launched a major public relations campaign to sell enlargement. But most Americans were not listening.[16] After four years of presidential speeches and summit meetings, only ten per cent of the public could name even one of the three countries admitted in the first wave – and granted an American nuclear guarantee.[17] Americans and their elected representatives did not exhibit isolationism, as some analysts feared. They just did not care.

The absence of an earlier and more searching Senate debate was also the product of design, not just apathy. The odd coalition that formed to support enlargement had a vested interest in preventing the Senate from probing too deeply. As mentioned above, the conservative branch of the coalition views enlargement as a military instrument for redividing Europe and keeping the Russians permanently out, while the liberal branch is using NATO as a political tool for building a united Europe – one that might well include Russia some day. Exposing these different objectives would have imperilled the pro-enlargement coalition. Both sides therefore swept the central issue of enlargement's aims under the carpet.

Finally, the Senate acted irresponsibly because a surfeit of American power enabled it to do so. The United States today enjoys uncontested global primacy. The result is not triumphalism or arrogance, as other powers sometimes claim, but a negligence born of complacency. Rather than husband American resources and apply them with measure and prudence, the Senate approved the whimsical exercise of power. Whether because of the country's current bounty or simple lack of interest, the Senate squandered precious commodities – American power and purpose.

James Madison warned in the Federalist Papers that without the judicious counsel of the Senate, 'the esteem of foreign powers will be forfeited by an unenlightened and variable policy'.[18] It now behoves the Senate to heed this warning. As the process of expanding NATO moves ahead, the Senate must give the issue the scrutiny it deserves and ensure the prudent and moderate exercise of American power intended by the founding fathers

Kosovo

NATO's successful battle to drive Serb forces from Kosovo seems, at least at face value, to vindicate the supporters of NATO enlargement. With European stability threatened by ethnic conflict in the Balkans, the United States rose to the occasion and took the lead in orchestrating NATO action. The United States effectively ran the war, kept recalcitrant allies in line, and contributed the lion's share of military assets to the bombing campaign.

The bigger picture, however, suggests anything but a new era of NATO crusades to preserve European stability and protect ethnic minorities. America's effort in the Balkans was at best half-hearted and enjoyed only razor-thin political support. From the outset, President Clinton blocked the use of ground forces, meaning that NATO got into a fight with one hand tied behind its back. Even after weeks of an air war that only exacerbated the humanitarian crisis NATO was supposed to resolve and increased the probability of a southward spread of the war, President Clinton maintained his veto. Moreover, he insisted that allied aircraft bomb from no lower than 15,000 feet to avoid being shot down.

Congressional opposition to the conflict only made matters worse. A month into a war that had not produced a single US casualty, the House nevertheless expressed grave misgivings, voting 290 to 139 to refuse funding for sending US ground troops to Yugoslavia without congressional approval. On the air war, the House was only a shade more adventuresome with a tie vote (213 to 213) on a resolution endorsing the bombing campaign. Congress's behaviour hardly represented a resounding confirmation of America's commitment to stability in the heart of Europe.

If the United States has a zero-tolerance for casualties in a region considered key to stability in south-eastern Europe, it will have no appetite whatsoever for engagements further afield. America fought the right war in Kosovo, and fortunately prevailed. But the sobering message left behind is that it is very unlikely to happen again.

NATO enlargement and the Kosovo conflict thus point to a troubling dilemma. Through enlargement and the intervention in Kosovo, the United States has taken the lead in building a new European house whose roof covers the continent's new and aspiring democracies. But it increasingly looks like a house of cards, built on an American polity that has a dwindling interest in footing the bill for construction and upkeep. America's commitments in Europe are expanding rapidly at the same time that the political appetite for robust internationalism is shrinking at an equal pace.

This mismatch between America's external policies and its internal politics was highlighted by the war in Kosovo. Clinton knew that a failure to confront Milosevic over Kosovo would likely jeopardize Macedonia and, with it, the entire Balkan peninsula. Doing nothing was therefore out of the question. At the same time, even before the conflict began, centrists from both main US political parties argued passionately that Kosovo did not involve America's vital interests and that Europe should assume responsibility for its own troubles. Former Secretary of State Henry Kissinger, hardly an isolationist, argued before the bombing campaign began that, 'the proposed deployment [of US troops] in Kosovo does not deal with any threat to American security as traditionally conceived. ... If Kosovo presents a security problem, it is to Europe.'[19]

Clinton responded by taking the middle road, authorizing an air campaign but nothing more. Coercion from the air did succeed in reining in Milosevic and compelling him to withdraw his troops from Kosovo. But the conflict should hardly be seen as a precedent for the future. NATO aircraft were able to do heavy damage to the Yugoslav army only after a Kosovo Liberation Army (KLA) offensive on the ground forced the Yugoslav army to concentrate in defensive and exposed positions. And throughout the conflict, Milosevic could easily have taken advantage of NATO's weakness on the ground to widen the war to Macedonia or Montenegro. Embarking on a massive air campaign without first putting a serious ground force in the region was not just short sighted, but also irresponsible. Rather than forcing American policy-makers and voters to confront the gap between increasing commitments and decreasing internationalism, NATO's war for Kosovo served only to reinforce the illusion that the United States can preserve global stability on the cheap.

Despite the facade of unity within NATO, America's deep ambivalence about the war did not go unnoticed in Europe. It is no coincidence that in the aftermath of Kosovo, the European Union has redoubled its efforts to forge a collective defence policy and a military force capable of operating independently of the United States. Europeans have been acting on the recognition that they may well be on their own when the next military crisis emerges on the continent. As British Prime Minister Tony Blair asserted in justifying the initiative, 'we Europeans should not expect the United States to have to play a part in every disorder in our own back yard'.[20]

Europe's renewed effort to forge a collective defence capability stems not just from fear of US disengagement. Many European politicians and military leaders had their confidence in US leadership shaken by the war over Kosovo. Despite the positive outcome of the war, the British and French in particular were critical of America's conduct of the war and especially its unwillingness to countenance casualties. Although NATO officials did a good job of maintaining a facade of unity there was behind the scenes a great deal of European criticism of America's strategy for prosecuting the war.

The war over Kosovo thus sent an ominous signal about America's dissipating willingness to be Europe's chief peacemaker and its protector of last resort. At the same time, it has committed the United States and its allies to a host of new commitments in southern Europe and only lengthened the list of candidates readying themselves for inclusion in future waves of NATO enlargement. The United States thus faces difficult dilemmas as it maps out a strategy for the future of NATO and the Atlantic community.

WHAT IS TO BE DONE?

At the end of the day, the impact of NATO enlargement on Europe's stability will turn not on the admission of Poland, Hungary and the Czech Republic, but on what comes next.[21] President Clinton is right that with the collapse of the Soviet Union, an historic opportunity exists to build a democratic Europe at peace. How to go about achieving that objective is the key question.

Now that NATO's first wave of enlargement into central Europe is complete, the coalition that formed to support enlargement is unravelling. Some staunch supporters of enlargement are already arguing that expansion should stop with the entry of Poland, Hungary and the Czech Republic; further enlargement would only dilute the alliance. In contrast, other supporters of enlargement – some looking to restrict further Russia's room for manoeuvre, others to promote the eastward spread of democracy – want the alliance to continue adding new members. The coalition that opposed enlargement is also coming apart. Some opponents are already arguing for a long pause or cessation after the first wave in order to mollify Russia. Others favour a rapid opening to the east in order to construct a pan-European security community.

I contend that, now that NATO enlargement has begun, sound strategic logic necessitates its continuation. Proceeding with enlargement is to establish NATO as *the* central vehicle for building a stable Europe. To stop its expansion at Poland's eastern border therefore makes no strategic sense. Indeed, NATO must now aim at drawing Russia into its ranks. As long as Russia continues down the path of democracy and succeeds in weathering its current economic woes, its ultimate inclusion in NATO is a logical necessity for three main reasons.

First, a new Europe must include Russia if it is to enjoy a durable peace. Russia has long been and will again become one of Europe's great powers. The central determinant of European stability in coming decades will be whether Russia exercises its power in a benign or malign manner. During this critical period in Russia's transition, the West should therefore be doing all it can to lock in democratic reform and to expose Russians to the norms and attitudes that underpin the responsible conduct of foreign policy. NATO's chief mission over the next decade should therefore be to embrace Russia and draw it into the West, not to amass the West's power against it.

Second, integrating Russia into NATO will help avoid the emergence of a new grey zone in the heart of Europe. Those states that now lie between an enlarged NATO and Russia – the Baltics, Romania, Bulgaria, Moldova, Belarus, Ukraine – are Europe's most fragile and vulnerable countries. To halt NATO enlargement after the first wave would only exacerbate their security predicament by leaving them in limbo. To the extent that a strategic vision now exists among NATO members, it calls for the gradual elimination of this grey zone through successive waves of NATO enlargement. But admitting these states into NATO sequentially from west to east will surely put Russia and NATO on a collision course. Russia neither should nor will stand by idly as every country on its western flank joins an opposing military bloc.

The only solution is to expedite Russia's own inclusion in NATO, thereby enabling Europe's grey zone to enter the West without steadily moving a new dividing line closer to Russia. Making it clear in deed as well as rhetoric that NATO's doors will be open to Russia simply cannot wait until the very end of the enlargement process.

Third, Russia's entry into NATO would give the Atlantic community far more influence over developments in the former Soviet space. And it is in Europe's east, not its centre, that the key challenges of the coming decades lie. At stake are the security of Russia's nuclear weapons and technology, Russia's relationship with China, the independence and stability of Ukraine, access to Caspian oil – interests that warrant deep Western engagement. In addition, Russia's relationship with its smaller neighbours would be subject to the restraining effects of NATO's co-operative rules and habits, helping to eliminate the residue of imperial ambition. Stopping NATO enlargement at the frontier between Poland and Belarus would thus restrict the alliance from engaging in those parts of Europe where its peace-causing effects are most needed.

The Clinton administration, at least in rhetorical terms, has not precluded Russia's eventual membership of NATO. In President Clinton's own words, 'NATO's doors will remain open to all those willing to shoulder the responsibilities of membership'.[22] In reality, however, most officials do not take seriously the notion of Russian membership of NATO. And those willing to entertain the idea put Russia at the end of a long queue, becoming eligible for membership only after virtually all countries to Russia's west are already inside the alliance.

Instead, Russian entry into NATO must become a top priority. To buy time for Russian democracy to deepen and for its economy to recover and mature, a small second wave of enlargement, one not provocative to Russia (Slovenia, Austria and Romania are prime candidates), should begin soon after the admission of the first three. But the third wave should include Russia – as long as its economic and political transition gets back on track – perhaps accompanied by its three Baltic neighbours. And in the meantime, NATO's links to Russia should be steadily deepened and the political groundwork laid for its eventual admission. Barring the collapse of the reform process, 2010 represents a reasonable target date for Russia's entry into NATO.[23]

Plans to integrate Russia into NATO face three main objections: (1) that Russia is not interested in NATO membership; (2) that Russia is for now a lost cause rapidly heading toward collapse, virtually precluding for the foreseeable future any consideration of its inclusion in NATO; (3) that Russia's entry into NATO would fundamentally change the character of the alliance.

As to the first objection, Russia remains uninterested in joining NATO in large part because it continues to see the alliance as an anti-Russian organization. This perception stems from NATO's persistence as a traditional military alliance and, despite its rhetoric to the contrary, its purposeful aggregation of capability against Russia. Were NATO to redefine its core mission, and in rhetoric and deed make clear its intention to embrace Russia, Russian perceptions of the alliance would change accordingly.

The claim that Russian reform has veered seriously off track is undeniable, especially since the financial collapse of August 1998. But it is way too soon to write Russia off. On the contrary, there are three potent reasons to remain cautiously optimistic about Russia's future and to take seriously the notion that the country could be ready for NATO within a decade.

First, contrary to conventional wisdom, Russia is not coming apart at the seams. Although the country's regions are growing more powerful at the expense of the central government, devolution is, on balance, contributing to the stability and integrity of the country. In certain regions, democratic accountability, interest group formation and pluralist debate, and entrepreneurship and market development are faring much better than at the national level. Indeed, the wealthier and more progressive regions may well emerge as the anchors of a decentralized Russian state. President Vladimir Putin is now in the midst of seeking to reassert the centre's control over the periphery. The relative strength of regional governors and municipal officials should, however, act as a check on any attempt to restore an authoritarian state.

Although the central government has lost its power more by default than by design, devolution is not about to become fragmentation. Moscow retains control of the military. It also remains the country's financial centre, ensuring that regional governments and firms still look to the centre for subsidies and capital. And even if residents in the regions want more autonomy, most do not want independence. Ethnic Russians, who comprise roughly 82 per cent of the population, remain firmly committed to an integral state. And most Russians are quite clear that theirs is a European, not a Eurasian, country. With about three-quarters of its population living west of the Urals and its history and culture rooted in the West, Russians look much more to Europe than to Asia as they imagine their future.

Second, democracy and civil society, although still primitive, have begun to take root. Elections are becoming a matter of course. Voters choose from numerous candidates, whose views range across the political spectrum. The media is relatively free and open debate the norm. Needless to say, Russia is far from a liberal democracy. But it has made great strides in the past decade. And there are good reasons to be confident that the liberalizing forces that have swept from Europe's west to east will with time take firmer hold in Russia.

Third, Russia is no longer an adversary of the West. It poses no military threat whatsoever to central or western Europe. Even ardent nationalists, who continue to urge Moscow to reassert control over some former Soviet republics, recognize that central Europe is gone for good. Although Russia has at times exercised its influence in the near-abroad through coercive means, it has by no means attempted to reconstitute by force an imperial zone of domination. Furthermore, the bark of Russian foreign policy is much worse than the bite. Russia and China decry American hegemony and call for a countervailing coalition, but do next to nothing to follow through. Despite confrontational rhetoric over NATO expansion, Iraq, and the Balkans, Russia has for the most part acceded to Western policy. Moscow vociferously condemned NATO's intervention in Yugoslavia and even sent a naval vessel to the Mediterranean. But its rhetoric far outpaced its actions. Russia honoured the arms embargo against Yugoslavia and left its troops in NATO's peacekeeping operation in Bosnia. Russian diplomacy played a critical role in convincing Milosevic to withdraw his troops from Kosovo. Far from being an intractable adversary, Russia is at worst a thorny bystander – and, as Kosovo made clear, at times an emerging partner.

Russia is anything but over the hump. A weakened state faces enormous challenges as it seeks to erect a viable system of taxation, reclaim the economy from corruption, and stabilize its finances. The flagging economy in turn increases the potential for the flow of nuclear material and technology to third parties. But Russia's current difficulties only make more urgent the need for Western efforts to help the country get economic and political reform back on course. The last message Russians should hear is that the West is turning its back or, worse still, enlarging NATO to ensure their exclusion from Europe. To be sure, NATO should readily return to its traditional mission of containment should the reform process collapse and Russia revert to an aggressor state. But until given compelling reasons to treat Russia as an adversary, the West should do all it can to facilitate the country's internal reform and its integration into Atlantic institutions.

It is true that Russian membership of NATO would dilute the alliance and alter its character. But Russian entry would only formalize changes in NATO that must come about if the alliance is to adapt to a new strategic landscape. Without an identifiable threat, NATO will make itself irrelevant if it remains a collective defence organization. Its focus on defending the territory of members needs to give way to an emphasis on peacekeeping and on deepening co-operation and trust among former adversaries. Automatic and binding defence guarantees should be replaced by looser and more informal commitments to protect common interests through common action. These changes should occur in step with the deepening of Russian democracy and the elimination of the need to hedge against the return of imperial ambition. If NATO is to be the vehicle of choice for building security across Europe, it must ultimately cease drawing new lines and focus instead on integrating all of Europe's democracies into a co-operative security community.

So too would a broader but looser NATO be more in keeping with domestic political trends in current NATO countries – especially in the United States. The ratification of enlargement by the US Senate should by no means be interpreted as a resounding confirmation of American internationalism. As mentioned above, most Americans and their elected representatives paid very little attention to the issue, in large part because the new commitments exist only on paper. The Balkans are a far better test case of Congress' willingness to put American lives on the line in Europe's centre. And Congress' reluctance to deploy and maintain US troops in Bosnia and Kosovo does not augur well for its willingness to stand behind the Article 5 commitments just extended to new NATO members. Hungary, after all, is just to Bosnia's north. It is troubling, to say the least, that most senators and representatives are so ready to grant nuclear guarantees to Hungary, but so reluctant to deploy US forces in the Balkans. Over the long term, the United States is far more likely to stay put on the Continent if it is able to pick and choose its fights than if it finds itself with treaty commitments to defend a host of new allies in Europe.

EUROPE WITHOUT ITS AMERICAN PACIFIER?

The success of Russia's reform efforts and its integration into Western institutions would complete one of the most important transformations of the modern era: the democratization and pacification of all of Europe's great powers. Paradoxically, the emergence of a democratic and stable Europe would put at risk one of the key sources of European peace – America's presence as an extra-regional balancer. The wider and deeper Europe's peace becomes, the more likely it is that the United States will focus its attention and strategic resources elsewhere.

As mentioned above, the battle for Kosovo has already raised the prospect of a diminishing American role in managing European security. The central issue, however, is not who will balance against Russia, but how the European project will fare if it can no longer rely on the United States as its strategic guarantor. In his 1986 article in *Foreign Policy*, 'Europe's American Pacifier', Joseph Joffe wrote that America's presence in Europe is central to preventing the return of national rivalries to Europe. Many contemporary analysts believe that Joffe's analysis still holds and that the viability of European integration continues to depend on America's continental commitment.[24]

But Europe cannot rely indefinitely on America's protective umbrella to ensure its security and pre-empt intra-European competition. The progressive pacification of Russia is only one of several factors that will induce the United States to lighten its load in Europe. The global diffusion of power, the end of unipolarity, and more inward-looking domestic politics in the United States all point to the retraction of American power in coming years.

America is still enjoying its unipolar moment, but a world of multiple centres of power is looming on the horizon. Economic output in the United States has fallen from one-half to one-quarter of global product over the last five decades, and secular processes of diffusion will continue to redistribute economic and military might in the years ahead.[25] A rising China and a Europe united by a single market and a single currency are emerging counterweights to American power. Assuming the European Union succeeds in deepening its level of integration and adding new members, it will soon have influence on matters of finance and trade equal to America's. A more balanced strategic relationship is likely to follow.

As NATO members look to the future, prudence thus necessitates that they forge a vision of European security that is less Atlantic and more European than in the past. Europe is in fact further along in developing such a self-sustaining regional order than is commonly recognized, especially in the United States. American power and purpose unquestionably made possible European integration. American guarantees enabled western Europeans to be comfortable with German recovery and rearmament. And NATO effectively took the weightiest security issues off the European agenda, allowing the European project to focus almost exclusively on economic and political integration.

But Europe is now to a significant extent running on its own steam, making the prospect of less reliance on its American pacifier far less worrying. The success of the European project stems from the fact that Europe integrated itself internally at the same time that it was integrated into the Atlantic community of capitalist democracies. Germany dealt with its past and made peace with its neighbours, paving the way for a collective process of integration that has produced dramatic results: the European Union. Europe stands in stark contrast to Asia, where Japan and other countries were integrated into the community of capitalist democracies, but the region failed to take advantage of American guarantees to pursue its own political integration. Unlike Germany, Japan neither confronted its past nor sought reconciliation with the victims of its aggression. This historical difference today leaves East Asia with a far more fragile and dangerous security environment than Europe.

The durability of the European polity stems in large part from the geopolitical transformation that has resulted from decades of integration. The Franco-German coalition has established itself as Europe's benign power centre, with smaller states arraying themselves in concentric circles around this core. The centripetal force of effective regional unipolarity has replaced the destructive jockeying that plagued Europe during its long decades of multipolarity. In addition, through a host of institutions and practices – a European parliament, a common market, a single currency – EU members have gradually pooled their sovereignty, enabling the national state to exist comfortably alongside a supranational union. That most of Europe's new democracies are now waiting impatiently for entry into the EU makes clear the appeal of this construction. And the prospect of entry in turn provides impetus behind reform and the resolution of disputes in central and eastern Europe.[26]

The tide also appears to be turning on the issue of common defence. British Prime Minister Tony Blair has made a top priority the creation of a more robust European defence capability. For a long time a brake on integration, Britain now appears to be casting its lot with a more unified and influential Europe. The EU is also pursuing a host of measures on the defence front. The EU's first-ever defence chief, Javier Solana, will be overseeing efforts to establish a crisis response force and develop a policy planning unit. The main impetus behind these initiatives is not, as some US critics charge, to undermine American influence in Europe. Rather, Europeans are becoming increasingly aware that their strategic dependence on the United States is untenable over the long term. Better to prepare now than be left in the lurch when the United States decides to pass on some future crisis in Europe.

Despite good reasons to be optimistic about the European project, it is also clear that the EU has much hard work ahead. Blair's noble intentions aside, formidable obstacles stand in the way of a more coherent foreign and defence policy.[27] Only a few years ago, Europe failed miserably when it tried to stop on its own the bloodshed in the Balkans. On the economic front, structural rigidities and an overextended state sector continue to produce low growth and high unemployment. And both Germany and France lack the political will needed to carry out structural reform. Indeed, Germany's new Social Democratic government has thus far only made matters worse. Economic stagnation and political stalemate, if they continue, will take a toll on the EU's coherence. So too does generational change pose a potential problem. For younger generations who lived through neither the horrors of the Second World War nor the formidable task of rebuilding Europe, escaping the past will no longer serve as a sufficient rationale for the European project. Elites will have to generate new arguments to ensure the integrity of the Franco–German coalition and the broader European polity.

As they build a stable Atlantic community for the future, both Americans and Europeans thus need to pay far more attention to locking in a European construction that will withstand the potential retrenchment of American power. At the same time that the United States takes the lead in expanding NATO and embracing Russia, it must also do what it can to strengthen the EU as an independent and durable centre of power. Even if it comes at the expense of US influence in Europe or trade across the Atlantic, a stronger and self-sustaining European polity is in America's long-term interests.

Washington can help strengthen Europe's core by dealing with Germany and France collectively. (Britain should be included in this troika down the road if Blair continues to move his country closer to Europe.) The United States should encourage, rather than look with suspicion, at efforts to strengthen Europe's own defence capabilities and at initiatives such as the joint visit of Helmut Kohl and Jacques Chirac to Moscow in 1998. The Clinton administration and a cohort of outside analysts should also drop their efforts to turn NATO into a vehicle for global military operations.[28] Rather than press European forces to join their US counterparts in battling common threats wherever they emerge, Washington should encourage Europe to shoulder more of the burden in its own neighbourhood. Europeans must consolidate peace on the continent before they can afford to focus their main attention elsewhere.

Washington can only do so much, however; it is primarily up to the Europeans themselves to prepare for a more balanced Atlantic relationship. Locking in the Franco-German coalition, especially as a new generation of leaders rises to power, is a top priority. The new German government must make unequivocal its commitment to solidarity with France, especially as all of Europe watches carefully the move of Germany's capital from Bonn to Berlin. France and Germany must not just ensure the smooth implementation of monetary union and other aspects of economic and political integration. They must also begin to address in earnest how to move forward on the defence front.

Reallocating defence spending is also a top priority. Europe spends way too much on troops, and way too little on capability. (Europe's collective defence spending is about 60 per cent of America's, but Europe maintains more forces under arms.) The EU needs to trade a large but hollow army for a smaller force with more capability, buy air and sea lift, consolidate its defence industry, and increase the technological sophistication of its weapons systems. Only then will the EU be a more complete partner of the United States and be capable of operating on its own should America choose not to engage in a future crisis in Europe.

CONCLUSION

My analysis should not be interpreted as a warning of America's impending departure from Europe. On the contrary, the United States is likely to remain engaged in managing European security well into the new century. At the same time, the current scope of America's preponderance – and the reliance of virtually every quarter of the globe on that preponderance – will not last. While they have the luxury of doing so, the United States and its European allies need to work towards a partnership in which responsibility and influence are more equally shared across the Atlantic.

This perspective necessitates both a short-term and a long-term strategy for the Atlantic community. In the short term, the United States should continue to guide NATO's enlargement and its internal reform, ensuring that Russia's eventual inclusion in the alliance becomes a top priority. The United States and its NATO allies must come to their senses and seize the historic opportunity to embed Russia in the Atlantic community. Over the long term, the United States and its NATO allies should take steps to facilitate the gradual devolution of increasing responsibility to the European Union. A more balanced relationship between the United States and Europe, and a European security order that is more European and less Atlantic, holds out the best hope for preserving a cohesive transatlantic community. As the twenty-first century progresses, America must become Europe's partner, no longer its pacifier.

NOTES

1. George F. Kennan, 'A Fateful Error', *New York Times*, 5 Feb. 1997.
2. For a succinct critique of enlargement, see Michael Brown, 'The Flawed Logic of NATO Expansion', *Survival*, Vol.37, No.1 (Spring 1995), pp.34–52.
3. See, for example, Richard Holbrooke, 'America, a European Power', *Foreign Affairs*, Vol.74, No.2 (March–April 1995), pp.38–51; and Henry Kissinger, 'Expand NATO Now', *Washington Post*, 19 Dec. 1994.
4. This interpretation of the evolution of policy is based in part on my own experience as a staff member of the National Security Council during 1993–94. I also draw on interviews with former colleagues after my departure from the NSC. For a published account of the evolution of enlargement, which is consistent with that presented here, see James Goldgeier, *Not Whether But When: The U.S. Decision to Enlarge NATO* (Washington, DC: The Brookings Institution, 1999). Goldgeier's book represents the most thorough study of the decision to enlarge NATO published to date.
5. Charles Kupchan, 'Strategic Visions', *World Policy Journal*, Vol.11, No.3 (Fall 1994), pp.112–21.
6. See, for example, Henry Kissinger, 'Not this Partnership', *Washington Post*, 24 Nov. 1993.
7. See, for example, 'Walesa Warns Communism May Reemerge', *Washington Post*, 4 Jan. 1994.

8. On the electoral importance of voters of central European extraction, see Dick Kirschten, 'Ethnics Resurging', *National Journal*, Vol.27, No.8 (25 Feb. 1995), pp.478–84.

9. President Clinton, Remarks on NATO Enlargement (Washington, DC: The White House, 3 July 1997).

10. See, for example, President Clinton's press conference at the Centro de Convenciones, Madrid, 9 July 1997.

11. Secretary of State Madeleine Albright's commencement address at Harvard University, 5 June 1997.

12. Secretary of State Madeleine Albright's Statement at North Atlantic Council Ministerial Meeting, Sintro, Portugal, 29 May 1997. Available at: http://secretary.state.gov/www/statements/

13. Cited in 'Arms Makers See Bonanza in Selling NATO Expansion', *New York Times*, 29 June 1997.

14. British American Security Information Council and the Centre for European Security and Disarmament, *NATO Expansion: Time to Reconsider*, Special Report (Washington, DC, 25 Nov. 1996). It is interesting to note that since joining NATO, Hungary has put off or cancelled several of the defence reforms that it had committed to undertake in preparation for admission.

15. On the debate over the League of Nations, see Thomas Knock, *To End All Wars: Woodrow Wilson and the Quest for a New World Order* (New York: Oxford University Press, 1992); and Ralph Stone, *The Irreconcilables: The Fight Against the League of Nations* (Lexington: University Press of Kentucky, 1970). For a succinct summary of the debate on NATO's formation, see Dean Acheson, *Present at the Creation* (New York: W.W. Norton, 1969), Chs. 31, 32.

16. As one senator told me, 'some of us have tried to elicit public interest in the issue. But when a flyer goes out advertising that Senator so-and-so is giving a talk on NATO enlargement at a local spot, no one shows up.'

17. Pew Research Center for the People and the Press, 'Public Opinion Leaders Favor Enlargement', 7 Oct. 1997. Available at: http://www.people-press.org/natoral.htm

18. James Madison, 'The Federalist Papers', No.63, 1 March 1788.

19. Henry Kissinger, 'US Intervention in Kosovo is a Mistake', *The Boston Globe*, 1 March 1999.

20. Tony Blair, 'NATO, Europe, Our Future Security', speech at the NATO 50th Anniversary Conference, 10 March 1999. Available at: http://www.number-10.gov.uk.

21. A version of this section of the essay originally appeared in 'Rethinking Europe', *The National Interest*, No.56 (Summer 1999), pp.73–9.

22. President Clinton, Remarks at NATO Summit Send-Off by America's Veterans, 3 July 1997. Available at: http://www.pub.whitehouse.gov.

23. For further discussion of Russia's integration into NATO, see James Goodby, *Europe Undivided* (Washington, DC: US Institute of Peace Press, 1998).

24. See Joseph Joffe, 'Europe's American Pacifier', *Foreign Policy*, No.54 (Spring 1984), pp.64–82; and Robert Art, 'Why Western Europe Needs the United States and NATO', *Political Science Quarterly*, Vol.111, No.1 (Spring 1996), pp.1–39.

25. During the second half of the twentieth century, America's economic output has fallen from roughly one-half to one-quarter of gross world product. See Jeffrey Frankel, *Regional Trading Blocs in the World Economic System* (Washington, DC: Institute for International Economics, 1997), p.6. Even if the US economy grows at a healthy rate, America's share of world product will continue to decline as other large countries develop.

26. For further discussion of the long-term implications of integration for European security and the transformation from multipolarity to unipolarity, see Ole Wæver, 'Integration as Security', in Charles Kupchan (ed.), *Atlantic Security: Contending Visions* (New York: Council on Foreign Relations, 1998), p.45–63; and Charles Kupchan, 'After Pax Americana: Benign Power, Regional Integration, and the Sources of a Stable Multipolarity', *International Security*, Vol.23, No.2 (Fall 1998), pp.40–79.

27. See Philip Gordon, 'Europe's Uncommon Foreign Policy', *International Security*, Vol.22, No.3 (Winter 1997/98), pp.74–100.

28. On the policy of the Clinton administration, see 'New Visions for NATO', *New York Times*, 7 Dec. 1998, p.A26. See also Robert Blackwill, *The Future of Transatlantic Relations* (New York: Council on Foreign Relations, 1999).

Boarding the NATO Train:
Enlargement and National Interests

RONALD J. BEE

International law springs from the relations between autonomous states. It is for this reason that what is absolute in it retains the form of an ought-to-be, since its actuality depends on the different wills each of which is sovereign.

Georg Hegel
The Philosophy of Right

This adapted NATO is not just an instrument through which Americans help Europeans secure Europe. Its purpose is to defend our common interest in transatlantic security.

US Secretary of State Madeleine Albright
Statement to the North Atlantic Council, Luxembourg, 28 May 1998

On 4 April 1949, Secretary of State Dean Acheson signed the North Atlantic Treaty, the first peacetime military alliance concluded by the United States since the adoption of the US Constitution.[1] After two world wars, a surprise attack at Pearl Harbor, and post-war Soviet expansion into eastern Europe, the United States determined that its own best national interests lay in providing western Europe with economic assistance via the Truman Doctrine and the Marshall Plan, cemented by a bona fide military security guarantee. A strong American economic and military presence in Europe would prove necessary for European economic recovery and the 'long-term, patient but firm and vigilant containment of Russian expansive tendencies'.[2] Western Europeans, too, saw American economic aid serving their best national interests as they struggled to rebuild their war-torn economies. Moreover, as they looked warily over their shoulder at the installation of communist governments in Czechoslovakia, Hungary and Poland, a Soviet blockade of West Berlin, and the first Soviet atomic test, western Europeans understood that a military alliance with America would be key to preventing another war.[3]

On 4 April 1999, NATO marked its 50th anniversary under far different circumstances by admitting the Czech Republic, Hungary and Poland to its ranks.[4] With the Warsaw Pact defunct and the Soviet Union dissolved, NATO accepted new member states even though the principal threat against which it originally organized no longer exists. Why? Because, under these new circumstances, national interests once again drove policy – this time US, western European *and* eastern European in origin. Just as these interests converged to enable the first wave of post-Cold War NATO enlargement,[5] so, too, will such a coalition of national wills be needed for any second-wave member states to join. As the fledgling Russian federation watches its former allies board the NATO train, Russians struggle to determine their own proper national interests, not yet shedding their Cold War distrust of the West on security matters. Most Russian attitudes regarding NATO remain visceral and negative, suggesting that since Russia is the successor to the Soviet Union, then NATO must still somehow be aligned against Russian interests.[6] This Russian fear of a runaway NATO train, this anti-NATO psychological baggage will have to be handled most carefully, proved wrong, and overcome if NATO enlargement is ultimately to achieve its objectives.[7]

US, WESTERN EUROPEAN, AND EASTERN EUROPEAN
INTERESTS AND NATO ENLARGEMENT:
BUILDING A POLICY CONSENSUS

US Interests: Keeping the Peace and Leadership of the Atlantic Alliance

> NATO Enlargement is critical to protecting and promoting our vital national security interests in Europe. If we fail to seize this historic opportunity to help integrate, consolidate, and stabilize Central and Eastern Europe, we would risk paying a much higher price later.
>
> Secretary of Defense William S. Cohen
23 April 1997[8]

How did the American NATO enlargement train get rolling, and what US rationale developed to fuel the engine? The democratic revolutions in eastern Europe and the disintegration of the Soviet Union called into question a number of key assumptions for the European security system and America's involvement in it. Yet, from the outset, American support for NATO stemmed from the judgement that US security had been threatened by war originating in Europe in the past and that future conflicts there thus must be deterred. Moreover, in 1949, US leaders reasoned that future US security would depend on Europe's continued peaceful and democratic evolution. That reasoning, at least for the near term, has not changed.[9] American support for and involvement in NATO enlargement stems largely from these same principles.

Furthermore, the US executive branch committed itself to maintaining a leadership role in European political–military affairs, and to playing a central role in the widening and deepening of European security arrangements. The US, in concert with its NATO allies, drew on past NATO rationale for extending a transatlantic security guarantee to an unstable region – this time central and eastern Europe, and this time, without the immediate threat of a major military force to counter it. For their part, central and eastern Europeans are reassured, like their western European counterparts 50 years ago, by the political presence and military promise of an American superpower. Eastern Europeans also see NATO membership as an important step towards economic integration with the European Union (EU). US Department of State documents emphasized how NATO enlargement will 'consolidate democracy and stability in Central Europe' and 'erase the Cold War dividing line'.[10]

In the US debate, opponents of NATO enlargement worried more about Europe's far east, the Russian Federation, interpreting this act as *creating* a new Cold War dividing line rather than erasing the old one. A number of prominent former American diplomats, including George Kennan, Jack Matlock and Jonathan Dean, argued against enlargement. Kennan went so far as to call the idea 'the most fateful error of American policy in the entire post-Cold War era'. He predicted the policy would ignite Russian nationalism, set back democratic reforms, bring back the Cold War, and imperil Russian ratification of the START II agreement, let alone future nuclear arms reductions.[11] A number of US academicians and international relations theorists also opposed the idea.[12] Certain political groups and pundits on the left and right urged the US to avoid getting involved in another 'entangling alliance' where the costs – financial and strategic – would be too high.[13] For opponents, the NATO enlargement train was destined to derail and wreck somewhere between Moscow and the US Treasury.

Yet, on 3 March 1998 the Senate Foreign Relations Committee approved by a vote of 16 to 2 a resolution giving the Senate's advice and consent to the admission of the Czech Republic, Hungary and Poland to NATO.[14] On 30 April 1998, the US Senate voted 80 to 19 to ratify the protocols of accession to make that possible. Certainly domestic politics played a role in the process. It is no wonder that major speeches in favour of NATO enlargement were not delivered in San Diego before the 1996 elections; President Clinton instead chose large mid-western cities with significant populations of eastern European immigrants – Cleveland in 1995 and Detroit in 1996. Clinton announced a timetable for admitting new NATO members just before the election.

The Republican Party's tactic on the issue insisted that Clinton was dragging his heels on NATO enlargement, thus playing into the hands of anti-democratic forces in Russia, while missing an opportunity to consolidate the gains of the end of the Cold War. By arguing about the pace of American leadership on the issue, and not the substance of admitting new NATO members, the clear implication was that Republicans supported enlargement. Moreover, the Republican 'Contract with America' called for Poland, the Czech Republic, Hungary and Slovakia to join NATO within the next four years. After the 1996 election, and before ratification hearings, majority leader Trent Lott established a NATO Observer Group to 'join the administration in its negotiations on NATO enlargement and to cut across party lines and committee jurisdictions'. Lott, in a *Washington Post* opinion-editorial, concluded, 'We stand ready to help President Clinton in this effort.'[15]

With both the Democratic and Republican leaderships in basic agreement, arguments for ratification of the accession protocols drew from a number of key political–military concepts that can be grouped along a past–present–future continuum. These arguments were also applied within the western European, and central and eastern European, debates over enlargement, albeit with different emphases which reflect different calculations of national interest. These concepts can be seen as self-reinforcing concentric circles, all revolving as much around the past, present and future perceptions of national interest as they do around 'national style'.

THE NATO PAST AS PRECEDENT

Remarkable generations of Americans invested in Europe's peace and freedom with their own sacrifice. They fought two world wars. They had the vision to create NATO and the Marshall Plan. The vigor of

those institutions, the force of democracy, the determination of people
to be free – all these helped to produce victory in the Cold War. But
now that freedom has been won, it is this generation's responsibility to
ensure that it will not be lost again, not ever.

President Bill Clinton[16]

Americans love winners, and NATO under American leadership is
widely perceived in the US and the US Senate as having played a central
role in rebuilding Europe, deterring the Soviets, keeping the peace, and
'winning' the Cold War. This positive perception of NATO's past
performance imbued a measure of confidence in its ability to face new
challenges now that the Cold War was over. The American post-Second
World War choice of policy engagement instead of abject indifference
paid off in terms of preventing renewed war in western Europe while
ensuring a thriving western European economic system that
complemented US interests in a liberal global economic order.

The Marshall Plan, which provided for the rebuilding of allied as
well as former enemy economies after the Second World War, worked
because it provided for the practical daily needs of real people, and
'against the hunger and poverty that breed desperation and chaos'.[17] It
worked because of a transatlantic political–military alliance that enabled
western Europe to rebuild and integrate its economies rather than refill
its graveyards. The Marshall Plan provided a set of organizing principles
to serve both US and western European interests at the outset of the
Cold War. It worked because it provided a psychological boost to
Europeans in need of rallying to their own economic recovery. These
principles of security and economic stability are at the heart of
proponents' arguments for the enlargement of NATO.

But what about the cost? Although the American cost of the
Marshall Plan over five years amounted to $13 billion, and containing
the Soviet Union over 40 years cost $13 trillion, these enormous sums
have been largely viewed as 'worth it', given the positive outcomes.
Although enlargement opponents tried to draw attention to the high
costs, that argument did not sway the US Senate. In fact, enlargement
proponents suggested that the US should continue its engagement in
Europe to protect, *inter alia*, its large past transatlantic investments –
financial and otherwise. Strobe Talbott, Deputy Secretary of State, put
it this way:

American internationalism in general and Atlanticism in particular are grounded in America's enlightened self-interest. We have learned that basic truth the hard way. The two world wars cost us the equivalent of over half a million Americans, while the Cold War cost us the equivalent of over 13 trillion dollars and brought us to the brink of the hottest war imaginable.[18]

Madeleine Albright argued further that a decision not to enlarge NATO would also carry an opportunity cost: 'it would constitute a declaration that NATO would neither address the challenges nor accept the geography of a new Europe. NATO would be stuck in the past, risking irrelevance and even dissolution. Those are costs we cannot afford'.[19]

NATO and the Marshall Plan are American success stories that provided historical precedents and strategic rationale for supporting NATO enlargement eastward. Further, it is no coincidence that the 1997 Madrid summit took place in the Spanish capital, formerly Franco's capital, to demonstrate that countries can successfully join the democratic community after a totalitarian past, and contribute to NATO's common defence. Italy and Germany were earlier examples. Greece and Turkey's incorporation into the Atlantic alliance has been viewed largely as playing a moderating influence on their mutual historical animosity. In effect, NATO's past has been invoked as an institutional precedent for addressing Europe's present and future security challenges.

For western Europeans, NATO's past also in large part served them well. Without NATO's, and in particular, the American security umbrella, the Cold War could have turned hot at many moments, and most likely at first on European territory. While some Europeans argue that peace prevailed 'despite the American presence', most acknowledge the key role that transatlantic military links, American troop deployments and nuclear deterrence played in securing their economic recovery, let alone reinforcing western European political stability over the longer term. Despite the periodic crises – among them, Suez in 1956, France leaving the NATO integrated military command in 1966, the Pershing II and Cruise missile deployment debates of the early 1980s – Europe as a whole has seen itself as better off with NATO than without it. This has proved true as well after the Cold War. West European affinities for NATO were reinforced by the Bosnian experience, and in particular the initial European failure to stop the carnage. Bosnia also served as a way of justifying a new mission for 'out of NATO area' conflicts, further extending future battlefields beyond allied territories, while engaging Americans, central Europeans and Russians in the military crisis management of a conflict no one wanted to see spread. An example had been set for regional security co-operation, one that drew on NATO's past institutional mechanisms to create a new mission that still served west European national interests.[20]

For the Czech Republic, Hungary and Poland, of course, NATO history meant something else. It did precious little as the Soviet sphere of influence, backed by the Warsaw Pact and Soviet nuclear weapons, spread to stifle and squelch all movements towards democratic capitalism. Denied Marshall Plan aid, the central Europeans had to wait out the end of Soviet communism to move towards that goal. When that door opened in 1989–91, and the Soviet sphere of influence disintegrated, the opportunity to reintegrate with the West, economically, politically, and yes, militarily proved compelling. Economically, the goal is integration within the EU. Politically, Visegrad wants to ensure that democratic freedoms and economic development evolve concomitantly to ensure that integration. And finally, while not always stated but always understood, the history of Soviet crackdowns in Hungary in 1956, Czechoslovakia in 1968, and Poland in 1981 plays an important role. That history drives current wishes for military integration with NATO as a hedge against a resurgent Russia, one that might wish to revive the old days under a different authoritarian but equally colonial banner. Such a hedge must include US participation, predominance, and preponderance of nuclear weapons in NATO to be credible. At this time, for central and eastern Europeans, nothing less will do.

THE NATO PRESENT AS PRACTICAL DUTY

> The dream of the generation that founded NATO was of a Europe whole and free. But the Europe of their time was lamentably divided by the Iron Curtain. Our generation can realize their dream.
>
> President Bill Clinton[21]

> Europe's institutional arrangements should be determined by the objective demands of the present, not the tragedies of Europe's past.
>
> Former Secretary of State Warren Christopher[22]

After the Cold War, US enlightened self-interest could also be extended to eastern Europeans for the first time without risking nuclear war. American proponents of NATO enlargement see this new environment as an opportunity to complete unfinished Western business vis-à-vis eastern Europe. It would be fruitless for the West to attempt to make amends for Yalta, or past Western inaction during past Soviet crackdowns. Yet NATO enlargement can assuage these regretful memories while acting to support present central and eastern European desires. By extending an umbrella of military reassurance to eastern Europeans, the West, out of historical duty and present practical interest, opens its institutions to those striving to join the Atlantic alliance. Pervasive US language on NATO enlargement about 'erasing Cold War dividing lines' and 'doing for Europe's East what it did for Europe's West' speaks to this duty. Before the Senate Appropriations Committee, Secretary of State Albright put it this way:

> The United States is a European power. If we have an interest in the lands west of the Oder River, then we surely have an interest in the 200 million people who live in the nations between the Baltic and Black Seas. We waged the Cold War in part because these nations were held captive. We fought World War II in part because they had been invaded. We know that half a continent cannot be secure if the other half is in turmoil. Now that the nations of central Europe are free, we want them to succeed and we want them to be safe.[23]

NATO necessarily began as a military alliance with a practical political dimension. It became the principal mechanism for American involvement and leadership in Europe. That has not changed. What has changed is the nature of the threat, and thereby the nature of NATO's mission. NATO's New Strategic Concept asserts that risks to allied security are less likely to result from calculated aggression against the territories of the allies, but rather from instabilities that may arise from serious economic, social and political difficulties. The Gulf War and particularly Bosnia made this abundantly clear. Secretary of Defense William Cohen has asserted, 'NATO operations in Bosnia are a prime example of the new missions that NATO must be prepared to undertake'.[24] In the Gulf and Bosnian cases, American political–military leadership proved crucial to bolstering NATO credibility; on the flip side, NATO remained key to demonstrating the value of post–Cold War

American leadership. The 1995 Dayton peace agreement, no matter how flawed for the long term, ended the war in Bosnia and thereby underscored the United States' continuing role as an important European power.[25]

Turmoil and US engagement in Kosovo illustrated this reality once again. By one State Department assessment, Kosovo represented the culmination of successive Balkan wars created largely by the ill will, military intervention, ethnic cleansing tactics and broken promises of Serbian leader Slobodan Milosevic.[26] Milosevic, the common denominator to the wars in Slovenia, Croatia, Bosnia-Herzegovina and now Kosovo, had defied Europe, the United States and the alliance that bound them together. Kosovo, like Bosnia before it, became a test case for the alliance's new strategic concept, for NATO's new role and mission in the post–Cold War era.

In January 1994, the Clinton administration proposed a three-pronged strategy for a new NATO: new missions, new members and new partnerships. First, NATO needed to strengthen its core mission of self-defence and adapt itself to take on 'new challenges to our security and to Europe's stability'.[27] Kosovo could certainly fit this general criterion. Second, NATO must reach out to new partners and take in new members from Europe's emerging democracies. With the acceptance of the Czech Republic, Hungary and Poland into NATO, this strategy had been initially achieved, although debate over the second wave of potential central European members was surely complicated by Kosovo. And third, NATO had to forge a strong co-operative relationship with Russia. Kosovo temporarily derailed this strategic track, as the Russians chose to withdraw from all NATO councils, associations and commitments after NATO began bombing Serbia.

While all three goals are linked, the first strategy speaks to maintaining NATO's military role amid new threat scenarios, and by implication, maintaining American leadership in carrying out those new missions. The second goal also implies the strengthening of NATO to field troops for those new operations; it is estimated that the Czech Republic, Hungary and Poland will add about 200,000 troops to the Atlantic alliance.[28] With the American military presence in Europe reduced from 300,000 troops to 100,000, central Europeans will in effect replenish the numerical difference. Although the third goal – co-operating with Russia – remains crucial to the long-term strategy, it clearly does not imply giving the Russians a veto over NATO actions.

During the early 1990s, the phrase 'out-of-area or out of business' became a mantra in the NATO wings of the Pentagon. This altered role and mission also signified a changed US political dimension and challenge *within* NATO. After the Cold War, the goal became not only to reassure former communists in Russia about the West's peaceful intentions, it also meant creating political coalitions inside NATO to support of out-of-area military activities. The United States, as a predominant NATO partner and superpower with global interests, still needs political allies within the alliance to act in support of those interests.

For example, the United States, under the Bush administration, whole-heartedly backed Helmut Kohl in his historic bid for the unification of Germany. At just about every private meeting with Americans since then, the German Chancellor has thanked the United States for its steadfast support of unification. As one likely consequence, Germany more readily agreed to the use of its military bases by US commanders to transfer American troops and war material to the Persian Gulf and later, Bosnia. While not expressly a quid pro quo arrangement, the value of US support for German unification proved huge to Chancellor Kohl. It is not inconceivable that he felt a responsibility to reciprocate the favour when American-led NATO military coalitions needed political and logistical support to carry out their missions. This appreciation for the American support of German unification probably also played a role in the German decision to send troops to Bosnia.[29]

If out-of-area American-led missions continue to be the NATO norm, political support for them within NATO will be needed. By championing the enlargement of NATO to the Czech Republic, Hungary and Poland, the United States can also expect to increase its intra-NATO political support by three votes. The political duty that Americans feel to extend a security guarantee to Visegrad may help create a reciprocal eastern European political duty to support the United States in future NATO deliberations over the use of force in out-of-area missions. While not a guaranteed quid pro quo, by admitting new passengers to the NATO train the United States may also gain political support for determining the alliance's future directions.

For Germans in particular, NATO enlargement represents a present and practical duty. Klaus Kinkel, German Foreign Minister, before the German Bundestag's 555 to 37 vote in favour of ratifying the NATO accession protocols, asserted, 'we see it as our historic and moral duty to aid them in their return to the European fold through membership in NATO and the EU'. Later in the same speech, Kinkel reminded his parliamentary colleagues of Germany's practical economic interest in enlargement: 'Today Germany exports more to central and eastern Europe than does the USA. According to current estimates, our exports to this region will reach DM150 billion by the year 2000, up 80 per cent from 1996.'[30] Volker Rühe, the German Minister of Defence, an early strong supporter of NATO enlargement, argued that Germany, too, had unfinished business. Germans, he argued, have a special responsibility for expanding the process that began with the fall of the Berlin Wall in 1989. German unification represented a precursor to European unification; NATO enlargement represented the next step towards that goal.[31] Moreover, enlargement would permit Germany finally to reconcile with Poland for past invasions by linking their common security together under the same alliance. What was accomplished with France via the European Coal and Steel Community and NATO could now be achieved with central Europe via NATO enlargement and the EU.

Economically, the sooner that central and eastern Europeans developed their economies and became integrated within the EU, the sooner Germany would see a reduction in the number of immigrants whose first stop west is the Federal Republic. Especially in light of gnawing economic burdens of German unification – large budget deficits, unemployment, and huge transfers to the five new eastern German states – support for the enlargement of NATO and the EU could easily be placed within a compelling domestic political context. Militarily speaking, for the first time since the end of the Second World War, NATO enlargement eastward gives Germany its own buffer. On the front lines during the Cold War, Germans can breathe easier now that NATO's forward defence will be moving to the eastern borders of Poland, the Czech Republic and Hungary. Now on the front lines of a new wave of immigration from east to west, Germany would prefer to see economically sound eastern neighbours than their citizens who seek to build a better life via a stronger currency called the Deutschmark.

Furthermore, within a broader European context, staunch German support for Visegrad joining the EU/European Monetary Union speaks to the practical and domestic political problem of supporting eastern European immigrants under difficult economic times. Now, Germany carries the bulk of that economic burden; the sooner central Europeans are under the European economic umbrella, the sooner all of Europe can help cost-share the burdens of central European transitions to a market-oriented economy.

France was not so much worried about missing the NATO enlargement train as it was about being in the caboose to help guide the locomotive's directions within the context of European integration. With the United States and Germany allied in support of NATO enlargement, and Germany being so important to European integration, France, for practical reasons, could not be opposed to new NATO members. Yet if NATO enlargement was a *fait accompli*, then by God, de Gaulle, and the Divine Right of Kings, there must be a French version of it. *L'enlargissement de l'OTAN*, then, had to include French candidates for membership, members that might be more inclined to side with France in future deliberations over European security. For this reason, among others, France argued for Romania to be included in the first wave of NATO membership. Moreover, if NATO admitted Romania, France might then have its own internal ally to argue in favour of French control over NATO's southern command.

The French, however, eventually dropped support for Romanian entry into NATO. Abandoned by the French, Romania has been placed in a double bind vis-à-vis future NATO membership by the Kosovo crisis. Eager to prove its trustworthiness as a *de facto* ally, Romania endorsed NATO's economic sanctions against Serbia. Since agreeing to do so, however, Romania, by autumn 1999, estimated the boycott cost it over $8 billion in lost trade.[32] With its foreign debt at about $8 billion, the Romanian economic burden effectively doubled. Romania thus may be diminishing its own chances to join NATO by adhering to NATO policy. While it claims its military is ready to board the NATO train,[33] its economy may not be ready to keep that train rolling. Kosovo has clearly complicated Romania's bid to the join the alliance. Driven by its national economic interests, Romania has asked NATO to compensate its losses incurred by loss of trade with Serbia. This approach – while understandable for reasons of Romanian domestic politics – may also raise questions about whether Romania is economically fit enough to join the NATO ranks.

Domestic politics also played a part in French views towards NATO, since the ruling coalition effectively split over NATO enlargement.[34] Since June 1997, France has been run by a socialist-led coalition under Lionel Jospin. The French socialists came to power by focusing on domestic issues; unemployment had reached almost 13 per cent and economic growth had slowed to two per cent. In such a charged political atmosphere, the estimated costs for NATO enlargement also become a political liability. While Jospin agreed to NATO enlargement in principle, he has criticized what he sees as the 'tendency to hegemony' in American European security policy, and has opposed French reintegration into NATO's command structure.[35] President Jacques Chirac, however, remains head of state. In 1996 Chirac firmly endorsed NATO enlargement, and has advocated the long-term goal of returning France to the integrated command structure. It is precisely the weak French economy, budget restrictions and defence cutbacks that influenced Chirac to move France towards reintegration in NATO. Without adequate resources, France's ability to conduct large-scale independent military missions has been compromised.[36] French goals and ambitions within the EU require co-operation with Germany; French roles and missions for its military require co-operation with NATO. For these reasons, French national interests require co-operation with the alliance decision to enlarge NATO.

Central European leaders, for their part, feel an overarching duty to help their citizens navigate and secure real practical political, economic and military benefits that arise from formal association with the West. Political and economic reforms in Poland, Hungary and the Czech Republic led to free elections and sweeping privatization programmes, requisites for Western aid, NATO membership, and eventual membership of the EU. For their economies to flourish, markets are needed for their goods; those markets are found primarily in the West. Furthermore, they have established firm civilian control of their militaries, agreed to resolve all outstanding border disputes, and committed to add some 200,000 troops to NATO, along with a range of airfields, ports and lines of communication. Why? Essentially for the same reasons NATO was founded in the first place. As Vaclav Havel explained, 'Has it not been established beyond doubt that even the most costly preventative security is cheaper than the cheapest war? Well, such an investment will hardly generate any return in the next elections, but it will be appreciated by generations to come.'[37]

In central Europe, however, making the present practical in economic and military terms is politically motivated by memories of the troubled past as much as it is by the prospects for a brighter future. If boarding the NATO train could feasibly move them towards that future (and away from that past) then central Europeans should buy their ticket now. Perhaps the most poignant sign of this was evidenced by central European leader discussions with President Clinton following on the opening of the Holocaust Museum in Washington, DC. As one US national security council employee put it, 'After the dedication of the Holocaust museum, we had a reception in the East Wing of the White House. We marched each Eastern European leader into meet the President one-on-one and each leader asserted that they wanted to join NATO. This made a strong impression on the President.'[38] Thus the phrase 'never again' not only resonates regarding the historical treatment of Jews, it also rang true for leaders like Vaclav Havel and Lech Walesa vis-à-vis the Soviet control over eastern and central Europe.

THE NATO FUTURE AS OPPORTUNITY

> And how this future Europe will look is going to depend on the quality of statesmanship – of thoughtfulness, of insight, of the balance of prudence and courage – that the many governments prominently involved, including our own, are able to bring to the shaping of it.
>
> George F. Kennan[39]

> NATO can do for Europe's East what it did for Europe's West: prevent a return to local rivalries, strengthen democracy against future threats, and create the conditions for prosperity to flourish.
>
> President Bill Clinton[40]

If you set a train in motion you should ensure that it leaves the station, gains speed, and that you have a clear sense of its final destination. Otherwise, present and potential passengers may question whether the ticket is worth the ride at all. So, too, with NATO enlargement. Proponents have accepted past and present itineraries to help guide their future objectives. For US leaders, NATO serves as the principal mechanism for American involvement in Europe, an involvement that remains crucial to US national interests. Europe hosts many of the world's most important democracies and market economies. By enlarging NATO, stability will be promoted by extending a safe haven to new members further to consolidate democratic and market-oriented reforms. The goal is not only to make good on missed opportunities created by the Cold War, it is to develop new friends and allies that can help integrate western, central and eastern Europe and help defend against new threats to that vision.

While enlargement of the EU is also key to encouraging stability, NATO, and US leadership of it, is viewed by Americans, western Europeans and central Europeans alike as a crucial link to preserving transatlantic security. To preserve it, however, means adapting NATO to a post-Cold War role and mission that includes central and eastern Europeans who are prepared to settle their differences and contribute to their political, economic, and military integration. The defence against 'out-of-area' threats will require political coalitions within NATO to implement joint military action; the United States, by championing three new passengers for the NATO enlargement train, may well have created a new block of political support for that future action.

If the train door is kept open, the hopes and NATO aspirations of other central and eastern European nations are kept alive. Perhaps most important, the open door policy buys time the longer-term political–economic reforms in central and eastern Europe to take hold, grow and become strong enough to resist anti-democratic forces. They will only become strong enough if measurable progress is made towards improved standards of living and political participation. All the developed NATO mechanisms like the Partnership for Peace, the NATO–Russia Founding Act, the NATO–Ukraine Charter, are designed to be inclusive, enlarging the opportunities for a NATO membership that ten years ago would have seemed laughable.

The end of the Cold War focused Western political attention on adapting NATO to meet new circumstances. Politicians and leaders innovate when new circumstances arise, fine-tuning and hedging as they go, drawing on their talents as problem-solvers to create plausible solutions. Those solutions need to have domestic and international political support, a patchwork of mutual interests that must be forged to ensure implementation. The first round of NATO enlargement fits this bill.

Certain social scientists or international relations theorists might call this flying blind while future historians may look back with 20/20 hindsight at these innovations as courageous political vision. Dumb luck also doesn't fit well into standard deviations. While academics are better at looking backwards than forwards, they play an important role in pointing out contradictions and providing conceptual frameworks for policy consideration. Few academics would make the leap of faith to suggest how better to shape the post-Cold War world. The fact that we don't yet have a description of the era in which we now find ourselves but 'the post-Cold War world' suggests that we are waiting for someone to create the nomenclature. That naming process will most likely be driven if not defined by those policy practitioners who innovate the programmes and policies that will define our participation in this new era of change. The policy-makers can learn from the academy but rarely can wait for academic debates to resolve themselves before having to shape the policies that will become the stuff of future academic debates.

One key to that train's ultimate destination, however, is Russia. Both proponents and opponents to NATO enlargement at least agree on that. NATO has engaged in a number of confidence-building measures with Russia in mind. Among the most important ones: the signing of the Partnership for Peace Framework Document (22 June 1994); the deployment of Russian troops supporting the implementation force (IFOR) in Yugoslavia (13 January 1996); and the signing of the Founding Act on Mutual Relations, Co-operation, and Security between NATO and the Russian Federation (27 May 1997). While the NATO bombing of Kosovo prompted Russia to withdraw from all NATO activities, Russia–NATO relations have warmed since Boris Yeltsin resigned on 31 December 1999. Vladimir Putin, now President of Russia, has made overtures of rapprochement. Whether this merely indicates a wish to keep Western aid flowing to Russia or represents a genuine interest in co-operative security remains to be seen. The main challenge to NATO and its plans to enlarge further is to work towards overcoming Russia's schizophrenia over NATO as both a threat and an opportunity.

Yet, under the current political–economic turmoil in Moscow, NATO enlargement is neither popular nor high on the Russian political agenda. When discussion does occur, the closer enlargement is proposed to the former republics of the Soviet Union, the more vehement the Russian opposition. After Kosovo, the phrase 'Partnership for Peace' has a hollow ring, suggesting to many Russians a one-way door through which NATO intends to interfere in national internal affairs.

Assuredly, some of this stems from resentment over losing the Cold War, and from the psychological baggage that comes from a shrunken superpower undergoing an extremely difficult transition. How will the NATO enlargement train proceed under Vladimir Putin? Will it sputter and stop at the borders of the former Soviet Union? Will it enlarge to other countries within central and eastern Europe? Will the enlargement train keep pace – and not pause – towards its goal of more members? These are among the most important questions that face NATO members after the first round of enlargement.

NATO has certainly established an infrastructure to keep the train rolling. Before Kosovo, the Partnership for Peace (PFP) and the North Atlantic Co-operation Council (NACC) had moved non-NATO members beyond discussions of co-operation into practical partnerships based on plans for joint operations. To reflect that change, after the Madrid summit of July 1997, PFP replaced the NACC with the Euro-Atlantic Partnership Council (EAPC). Madrid also created the NATO–Russia Permanent Joint Council (PJC) and the NATO–Ukraine Commission to keep Russia and Ukraine engaged in the process. At the Washington summit of April 1999, NATO approved the New Strategic Concept and began a Defence Capabilities Initiative to improve interoperability among alliance forces, and where appropriate, between NATO and PFP members. A Membership Action Plan (MAP) was created as another mechanism to underscore NATO's open door policy, but MAP was only offered to nine of the 24 members of the PFP.[41]

By differentiating among the PFP members, the Washington summit posed a serious challenge, a new dividing line that will have the effect of slowing enlargement. Most see it implausible that nine new members will be admitted to NATO any time soon. Nonetheless, NATO has created expectations for its MAP members. If progress towards membership is not visible and forthcoming, those aspirants will become disillusioned sooner rather than later. Three MAP members include the Baltic states. Russia will pay particular attention to any former Soviet republic, and especially a Baltic state, that wishes to join NATO as this will bring the alliance directly to the Russian border. In effect, it may be easier for the Baltic states to join the EU before they join NATO.

The calculus and pace of NATO enlargement was complicated by Kosovo. While it is yet unclear whether the war in Kosovo will serve as a catalyst or impediment for further NATO enlargement, it is almost certain that it will slow it down.[42] The issue of which NATO members will pay how much to rebuild Yugoslavia may also serve to delay future enlargement. NATO member states will have to work hard to ensure that the promises and process of enlargement proceed in a timely fashion.

Decisions about boarding and promoting the NATO enlargement train revolved around the calculation of national interests. For the United States, NATO enlargement translated, *inter alia*, to maintaining its leadership of the alliance. Germany largely saw the process as securing its eastern border with an eye towards expanding eastern export markets. France envisaged more leadership at less cost. Central and eastern Europeans wanted to join the alliance as a hedge against Russia and a door to the EU. For Russia, the seats of this train remain uncomfortable for an ex-superpower accustomed to NATO as an enemy, but those freight cars of Western aid certainly remain attractive.

In the final analysis, three new passengers climbed aboard the NATO train in 1999, with more aspiring ticket-holders waiting on the platform. That journey, the passports and entrance to the club car are predicated on a convergence of national interests – US, western European, central European and eastern European. All aboard?

NOTES

1. See Harry S. Truman's Memoirs, Vol.II: *Years of Trial and Hope* (Garden City, New York: Doubleday, 1956), p.240. In view of America's traditional isolationism in foreign affairs, much importance must be attached to the US Senate's Vandenberg Resolution, passed in June 1948, that authorized alliances outside the American continent in peacetime.

2. George F. Kennan, 'X, the Sources of Soviet Conduct', *Foreign Affairs*, Vol.25, No.4 (July 1947), pp.566–82. For reviews of Cold War containment policy, see John Lewis Gaddis, *Strategies of Containment: A Critical Appraisal of Postwar American National Security Policy* (New York and Oxford: Oxford University Press, 1982) and Terry L. Deibel and John Lewis Gaddis (eds.), *Containment: Concept and Policy* (Washington, DC: National Defense University Press, 1986).

3. See Winston S. Churchill, *Memoirs of the Second World War* (Boston: Houghton Mifflin, 1987), pp.1002–4. For French and German initial thinking on NATO, see Roy Willis, *France, Germany and the New Europe, 1945–67* (Stanford, CA: Stanford University Press, 1968).

4. This required that all 16 NATO member states ratify the accession protocols. See Sean Kay and Hans Binnendijk, 'After the Madrid Summit: Parliamentary Ratification of NATO Enlargement', *Strategic Forum* (National Defense University, Institute for National Strategic Studies), No.107 (March 1997).

5. Throughout this article the term 'enlargement' is used instead of 'expansion'. This decision was based on the origin of the policy articulated by Anthony Lake in 'From Containment to Enlargement', *Vital Speeches of the Day*, Vol.60, No.1 (15 Oct. 1993), pp.13–15; for the evolution and application of Lake's enlargement idea to NATO, see James M. Goldgeier, 'NATO Expansion: The Anatomy of a Decision', *Washington Quarterly*, Vol.21, No.1 (Winter 1998), pp.85–102, and James M. Goldgeier, *Not Whether But When: The U.S. Decision to Enlarge NATO* (Washington, DC: Brookings Institution, 1999). See also Gale A. Mattox, 'The U.S. Role in Europe: The Decision to Enlarge NATO', *Miller Center Journal* (University of Virginia), Vol.5 (Spring 1998), pp.115–30.

6. For Russian attitudes and arguments against NATO enlargement, see Alexander Velichkin, 'NATO as Seen through the Eyes of the Russian Press', *NATO Review*, Vol.43, No.2 (March 1995), pp.20–3; Sergey Rogov, 'Russia and NATO's Enlargement', Occasional Paper MSIC 194 (Alexandria, VA: Center for Naval Analysis, Nov. 1995); Dimitry V. Trenin, 'Russia and the West: Avoiding Complications', *International Affairs*, Vol.42, No.1 (Jan.–Feb. 1996), pp.30–8; Senator Joseph R. Biden, *Meeting the Challenges of a Post-Cold War World: NATO Enlargement and U.S.–Russia Relations*, Report to the Senate Foreign Relations Committee, 105th Congress, 1st session, Washington, DC, May 1997; Tatiana Parkhalina, 'Of Myths and Illusions: Russian Perceptions of NATO Enlargement', *NATO Review*, Vol.45, No.3 (June 1997); 'Comments by

Alexei Arbatov on NATO Expansion and Russia' (Washington, DC: Center for Political and Strategic Studies, 21–27 March 1998); and Steven Woehrel, 'NATO Enlargement and Russia', *CRS Issue Brief* 97-477 (US Library of Congress, Congressional Research Service, Foreign Affairs and National Defense Division) (14 April 1998).

7. See Zbigniew Brzezinski, 'On to Russia', *Washington Post*, 3 May 1998, p.C7.

8. As quoted in *The Enlargement of NATO: Why Adding Poland, Hungary, and the Czech Republic to NATO Strengthens American National Security* (Washington, DC: US Department of State, Bureau of Public Affairs, Publication No.10533, Feb. 1998), p.5.

9. See Ronald J. Bee (ed.), 'The Future of NATO and U.S. Interests', *ACCESS Security Spectrum*, Vol.V, No.3 (Dec. 1991); Catherine McArdle Kelleher, *The Future of European Security: An Interim Assessment*, Brookings Occasional Papers (Washington, DC: Brookings Institution, 1995); Richard C. Holbrooke, 'The Future of NATO and Europe's Changing Security Landscape', *US Department of State Dispatch*, Vol.6, No.16 (17 April 1995); Warren Christopher, 'Fulfilling the Founding Vision of NATO', *US Department of State Dispatch*, Vol.7, No.50 (9 Dec. 1996); Madeleine Albright, 'NATO Expansion: Beginning the Process of Advice and Consent', *US Department of State Dispatch*, Vol.8, No.8 (Oct. 1997).

10. See *The Enlargement of NATO* (note 8 above); see also Joseph Fitchett, 'NATO Expansion Is Not Intended to Move the Iron Curtain Eastward', *International Herald Tribune*, 16 Jan. 1997, p.6; President Bill Clinton, 'The Lessons of the Marshall Plan: The Expansion of NATO', Address given at the Hague, *Vital Speeches*, Vol.63, No.18 (1 July 1997); Albright, 'NATO Expansion: Beginning the Process of Advice and Consent'; Paul E. Gallis, 'NATO Enlargement: Pro and Con Arguments', *CRS Report to Congress* 97–718 (US Library of Congress, Congressional Research Service) (14 April 1998); *Top Ten Questions on NATO Enlargement*, Fact Sheet released by the NATO Enlargement Ratification Office (Washington, DC: US Department of State, 19 Feb. 1998); Gerald B. Solomon, *The NATO Enlargement Debate* (Washington, DC: Center for Strategic and International Studies, 1998); and Kenneth W. Thompson (ed.), *NATO Expansion*, Vol.4, Miller Center Series (Landham, Maryland: University Press of America, March 1998).

11. See George Kennan, 'Fateful Error', *New York Times*, 5 Feb. 1997; Jack F. Matlock, Jr., Testimony Before the Senate Foreign Relations Committee, 3 May 1995; Jack F. Matlock, Jr., 'It's a Bad Idea; Vote Against It', *Global Beat*, 3 March 1998; Jonathan Dean, 'No NATO Expansion Now', *Bulletin of the Atomic Scientists*, Vol.52, No.3 (May–June 1996), pp.18–19; Jonathan Dean, 'The NATO Mistake: Expansion for All the Wrong Reasons', *Washington Monthly*, Vol.29, No.7 (July–Aug. 1997), pp.35–8.

12. For example, Kenneth Waltz, Ernest Haas and Vinod Aggarwal each argued enlargement was a bad idea at a conference held at UC Berkeley on 9–10 March 1998 entitled 'The Debate over NATO Expansion: Views from Berkeley, Washington, Bonn, Prague, Kiev, and Moscow' sponsored by the Center for German and European Studies and the Center for Slavic and East European Studies; see also Michael Mandelbaum, 'Preserving the Peace: The Case against NATO Expansion', *Foreign Affairs*, Vol.74, No.3 (May–June 1995), pp.9–13; Michael Mandelbaum, *The Dawn of Peace in Europe* (New York: Twentieth Century Fund, 1997); Paul Kennedy, 'The False Pretense of NATO Expansion', *New Perspectives Quarterly*, Vol.14, No.3 (Summer 1997), pp.62–3.

13. See Eugene J. Carroll, Jr., Center for Defense Information, 'NATO Expansion Would Be an Epic Fateful Error', *Los Angeles Times*, 7 July 1997; Jeremy Stone, Federation of American Scientists, 'NATO Expansion is a Pandora's Box', *F.A.S. Public Interest Report*, Vol.50, No.2 (March–April 1997), pp.1–2; Patrick J. Buchanan, 'NATO Expansion: A Dangerous Folly', *Washington Times*, 5 Feb. 1997; Amos Perlmutter and Ted Carpenter, 'NATO's Expensive Trip East: The Folly of Enlargement', *Foreign Affairs*, Vol.77, No.1 (Jan.–Feb. 1998), pp.2–6; Ted Carpenter and Barbara Conry (eds), *NATO Enlargement: Illusions and Reality* (Washington, DC: Cato Institute, April 1998). For the Clinton administration's response on the cost criticisms, see Lawrence Summers, 'The Economic Benefits of NATO Expansion', Remarks to the US Chamber of Commerce, 11 April 1997; and Madeleine Albright, 'NATO Expansion: A Shared and Sensible Investment', *US Department of State Dispatch*, Vol.8, No.9 (Nov. 1997), pp.12–18.

14. Treaty Document 105-36; see also 'The Senate Resolution on NATO Expansion: Complete Text of the Resolution', *Arms Control Today*, Vol.28, No.3 (April 1998), pp.14–21.

15. Trent Lott, 'The Senate's Role in NATO Enlargement', *Washington Post*, 21 March 1997, p.A27. See also, Simon Serfaty, *Stay the Course: European Unity and Atlantic Solidarity*, The Washington Papers/171 (Washington, DC: Center for Strategic and International Studies, 1997); John O'Sullivan, 'Sold on NATO: The Case for Expansion', *The American Spectator*, June 1998, pp.25–8.

16. Remarks by the President to the People of Detroit, Fisher Theater, Detroit, Michigan (Washington, DC: Office of the White House Press Secretary, 22 Oct. 1996).

17. See George C. Marshall's commencement address at Harvard University, 5 June 1947. In *Foreign Affairs*, special commemorative section Vol.76, No.3 (May–June 1997), pp.160–1.

18. Strobe Talbott, 'The United States, Germany, and the Idea of Europe', an address made at the American Academy of Berlin, New Traditions Conference II: Intellectual Leadership for the New Century, 20 March 1998, p.2.

19. Madeleine Albright, 'Enlarging NATO: Why Bigger Is Better', *The Economist*, 15 Feb. 1997, p.22.

20. For European views on NATO enlargement, see Paul E. Gallis, 'NATO Enlargement: The Process and Allied Views', *CRS Report for Congress* (Library of Congress, Congressional Research Service), 97-666F (1 July 1997).

21. Remarks by the President on the National Interest for Enlarging NATO (Washington, DC: Office of the White House Press Secretary, 20 March 1998).

22. Quoted in Strobe Talbott, 'Why NATO Should Grow', *New York Review of Books*, 10 Aug. 1995.

23. Madeleine K. Albright, *NATO Enlargement*, Statement before the Senate Appropriations Committee, 21 Oct. 1997, p.3. For more on this theme, see also Richard Holbrooke, 'America, A European Power', *Foreign Affairs*, Vol.74, No.2 (March–April 1995), pp.38–51.

24. Secretary of Defense William Cohen, *Shaping NATO to Meet the Challenges of the 21st Century*, Remarks to the NATO Defense Planning Committee, 11 June 1998.

25. See Michael Brenner, *Terms of Engagement: The United States and the European Security Identity*, The Washington Papers/176 (Washington, DC: Center for Strategic and International Studies, 1998), pp.85–91; and particularly, Richard Holbrooke, *To End A War* (Modern Library Paperback Edition, 1999), section entitled 'America, Still A European Power', pp.366–72.

26. Remarks of Dan Hamilton, US State Department Policy Planning, to IGCC MacArthur Scholars conference, 'The Future of Europe', 13 April 1999, Washington, DC.

27. See Remarks by the President on the National Interest for Enlarging NATO (note 21 above). See also Remarks by the President to the People of Detroit (note 17 above).

28. See *The Enlargement of NATO* (note 8 above), p.8.

29. See in particular press conference by President Clinton and German Chancellor Kohl, City Hall, Milwaukee, Wisconsin, 23 May 1996, where President Clinton lauds Germany's decision to deploy 4,000 troops to Bosnia in support of the Dayton peace accord. Clinton remarked, 'Germany is shouldering its security responsibilities in the post-Cold War world, and we are all grateful for that'. Chancellor Kohl indicated at the same press conference, however, that Germany was hosting 350,000 refugees from the former Yugoslavia, and had spent DM10 billion to assist them. This fact also certainly played a role in the German decision.

30. 'Bundestag Approves NATO Expansion', *This Week in Germany*, 27 March 1998, p.2; See also *Rede anlaesslich der zweiten Beratung und Schlussabstimung des Gesetzes zu den Protokollen vom 16. Dezember 1997 zum Nordatlantikvertrag ueber den Beitritt Polens, der Tschechischen Republik und Ungarns*, Bundesminister des Auswaertigen Dr. Klaus Kinkel im Deutschen Bundestag am 26 März 1998, Pressemitteilung des Auswaertiges Amtes vom 26 März 1998. (Speech given by German Foreign Minister Klaus Kinkel on 26 March 1998, in consideration of the ratification of the North Atlantic Treaty Organization Protocol dated 16 December 1997 regarding the accession of Poland, the Czech Republic and Hungary. Press release of the German Foreign Ministry, 26 March 1998.)

31. See *Intervention des Bundesministers der Verteidigung, Volker Ruehe, im Deutschen Bundestag gelegentlich der zweiten und dritten Lesung des Ratifizierungsgesetzes zum Protokoll des NATO-Beitritts von Polen, Ungarn und der Tschechischen Republik am 26. März 1998*, Pressemitteilung des BMVg vom 26. März 1998. (Intervention of the German Minister of Defence, Volke

Ruehe, in the German Parliament on the occasion of the second and third reading of the ratification law concerning the NATO Protocol admitting Poland, Hungary, and the Czech Republic. Press release of the German Ministry of Defense, 26 March 1998).

32. This issue was raised publicly in Romania at a joint press conference with American Secretary of State Madeleine Albright and Romanian Foreign Minister Andrei Plesu on 22 June 1999. See Remarks at Joint Press Conference, Presidential Palace, Bucharest, Romania, 22 June 1999, as released by the Office of the Spokesman, US Secretary of State. See also Mirel Bran, 'Le Commerce fluvial en Roumanie etrangle par l'embargo contre la Yougoslavie' (River Commerce in Rumania Strangled by the Embargo against Yugoslavia), *Le Monde*, 10 Sept. 1999. The theme of NATO compensation was prevalent among a group of Romanian senators and members of the Chamber of Deputies, who visited the IGCC at UC San Diego on 12 Oct. 1999 as part of a USIA programme on 'Military Reform'. That group included Senators Alexandru Radu Timofte, Cornel Boiangiu, Dumitru Badea, Costei Georghiu and Karoly-Ference Szabo, and Deputies Mihail Nica, Gheorghe Ana, Mircea Valcu, Sandu Alecu, and Paul Adrian Dumitrescu.

33. See, for example, Ion Ratiu, *Les Forces Armées Roumaines: Un Partenaire Fiable au Seuil de l'OTAN* (The Rumanian Armed Forces: A Reliable Partner in NATO), NATO Parliamentary Assembly, Committee Reports, Commission de la defense et de la securite, Sous-commission sur l'avenir des forces armées, 9 April 1999. See also Adina Stefan, 'Romania's Engagement in Sub-regional Co-operation and the National Strategy for NATO Accession', *Harmonie Papers* (The Netherlands: Centre for European Security Studies), No.10 (Dec. 1999).

34. See Gallis, 'NATO Enlargement: The Process and Allied Views', pp.11–14; and Gallis, 'France: Current Foreign Policy Issues and Relations with the United States', *CRS Report for Congress* (Library of Congress, Congressional Research Service), 96-794 (26 Sept. 1996).

35. 'M. Jospin critique la reintegration de la France dans l'OTAN' (Mr. Jospin critiques the reintegration of France into NATO), *Le Monde*, 5 Feb. 1997, p.5; see also Paul-Marie de la Gorce, 'L'alliance atlantique, cadre de l'hegemonie americaine' (The Atlantic Alliance: Framework for American Hegemony), *Le Monde Diplomatique*, April 1999, pp.4–5.

36. See Gallis, 'France: Current Foreign Policy Issues', pp.7–9.

37. Vacalav Havel, 3 Oct. 1997, quoted in *The Enlargement of NATO* (note 8 above), p.11; in 1996, the Polish Prime Minister stated that Poland's reasons for wanting to join NATO 'are guided by our own historical experience': see Wlodzimierz Cimoszewicz, 'Building Poland's Security: Membership of NATO a Key Objective', *NATO Review*, Vol.44, No.3 (May 1996), pp.3–7.

38. Conversation between the author and Charles Kupchan. See also Goldgeier, 'NATO Expansion: The Anatomy of a Decision'.

39. George F. Kennan, *At a Century's Ending, Reflections 1982–95* (New York: W.W. Norton & Co., 1996), p.169; published originally as 'NATO and the Warsaw Pact', *Washington Post*, 12 Nov. 1989.

40. Remarks from the President on the National Interest in Enlarging NATO (note 21 above); also Quoted in *Top Ten Questions on NATO Enlargement* (note 10 above), p.1; the same language, verbatim, is also used in Anthony Lake, 'The Challenge of Change in Russia', speech given 1 April 1996 to the US–Russia Business Council (Washington, DC: Office of the White House Press Secretary, 3 April 1996); in Anthony Lake, Remarks to the Chicago Council on Foreign Relations, 24 May 1996. Available at: http://www.whitehouse.gov/WH/EOP/NSE/html/speeches. For a close paraphrase, see also Albright, 'Enlarging NATO: Why Bigger Is Better', p.22.

41. The MAP partners are Albania, Bulgaria, Estonia, Latvia, Lithuania, Macedonia, Romania, Slovakia and Slovenia. The 15 non-MAP countries include Armenia, Austria, Azerbaijan, Belarus, Finland, Georgia, Kazakhstan, Kyrgystan, Moldova, Russia, Sweden, Switzerland, Turkmenistan, Ukraine and Uzbekistan.

42. See Jeffrey Simon, 'Partnership for Peace: After the Washington Summit and Kosovo', *Strategic Forum* (National Defense University, Institute for National Strategic Studies), No.167 (Aug. 1999).

PART V: CONCLUSION

Explaining NATO Enlargement[1]

ROBERT W. RAUCHHAUS

Over the past few decades, a divide has grown between scholars who build and refine theory, and those who try to explain real-world foreign policy outcomes. In an effort to break this trend, the authors of the preceding essays use and, when necessary, modify international relations (IR) theory to explain a topic that is both ongoing and important. When this endeavour first began, there was very little theoretical work on the enlargement of the North Atlantic Treaty Organization (NATO). When IR theory was applied, it was largely done so for the purposes of evaluating the pros and cons of enlargement, or for explaining how a particular country came to hold its policy position on enlargement.[2] The essays in this volume, therefore, represent some of the first efforts directly to ask and answer the question, why is NATO enlarging?

Given this volume's purpose, it is important to ask a number of questions. For example, how well do the preceding essays explain the motivations behind NATO enlargement? Is there a coherent unified account of these motivations, or do the essays contradict one another and offer mutually exclusive explanations? Was IR theory ultimately able to keep pace with NATO's enlargement, or was it of little use? Did the authors perform better when they abandoned IR theory for *ad hoc* explanations?

The purpose of this essay is to integrate the volume's findings and evaluate whether the volume, when considered in its entirety, offers a unified answer or whether the individual essays reach contradictory conclusions. Surprisingly, despite the divergent approaches taken by the authors, this volume does offer a rather unified explanation. Many of the essays indicate the same key issues, regardless of the type of approach that the author employed. There are, of course, some points of disagreement that require further examination. But often what appears as disagreement is actually caused by differences in the essays' purposes. For example, while some essays explain the timing of enlargement, others explain why alliance expansion is chosen over alliance deepening. Similarly, the different theories used by the authors often highlight the significance of different causal variables. Overall, however, there is broad agreement on several of the most important issues, and the volume's findings can be synthesized.

EXPLAINING NATO ENLARGEMENT

Why is NATO offering membership to its former Cold War adversaries? Is it due to the current international distribution of power and an effort by the US or the West to extend its influence into eastern Europe? Is it due to NATO's unique organizational attributes and the initiative of NATO officials? Or is it due to other factors, such as new preferences that have resulted from the evolution of a transatlantic security community? Others might look more to causes found at the domestic level within the US and other key members of the alliance. Did some sort of ideology, such as Wilsonian Liberalism, drive enlargement? Or is the reason simply that key members of the Clinton administration wanted enlargement to occur?

Despite the variety of analytic frameworks used in the preceding essays, a clear first-cut answer emerges: the main reason that NATO offered membership to Poland, Hungary and the Czech republic is that United States wanted the alliance to expand eastward. The US initiated the policy and pushed it through over the opposition of key allies, determining most of the details, including when the alliance would expand and who would be admitted. Even in the weeks leading up to the Madrid summit, NATO enlargement remained a contentious issue. The only European ally that supported the Clinton administration's policy from the start was Germany, but even Germany's support was moderate at best.[3] During the Madrid summit when the final decision was made, there still remained considerable disagreement among NATO allies.[4] Most realized that opposing enlargement was pointless, and the central debate then shifted to which countries would be admitted.[5] However, the US prevailed on this issue too. The alliance ultimately offered membership only to the US's three preferred choices – Poland, Hungary and the Czech Republic – the countries that other NATO members supported would have to wait until the next round of enlargement.[6]

Two types of counter-arguments, if correct, could potentially undermine this conclusion. First, some might argue that the policy was somehow inertial or inevitable and that enlargement would have occurred even if the US had not played a leadership role. It is important to remember that from the vantage point of the early 1990s, not only were NATO members quite reluctant to consider expanding the alliance eastward, but they were even reluctant to consider other sorts of security partnership with the newly independent states. Most of the reasons why NATO members were opposed to the alliance's expansion are well known: they are the same sorts of concerns about political and economic costs raised today by critics of the alliance's expansion. However, in addition to these concerns, in the years following the collapse of the Soviet Union, many decision-makers and policy analysts believed that NATO expansion was impossible because of agreements made with the Soviet Union and, later on, with Russia. In an effort to hasten the demise of the Soviet Union and facilitate the transition to democracy, the Bush administration and the governments of European states wanted to avoid actions that might seem opportunistic or provocative.[7]

A second type of counter-argument might claim that NATO is expanding because of the lobbying efforts of eastern European states, or because of their clever use of the Partnership for Peace (PFP) as a way to gain full access to NATO. While this type of argument has some merit, several of the preceding essays make it clear that in the US there was also a separate and indigenous effort to enlarge the alliance. Although in the early 1990s a number of eastern European countries were knocking on NATO's door, either no one was listening, or, if they were, no one was willing to admit them. The efforts of a few key individuals in the Clinton administration appear decisive for explaining how the enlargement process began, and these ideas appear to have formed independently of the lobbying efforts of eastern European states.

That the US was the main driving force behind enlargement and ultimately prevailed on the major decisions, such as the timetable for enlargement and who would be admitted, should not come as a surprise. As other members of the alliance have themselves noted on a number of occasions, NATO is, for better or for worse, an American-run show.[8] Despite the absence of a menacing Soviet threat and the enhanced bargaining position of an increasingly unified Europe, today NATO continues to rely on America's leadership and support. There have, of course, been many efforts over the years to create greater balance in the organization. While at times the US encourages Europe to share more of the burden and take more of a leadership role in the organization, it often subsequently stifles or sabotages Europe's efforts to do so. This mixed message was recently apparent again when the US prodded its European allies to assume more responsibility in NATO, but then blocked their efforts to create greater balance in NATO's command structure.[9] Similarly, following the Clinton administration's criticism of Europe for failing to monitor its own back door and take a leadership role in Kosovo, the US demanded the reins when NATO finally did intervene.

While there is broad consensus by the contributors to this volume that the US was the main force behind NATO enlargement, this does not deny the importance of other factors. For example, many of the contributors found that NATO's unique organizational attributes were very important for explaining the outcome, and so too were the actions of other key NATO members. Nevertheless, it is important to note this volume concludes that in order to understand why NATO is enlarging, it is critical to understand why the US wants NATO to expand. Most of the preceding essays, therefore, either implicitly or explicitly ask why the US wants NATO to enlarge.

This first-cut answer raises as many questions as it answers, and it forces us to recast the questions that we asked above. Is the US's preference for enlargement due to its current position in the international system as the only remaining superpower? Or is it due to a commitment to multilateralism brought about by the creation of the transatlantic security community? In contrast, others might believe that the US preference was driven by purely domestic factors. To what extent did lobbying groups, party politics, or perhaps even the independently held views of key decision-makers drive the expansion policy?

INTERNATIONAL DETERMINANTS

While most of the preceding essays find that both domestic and international factors mattered, most also viewed America's current status as the world's only remaining superpower as a key factor explaining America's preference for alliance expansion. With American power currently unchecked, it seems very likely that the United States, or any country similarly situated, would try to take advantage of its position. Expanding NATO eastward is in effect America's way of attempting to consolidate its Cold War victory.

While the US's current position as the world's sole superpower is central to understanding why NATO is enlarging, it clearly is not a sufficient explanation. History is ripe with examples of states that were similarly situated yet failed to take advantage of their positions. Consider, for example, the US during the interwar period. Although the US was wealthy enough to stabilize the international economy and powerful enough to stop Nazi aggression, it lacked the will to do so because of domestic constraints.[10] Clearly a state's position in the international system cannot by itself explain why it selects a particular foreign policy.[11] With examples of reluctant great powers in mind, the contributors recognize that a variety of other factors are also necessary to give a thorough account of why the US is willing to continue playing a leadership role. This said, it is nevertheless important to note that America's current position was broadly identified as a critical part of the explanation.

The preceding essays also tend to agree on several other key points. There is a general consensus that NATO's unique organizational attributes are an important part of the explanation. From its inception, NATO was designed to deal with security issues, broadly defined, including important political and economic issues that ensure domestic stability. Unlike traditional alliances, NATO did not have a narrowly defined military objective.[12] There are also important institutional and procedural differences between NATO and most military alliances. In many ways, NATO more closely resembles a regional or international organization than it does a traditional military alliance.[13] As organization theorists are quick to note, NATO is not just an *ad hoc* agreement between states; instead, NATO is a large organization, comprised of hundreds of officials and bureaucrats whose livelihood depends on the organization's survival. These officials have a degree of autonomy that allows them to pursue goals that help keep the organization alive. Add to this the inertia generated by a 40-year good track record – something few alliances have ever attained – it becomes clear why treating NATO as a traditional military alliance may lead one astray. While scholars in the field often apply alliance theory to NATO, none of the contributors found it useful here.[14]

How do NATO's organizational attributes matter? Organization theory would posit that NATO survives because the organization is greater than the sum of its parts and it has taken on a life of its own. The individuals who work for the organization have vested interests in the organization's survival. Their interests may be attributed to selfish motives such as keeping their own jobs, or they may be the result of a genuine altruistic desire to see the organization survive and prosper for its own sake or for the sake of European security.

Several of the volume's contributors took issue with this conventional characterization of international organizations. For example, in essay 5, Ernst B. Haas traces organization theory's problems to the substantive issues from where it finds its roots. Originally developed in the fields of sociology and business, organization theory was intended to explain the behaviour of bureaucracies, businesses, and other organizations that are comprised of individuals. Organization theory is very effective when used properly, such as for explaining the evolution and survival of the March of Dimes. As Kenneth N. Waltz notes in essay 2, when organizations such as the March of Dimes accomplish their mission, they do not simply close up shop: the individuals who run these organizations have vested interests and will search for new missions, find new ways of raising money, and evolve or mutate the organization so that it will survive past its original purpose. However, while NATO officials were interested in finding new post-Cold War missions, they generally were not enthusiastic about enlargement because they feared it would dilute the alliance and make management more difficult.

The question then remains, how does organization theory apply to international organizations such as NATO? Whereas most organizations are comprised of individuals, international organizations such as NATO are comprised of states. This imposes certain limits on an organization's ability to go out and recruit new members. Voluntary organizations that are comprised of individuals can just go out and recruit new members. Non-voluntary organizations can force their members to contribute – national governments, for example, have become quite good at extracting resources from their citizenries. In contrast, international governance structures, such as NATO, lack the power to tax or coerce their members.[15] They therefore have much greater difficulty adapting because they remain highly dependent on the voluntary support of the members that found and comprise them. Without members' continued voluntary support, not only do international organizations lack a source of revenue, they also have no services to provide to prospective members. What kind of security guarantee could NATO provide eastern Europe without the support of key members such as the United States? Without its member states, there is no NATO. The officials that comprise NATO cannot simply abandon their old constituency and find a new one. NATO officials, therefore, operate in a much more constrained environment.

Why did the US prefer NATO as its vehicle for incorporating formerly communist states into the West? Vinod Aggarwal (essay 4) and Beverly Crawford (essay 3) offer two accounts of why NATO beat out its competitors and why expansion was preferred over other post-Cold War adaptations for the alliance. The answer rests both with the strengths of NATO and with the weaknesses of the available alternatives. The Organization for Security and Co-operation in Europe (OSCE), for example, remains institutionally weak. It suffers the fate of most organizations that have large and diverse membership, namely, that it is difficult or impossible to obtain a consensus on important issues. The only alternatives that would avoid the problems of the OSCE or other large regional organizations would be ones such as the Western European Union (WEU), but such schemes exclude the US and reduce America's influence on European affairs.

A key advantage held by NATO, as Crawford argues, is that NATO served the dual purpose of increasing America's influence in Europe while limiting Russia's influence. This shows that geostrategic concerns played an important role in NATO expansion. Washington was especially concerned about Russia's efforts to thwart the West's attempt to bring an end to hostilities in former Yugoslavia. And as Aggarwal argues, expanding NATO also served another important end: in the early 1990s there was a growing sense that the alliance was falling into disuse and required rejuvenation. Here again expansion was the best available alternative. Widening the alliance was cheaper than deepening it, and, in addition to giving the alliance a new sense of purpose, it might address some of the needs of eastern European countries.

DOMESTIC DETERMINANTS

There are a number of useful ways to characterize different approaches to domestic politics. Two distinctions are particularly important here. First, a separation exists between approaches that are fundamentally society-centred and those that are state-centred. A second useful distinction can be drawn between approaches that operate at the group or national level of analysis (second-image), and those that operate at the individual or decision-making level (first-image).[16]

Most of the contributors to this volume adopted state-centred approaches. It is interesting to note, though, that many of the volume's contributors also found it important to augment their analyses with explanations located at the decision-making level. President Clinton and several of his key advisers play a very important role in explaining NATO enlargement. While it is possible or even likely that this policy would have eventually come about if a different administration had been in place, several of the essays conclude that, at minimum, Clinton and his advisers determined the timing and rapid pace of enlargement.

Society-Centred Approaches

Society-centred approaches posit that state policy can be reduced to the interests of dominant domestic groups. In effect, the state is little more than a scale or calculator that adds up the strengths and weaknesses of various societal actors. State policy, therefore, is not the result of the state's independent interests, but rather it reflects the underlying distribution of power among domestic groups.

More sophisticated society-based approaches may also try to incorporate how state structure or elite leadership affects the aggregation of domestic actors' preferences. For example, approaches that grapple with the role of the state often do so by examining how state structure can channel and influence domestic groups. Parliamentary democracies, for example, might aggregate preferences in a different way from that of presidential systems; similarly, countries with extensive legislative committee systems might aggregate preferences in ways different from *dirigiste* states where executive agencies play a much greater role. A state's structure may affect the balance of power between domestic groups, their opportunities for striking coalitions, and their ability to construct issue-linkages. However, regardless of how the state's structure may shape and channel domestic interests, it is important to note that these domestic actors still provide the motor behind policy outcomes. The state, therefore, is not an independent actor in its own right.

Society-centred approaches may also try to incorporate a role for political entrepreneurship. While political elites do not themselves drive or determine the policy outcome, they can play an important role in helping domestic interests find their voice. In extreme cases, some issues may remain dormant altogether until a political entrepreneur brings attention to them. In most cases, however, political elites just help to define the problem better and narrow or channel interests towards a certain policy outcome.

Regardless of whether a society-centred approach is simple or more sophisticated, all share the belief that state policy is reducible to the interests of the dominant domestic actors, which may stem from social status, wealth, religion, party affiliation, ideology, commercial interests, or any number of other factors. Two key constituencies – the arms industry and groups that represent eastern European immigrants and their descendants – lobbied the Clinton administration and key members of Congress.

There is clear evidence of an extensive lobbying effort by the arms industry on the issue of NATO enlargement, but its effects seem rather limited.[17] In the two years leading up to the Madrid summit, the six largest military contractors in the US spent over $51 million lobbying the US government. NATO enlargement was one of the issues on their agenda.[18] Given that the arms industry has faced difficult times in recent years, the possibility of expanding arms sales to eastern Europe represented an important opportunity. NATO membership would require eastern European countries to purchase military hardware, most of which would come from American companies. According to Senator Tom Harkin (D-Iowa), the lobbying efforts of the arms industry have turned NATO enlargement into 'a Marshall Plan for defense contractors'.[19] Indeed, NATO enlargement is big business. Poland, for example, is considering buying 100 to 150 Boeing F-18s or Lockheed Martin F-16s. At a price tag ranging from $45 to $60 million per plane, these sales would generate substantial revenues.

Groups that represent eastern European immigrants and their descendants are another key constituency that have lobbied the President and Congress.[20] Unlike the arms industry, however, these groups were not as aggressive about pressing their demands. Whereas the arms industry was self-organized and lobbied the government on its own accord, political entrepreneurship played an important role in mobilizing these groups.

Election-year politics may also have played an important role in the President's decision to support the policy. Clinton and his staff hoped that the policy would allow the President to appeal directly to ethnic eastern European voters and offset the administration's recent failures in eastern Europe, especially in former Yugoslavia. Clinton announced his support for the policy during campaign stops in key states with large Polish and Czech constituencies, such as Illinois and Michigan in the mid-west, and Pennsylvania and New York in the north east. In addition to the entrepreneurship of politicians, other groups helped to organize and mobilize these groups. The arms industry, for example, was eager to fund these groups and encourage them to lobby the Clinton administration and Congress for the specific purpose of NATO enlargement.[21]

These two groups certainly provide some of the explanation of why NATO is enlarging. However, it is clear that key figures in the Clinton administration favoured the enlargement of NATO prior to, and independent of, the pressures brought to bear by key domestic groups. Without the Clinton administration's political entrepreneurship, lobbying groups that represent eastern European immigrants and their descendants would not have exerted much pressure. Similarly, while the arms industry did actively lobby the administration and Congress, their efforts did not seem to have much effect. Nevertheless, while organized domestic interests may not explain why the policy enjoyed widespread support, they do help explain why policy-makers who were otherwise indifferent towards the policy decided not to stand in its way.

State-Centred Approaches

Society-centred approaches contend that dominant societal interests determine state policy. State-centred approaches, in contrast, place much greater causal weight on the state as an independent actor. While many state-centred analyses appear to anthropomorphize the state, it is important to remember that the state is obviously not an actor in the same sense that an individual is an actor. When analysts make reference to state interests and state actions, what they are actually referring to is the group of individuals who act on the state's behalf.

This raises an important question. How much autonomy do decision-makers have? The answer can place state-centred analyses in one of two categories. Some state-centred approaches assume that decision-makers enjoy a very high degree of autonomy. If this is the case, then, in order to understand why NATO is expanding, this school would argue that it is necessary to know something about the goals and personalities of the individuals involved in the decision-making process. Other state-centred approaches believe that knowing the particular decision-maker is less important because decision-makers operate in highly constrained environments. Decision-makers represent the state's interests or the interests of their particular agency or department.

The difference between these two types of approaches becomes especially clear when one thinks counterfactually. State-centred approaches that believe decision-makers are highly constrained would posit that foreign policy outcomes will remain the same, or very similar, even if there were different decision-makers in place. In contrast, approaches that assume decision-makers have autonomy and wide latitude believe that the beliefs and views of individual decision-makers are very important for explaining foreign policy outcomes.

Regardless of where one finds the root source of decision-makers' preferences, the common theme in all state-centred approaches is that the individuals who act on the state's behalf have interests that cannot simply be reduced to the underlying interests of dominant domestic groups.

Internationalist Ideology. Is the Clinton administration the driving force behind NATO enlargement, or would another administration have pursued the same policy? A good case can be made that a different administration also would have pushed for NATO enlargement. A state-centred analysis that believes decision-makers are highly constrained would highlight the attitudes and beliefs that are shared by elites. In the US today, it is important to note that a common internationalist ideology bridges the two dominant political parties, as well as different branches of government.

Following the collapse of the Soviet Union, many expected American foreign policy, without an external threat, to become much more contested. It seemed very reasonable to expect more partisan conflict over foreign policy, as well as more conflict between branches of the government. For example, without a menacing communist threat, it seemed likely that Congress might become more parochial and begin diverting funds from national defence to local constituent interests. In peacetime, conflict over foreign policy has generally emerged between an inward-looking Congress and an outward-looking executive. However, in the period following the end of the Cold War this, for once, did not happen. Although defence spending was drastically reduced, there was broad agreement between the White House and Congress on many of the most important issues. On potentially contentious issues, such as military base closures, the Clinton administration and Congress decided to farm the issue out to a special commission rather than make tough choices themselves. Both branches were more concerned about avoiding risk and insulating themselves politically than with advancing their own agenda.

Significant partisan disagreement over foreign policy also failed to materialize after the collapse of the Soviet Union. Many expected that the election of a Democrat to the White House in 1992 would mark a change in American foreign policy. However, once in office, the Clinton administration began supporting a number of Bush administration policies, including the North American Free Trade Association (NAFTA) and Most Favored Nation (MFN) trade status for China. Overall, there was considerable continuity between the two administrations' foreign policies.

In addition to the changes that were anticipated with the election of a Democratic president, there was also some talk that the end of the Cold War might allow paleo-Republicans, such as Pat Buchanan, to return the Republican party to its interwar policies of isolationism and protectionism. Buchanan's two failed bids for president illustrate just how little this rhetoric rallies modern Republicans. During the 2000 election cycle, so few Republicans were receptive to this message that Buchanan decided to run for the Reform Party's nomination.

There are, of course, important differences between attitudes in Congress and the executive branch, and between Republicans and Democrats. But the variation within each party is nearly as large as the variation between them. When compared to other democracies, the differences that exist between American political parties are rather small. Most disagreements in the US are over how to do something, not whether it should be done. NATO enlargement nicely illustrates this point. While President Clinton and some key Democrats were calling for NATO enlargement, the Republicans included it in their *Contract with America*.[22] The only difference between parties was on details, such as when the alliance should expand, who should be admitted first, and who should cover the financial costs of enlargement.

The reason for this new internationalism is open to debate. It may be due to learning from pre-First World War and pre-Second World War failures.[23] If one believes the rhetoric behind PFP and NATO enlargement, then it is clear that political elites do believe that what happens in eastern Europe is likely to have far-reaching consequences for the United States. But in addition to the learning that has taken place, the internationalist ideology which was generated by more than half a century of the Cold War is undoubtedly also playing an important role.

Although many of the contributors believed that the US has primarily benevolent motives, this need not be the case. The Clinton administration might be motivated by the desire to consolidate America's Cold War victory. As Ernst B. Haas recognizes in essay 5, NATO enlargement may well be an attempt by the US to 'perpetuate unilateral hegemony'. On this point, Kenneth N. Waltz agrees. Enlargement may be viewed as another 'tool for lengthening America's grip on Europe'. While an international ideology and the potential altruism that it breeds may be a part of the explanation, clearly a number of self-interested motives, or perhaps even selfish motives, are also present.

The Clinton Administration. It is important to recognize that internationalism does not necessarily translate into any particular policy. Despite shared commitment to internationalism across parties and between branches of government, there was widespread opposition when the idea to expand NATO was first floated.

Some of the harshest criticisms of enlargement came not from isolationists or those opposed to internationalism, but from internationalists who believed that NATO enlargement would undermine other internationalist goals.[24] Conservative internationalists were particularly concerned that enlargement would hurt US–Russia relations and efforts to co-operate on arms reductions and preventing nuclear weapons proliferation. Many liberal internationalists criticized the policy because they believed it would weaken and dilute the alliance.

There was also widespread opposition to enlargement within the bureaucracy. A number of key career professionals in the State Department and Pentagon did not support the policy.[25] Even a number of key political appointees were opposed to the policy – especially early on – including Secretary of Defense Les Aspin and Chairman of the Joint Chiefs of Staff General Shalikashvili. In 1993, a bureaucratic politics analysis would have lead one to believe that the administration would not begin supporting NATO enlargement any time soon.[26]

While internationalism and learning may have inclined any administration to do something about eastern Europe, there were many alternatives to expanding NATO, including bilateral agreements, the PFP, or prodding the EU to assume a greater role.

In essay 8, Charles Kupchan identifies a small group of policy-makers in the Clinton administration who played a critical role in initiating the enlargement. One of the key players who helped advance the policy was Anthony Lake, the national security adviser during the first Clinton administration. Lake was also joined by several proponents of the policy, including Assistant Secretary of State Richard Holbrooke and, later on, Deputy Secretary of State Strobe Talbott. Although in the minority, this group of enlargement supporters was able to overcome widespread bureaucratic opposition by encouraging the President to issue public statements about the future of NATO and eastern Europe. The speeches made by the President were then used to muster support for the policy. Lake's internal policy review and smart manoeuvring in the bureaucracy helped transform the President's words into a *de facto* foreign policy, despite the fact that a high-level policy meeting had never taken place to discuss the merits of the issue.

This raises a number of important questions. Why was the President receptive to the individuals pushing for NATO enlargement? Why did he decide to support their agenda? Was it due to his own personal views or his trust in some of the individuals closest to him? Would any president have come to the same conclusion about expanding the alliance?

The reasons for President Clinton's decision to champion the policy remain elusive. Certainly his relationship with Anthony Lake and other supporters of the policy played an important role. Clinton also received advice from a number of individuals with eastern European roots, including Madeleine Albright, Charles Gati, and others. A series of meetings late in 1993 with key leaders from eastern Europe, including Lech Walesa and Vaclav Havel, are also reported to have made a strong impression on him.[27] The administration's floundering policy in the Balkans and NATO's inability to stop the bloodshed also seems to have created the sense that something needed to be done to show that the administration was serious about stabilizing eastern Europe. This need was made all the greater by continued Republican attacks in the months leading up to the election. As noted earlier, NATO enlargement had the virtue of solving two problems at once. Alliance expansion could simultaneously address some of the needs of transitioning states in eastern Europe, while also helping to revitalize NATO. At minimum, the policy would send a signal that the administration was serious about doing something about eastern Europe.

While the exact motivation behind Clinton's support of NATO expansion remains difficult to determine, something did convince the President in late in 1993 that NATO enlargement was worth considering.[28] By mid to late 1994 he was fully on board. As I argue above and in the introduction, the administration's decision to push for NATO enlargement came as a surprise. Only months before administration officials began publicly floating the idea, no one thought that NATO enlargement was a real possibility. Perhaps over time, more interviews, along with the release of public records and the publication of the memoirs may shed more light on how Clinton came to support the policy. However, what we can say for now is that the President's support of the policy and his public statements were the catalysts that brought the policy into being. While support for the policy may have eventually emerged in any administration, President Clinton and several of his key advisers, at minimum, made the policy happen years sooner than it otherwise would have happened.

THE 'OPPOSITION'

As Kupchan argues in essay 8, in addition to knowing the proponents of a policy, it is also important to become familiar with a policy's opponents. This is because a support base exists for almost any conceivable policy, and a policy that enjoys considerable support may still be blocked or derailed if those opposed to the policy are more vocal, better funded or better organized. To understand why a policy such as NATO enlargement is adopted, it is also necessary to understand why the opponents of the policy failed to prevent its adoption.

While the President and key members of his foreign policy team wanted NATO to grow, there are many points at which the policy could have been derailed. Prior to the Madrid summit, many analysts and pundits predicted that NATO enlargement would trigger a lengthy and heated public debate in the US. In the months leading up to the Madrid summit when the policy first began to receive public attention in the *New York Times* and other leading newspapers, it seemed as though the policy would indeed face considerable opposition. Criticism came from current and former policy-makers, as well as many leading academics and influential business leaders.

One of the main assaults on the policy came in June 1997, when 50 current and former members of the foreign policy establishment signed an open letter to the President that was critical of the policy (see Appendix 4). The letter's long and distinguished list of signatories, included former Senator Sam Nunn, (D–Georgia), and former Secretary of Defense Robert McNamara.

In addition to receiving criticism from many in the foreign policy community, the proposal also received heavy criticism from academics. The proposal provoked George F. Kennan's often-quoted warning that NATO enlargement is the 'most fateful error of American policy in the entire post–Cold War era'.[29] In a similar vein, John Lewis Gaddis called NATO enlargement a 'blunder of historic proportions'.[30] While academics are generally divided on most issues, NATO enlargement affords one of the few opportunities where there appears to have been a general consensus. As Gaddis noted, although 'Historians normally don't agree on much', he had 'difficulty finding any colleagues who think NATO expansion is a good idea'.[31] The same could be said of political scientists. At a conference held at the University of California at Berkeley during the spring of 1998, the panel was stacked against NATO enlargement 12 to 3, despite considerable effort by the organizers to recruit pro-enlargement scholars. Some of the participants who initially committed themselves to supporting the policy changed their mind by the time the conference was held. And as the preceding essays indicate, even scholars who support the policy often have reservations and limited expectations. Many concluded that NATO enlargement was the right thing to do, not because it was a great policy, but because the policy was 'too far along' to stop or because it was the 'best available alternative' and might make 'modest contributions' to European security.

Opposition to the policy also appeared to be mounting in the US Senate. Early in 1998, 20 senators signed an open letter to the President asking that the administration answer a number of tough questions. Given the letter's tone and who the signatories were, many saw it as more of a signal to the White House than a request for information – it was potentially a round robin.

Despite all the early signs of an impending heated debate over the policy, it never materialized. Both the Senate and the public reacted to the proposal with a collective yawn. To say that there was even a real debate may indeed be an overstatement. Aside from *Foreign Affairs* and a few leading newspapers such as the *Washington Post* and the *New York Times*, the policy never captured much attention.

Why did the policy fail to generate much debate? Two types of answer are advanced to explain why the policy never triggered a wave of real opposition. The first relates to the discussion above about learning and an internationalist ideology. It is possible that the vast majority of the American public and elites believe that NATO enlargement was the right thing to do. Eastern Europe has, after all, borne the brunt of two world wars and the Cold War. There might be a general sentiment that the West should help ensure stability in eastern Europe and see to it that history does not repeat itself.

The second explanation is much less flattering. Perhaps the American public and political elites are simply too apathetic or preoccupied really to care about the policy. Things are going very well domestically. With the economy booming, the Dow and National Association of Securities Dealers Automated Quotations (NASDAQ) climbing and the budget 'balanced', Americans do not appear to be worried about the immediate costs of expanding the alliance. Perhaps recent events in Yugoslavia will change this, especially if the NATO peacekeeping effort underway runs into difficulty, which is likely to happen.

While the lack of public debate is perhaps understandable, the Senate's failure adequately to debate the strengths and weaknesses of the policy is not. Regardless of whether one is for the policy or against it, the US Senate's decision not to give the policy more serious consideration is alarming. There are, of course, many good reasons for supporting the policy. Nevertheless, the issue here is not that the Senate ultimately approved enlargement, but rather that it did so without even forcing the administration to answer any tough questions about NATO expansion.

The final 'debate' in the Senate was friendly and congenial.[32] Few senators even raised the questions first asked in their open letter to the President, despite the fact that the administration never answered most of them. Some have been quite harsh in their criticism of the Senate. *New York Times* columnist Thomas Friedman, for example, asserts that 'Senators Jesse Helms, Joe Bidden, & Co. rolled over like puppies having their bellies rubbed'.[33] This stems from the fact that even the administration's cost estimates, which were roundly criticized in the press for failing to offer serious assessments, failed to receive much scrutiny in the Senate.[34] The Protocols on enlargement (see Appendix 3) ultimately were passed out of the Foreign Relations Committee on 4 March 1998 by a vote of 16 to 2; it was passed by the full Senate on 30 April by a vote of 80 to 19.

Why did the Senate fail to debate the policy seriously? Some have been very cynical about the political motives of some senators. At the Madrid summit, Jean Chretien, Prime Minister of Canada, summed up the Senate ratification process in the following way: '[US Senators] are selling their votes, *they are selling their votes* ... "You want me to vote for NATO? Don't forget the bridge in my district" ... It's incredible. In your country or mine, all the politicians would be in prison'.[35] Of course when the Prime Minister made these remarks, he was unaware that microphones were recording his conversation with Belgian Prime Minister Jean-Luc Dehaene.

This brings up the important point raised by Charles Kupchan in essay 8. Although the benefits or pay-offs for voting for NATO enlargement might be overstated, it is clear that the political calculus would lead a senator to support NATO enlargement anyway. Even if there were few or no positive benefits for voting for expansion, there were certainly costs associated with voting against it. Although voting for the policy might not directly lead to money or more votes, voting against the policy could certainly anger some constituents and interest groups. In contrast, voting for the policy, given the overall apathy of the public, could anger only a very small group of scholars, foreign policy experts and political pundits. In other words, whereas a vote for enlargement could be based on short-term political calculations, a vote against enlargement would require a more abstract and subjective consideration of how enlargement might affect national security in the long run. At a time when America has domestic prosperity and faces few challenges abroad, this asks a lot from politicians.

SUMMARY

America's current status as the world's only remaining superpower and its dominant position in NATO are key to understanding why the alliance is expanding. NATO's unique organizational attributes and good track record also help explain why NATO became the preferred vehicle for advancing American interests. The failure of the OSCE and other organizations to manage problems in former Yugoslavia made it clear that NATO still remained America's best option in Europe. In addition, by expanding the alliance, the US was able to extend its influence further into eastern Europe while simultaneously reducing Russia's influence in the region.

A number of domestic factors also help explain why NATO is enlarging. America's superpower status and more than half a century of internationalism have created a domestic consensus that the US must continue to play a leadership role in international politics. This view is shared by the public and elites alike, and by both Republicans and Democrats. The Clinton administration also felt pressure from special interests, including groups that represent eastern European immigrants and their descendants, as well as from the arms industry. Although these domestic groups did not drive the policy, they certainly did raise the immediate political costs for opposing it.

While many factors point in the direction of NATO enlargement, the policy was not over-determined or inevitable. There is good reason to believe that another administration would have delayed enlargement or prevented it all together. Most members of the foreign policy establishment were against the policy. There was widespread fear that the policy was too costly and would damage Russia's relations with the West. Whereas the Clinton administration turned the PFP framework into a fire-ladder that facilitated the entry of eastern European countries into NATO, other administrations may have used the PFP as firewall to keep them out. Even if one believes that enlargement was inevitable, several of the preceding essays make it clear that President Clinton and his key advisers ensured that the policy happened much sooner than it would have, perhaps by as much as a decade.

The preceding essays take a step towards filling the gap that currently exists between the realm of international relations theory and the study of foreign policy. This volume was fundamentally motivated by trying to answer a series of questions about an important foreign policy outcome; it was not motivated by the desire to advance any particular theory for its own sake. Various approaches were applied in a non-dogmatic way, often treated more like conceptual frameworks than theories. While some might be uncomfortable with combining, modifying, or even stretching theories, this is better than the common alternative, which is to force the facts to fit the theory. In many ways, by being problem-driven rather than theory-driven, the strengths and weakness of IR theory become even more apparent. No approach to international relations could be taken off the shelf and applied to this important event without significant modification and, in most cases, without being supplemented by another approach.

In the case of NATO enlargement – as is the case in all foreign policy outcomes – variables operating at all three levels of analysis are at work.

While this point is simple and should not come as a surprise, it is often overlooked or obscured because of how various debates have unfolded. All too often, constructing and refining theory is more highly regarded than making sense of an important event. This is unfortunate since IR theory – by design – offers only partial explanations. Asking which approach is better or which level of analysis is most useful is important, but all too often this endeavour has crowded out other pursuits. It is also important to learn how to use existing approaches together in order to offer more thorough and complete explanations of important events. This volume takes a step in that direction.

NOTES

1. For their valuable comments and suggestions, I thank Ashlee Bailey, Beverly Crawford, Kevin Donovan, James M. Goldgeier, Christine Lau, Kenneth P. Miller, Kenneth N. Waltz and two anonymous reviewers. The views expressed here are those of the author and do not represent the views of any organization with which the author is affiliated.

2. There are now a number of books and articles on NATO enlargement that focus on why the policy was adopted in the US. Most of these efforts do not develop or apply theory. See, for example, Gerald B. Solomon, *The NATO Enlargement Debate, 1990–1997: The Blessings of Liberty* (Westport, CT: Praeger, 1998); James M. Goldgeier, 'US Security Policy Toward the New Europe: How the Decision to Expand NATO Was Made', lecture delivered to the American Political Science Association, Washington, DC, August 1997, is one of the few efforts to evaluate whether international relations theory explains why the US decided to support enlargement; also see Goldgeier, *Not Whether But When: The U.S. Decision to Enlarge NATO* (Washington, DC: Brookings Institution, 1999).

3. While Volker Rühe was one of the first and most vocal advocates of enlargement, his enthusiasm was not shared by other members of his government. Even at the time of the Madrid summit, the German government was still divided on the issue of enlargement, especially over which countries should be included in the first round.

4. There remained considerable disagreement about who should be included in NATO. While it was clear that the Baltic republics and some of the other tougher choices could be delayed, there remained disagreement over Bulgaria, Romania, Slovakia and Slovenia. France supported the admission of Romania, Italy pushed for Slovenia, and Turkey supported Bulgaria. Spain, Belgium, Luxembourg and Canada also wanted more than three states admitted in the first round. See Philip Shenon, 'U.S., Defying Allies, Insists NATO Limit Expansion to 3', *New York Times*, 13 June 1997; also see Craig Whitney, 'NATO Invitations Snarled by Splits among Allies', *New York Times*, 15 June 1997.

5. In addition to realizing that enlargement would happen despite their objections, European leaders also began recognizing advantages in NATO enlargement. During this same period, the EU found itself under increasing pressure to offer membership to eastern European countries. NATO enlargement was a less costly way of incorporating eastern European countries into the West, and it simultaneously allowed the EU to put off this tough choice.

6. Iceland, Norway, Denmark, Britain and Portugal also supported the US's position on limiting the first round of expansion to Poland, Hungary and the Czech Republic.

7. Many involved with US–Soviet negotiations at the conclusion of the Cold War, especially during the 2 + 4 Talks over German unification, believed that the US pledged not to expand NATO eastward. Baker's promise that there 'would be no extension of NATO's current jurisdiction eastward' came as the Bush administration was playing a key role in German reunification. Similar promises were also made by European members of the alliance. Hans-Dietrich Genscher, the Foreign Minister of Germany, eager to assuage Soviet fears and reunify Germany, delivered the same message and also promised that there would be 'no expansion of NATO territory eastward'. See Michael R. Gordon, 'The World: Anatomy of a Misunderstanding', *New York Times*, 25 May 1997. American and European policy-makers now claim these remarks are taken out of context. The pledges that were made concerned the stationing of NATO troops in eastern Germany; there were no promises made about expanding eastward. Russian participants in the meetings, however, have a very different view. Russian Foreign Minister Yevgeny Primakov, for example, stated that 'In conversations with Mikhail Gorbachev, Eduard Shevardnadze and Dmitri Yazov, held in 1990–91, i.e., when the West was vitally interested in the Soviet troop withdrawal from the German Democratic Republic, ... Francois Mitterand, John Major and [James] Baker, all of them said one and the same thing: NATO will not move to the east by a single inch and not a single Warsaw Pact country will be admitted to NATO. This was exactly what they said.' See 'A Minister Who Is Not under Opposition's Fire', *Obshchaya Gazeta* (Moscow), 19 Sept. 1996, quoted by Stanley Kober in 'Russia's Search for Identity' (paper presented at Cato Institute conference 'NATO Enlargement: Illusions and Reality', 25 June 1997, F.A. Hayck Auditorium, Washington, DC).

8. For a book that documents the role of the US, see Lawrence S. Kaplan, *NATO and the United States: The Enduring Alliance* (Boston: Twane Publications, 1988).

9. Craig R. Whitney, 'Paris Blames U.S. Position for Setback over NATO', *New York Times*, 13 Oct. 1996; Gail Russell, 'Paris Tries to Direct NATO's Club Med', *Christian Science Monitor*, 9 Dec. 1996.

10. On America's failure to assume leadership of the world economy during the interwar period, see Charles P. Kindleberger, *The World in Depression, 1929–1939* (Berkeley: University of California Press, 1973). For a good overview of the reasons for the US's unwillingness to take on greater political and military roles, see Hans J. Morgenthau, *Politics Among Nations: The Struggle for Power and Peace*, 5th ed. (New York: Knopf Press, 1978).

11. For an informative review of the inherent limits of third-image theory, see Kenneth N. Waltz, *Theory of International Politics* (New York: McGraw Hill, 1979), p.121. In regard to balance-of-power theory, Waltz notes that 'The theory explains why a certain similarity of behavior is expected from similarly situated states. To explain the differences in national responses, a theory would have to show how the different internal structures of state affect their external policies and actions.' Third-image theories cannot, by design, explain particular foreign policy outcomes.

12. NATO's unique attributes drew attention from its inception. For one of the first efforts to examine these important differences, see Karl W. Deutsch *et al.*, *Political Community and the North Atlantic Area* (Princeton: Princeton University Press, 1957).

13. Most of this stems from provisions under Article 9 of the North Atlantic Treaty. See Appendix 1.

14. Cf. Robert B. McCalla, 'NATO's Persistence after the Cold War', *International Organization*, Vol.50, No.3 (Summer 1996), pp.445–75.

15. International organizations may nevertheless share some common features with national governments. For example, the International Monetary Fund (IMF) may create incentives for members to take certain actions by providing funds. While international organizations often have some positive inducements or 'carrots' for eliciting a desired behaviour, they have few or no 'sticks' for punishing unwanted behaviour. In most instances, the largest stick that an international organization possesses is the carrot that it can withhold. Coercive capabilities are often limited to public shaming.

16. Kenneth N. Waltz draws a distinction between third-image theories that operate at the systemic or international level, second-image theories which include domestic determinants such as regime type and economic system, and first-image theories that examine human nature or

individual decision-makers: see *Man, the State, and War* (New York: Columbia University Press, 1959).

17. See William D. Hartung, 'Welfare for Weapons Dealers 1998: The Hidden Costs of NATO Expansion' (New York: New School for Social Research, World Policy Institute, March 1998). Jeff Gerth and Tim Weiner, 'Arms Makers See Bonanza in Selling NATO Expansion', *New York Times*, 29 June 1997, p.1.

18. Katharine Q. Steelye, 'Arms Contractors Spend to Promote an Extended NATO', *New York Times*, 30 March 1998.

19. Ibid.

20. On the growing importance of voters that are of eastern European origin or descent, see Dick Kirschten, 'Ethnics Resurging', *National Journal*, Vol.27 (25 Feb. 1995), pp.478–84.

21. Steelye, 'Arms Contractors Spend to Promote an Extended NATO'.

22. Ed Gillespie and Bob Schellhas (eds), *Contract with America: The Bold Play by Rep. Newt Gingrich, Rep. Dick Armey and the House Republicans to Change the Nation*, 1st ed. (New York: Times Books, 1994).

23. This question has received little attention. For a good review of learning and foreign policy, see Jack S. Levy, 'Learning and Foreign Policy: Sweeping a Conceptual Minefield', *International Organization*, Vol.48, No.2 (Spring 1994), pp.279–312.

24. George F. Kennan and John Lewis Gaddis, both internationalists, were among the harshest critics of the policy. Also see the signatories of the 'Open Letter to the President', Appendix 4.

25. See Kupchan, essay 8.

26. See Goldgeier. The article nicely illustrates how the President can often overcome bureaucratic obstacles. Goldgeier's findings support Richard Neustadt's work on the presidential power, rather than Graham Allison's work on bureaucratic politics. See Richard Neustadt, *Presidential Power: The Politics of Leadership with Reflections on Johnson and Nixon* (New York: John Wiley & Sons, Inc., 1976), p.107. Cf. Graham Allison, *Essence of Decision: Explaining the Cuban Missile Crisis* (Boston: Little, Brown, 1971).

27. 'Walesa Warns Communism May Reemerge', *Washington Post*, 4 Jan. 1994. Meetings with these two leaders seem to have had a profound influence on many senators as well. After meeting with Vaclav Havel, the Czech President, a US senator who was inclined to vote against enlargement, Senator Wellstone, noted that 'of all the decisions I've made as a Senator, this is the most difficult one'. The reason, he claimed, was that Vaclav Havel 'is a hero to me'. 'Key Senate Panel Passes Resolution to Expand NATO', *New York Times*, 4 March 1998.

28. Some have argued that NATO enlargement is only one example of a general pattern of the Clinton administration. As R.W. Apple Jr. notes, the decision to enlarge NATO was made 'in characteristic Clinton administration style, without a structured evaluation of competing viewpoints, without political debate, and over the initial objections of senior military officials'. R.W. Apple Jr., 'Road to Approval Is Rocky, and Gamble Is Perilous', *New York Times*, 15 May 1997. During the months leading up to the Madrid summit, Thomas Friedman and others have also noted that 'the Clinton Administration has never had an integrated foreign policy'. See Thomas Friedman, 'Foreign Affairs: Madeleine's Folly', *New York Times*, 17 Feb. 1998, p.A19.

29. George F. Kennan, 'A Fateful Error', *New York Times*, 5 Feb. 1997.

30. John Lewis Gaddis, 'The Senate Should Halt NATO Expansion', *New York Times*, 27 April 1998.

31. Ibid.

32. This was especially obvious when several amendments were proposed that would limit the number of members or place a cap on the costs that the US would be pay for expansion. For example, Senator John Warner and Senator Daniel Patrick Moynihan co-sponsored an amendment to delay a second round of enlargement for three years. All of these amendments were dropped at the administration's request after little consideration and debate.

33. Thomas Friedman, 'Foreign Affairs; Ohio State II', *New York Times*, 3 March 1998.

34. William D. Hartung, 'NATO's Hidden Costs', *Washington Post*, 27 March 1998; Alison Mitchell, 'Senate Panel Hears Costs and Benefits of Bigger NATO Debated', *New York Times*, 10 Oct. 1997.

35. 'Oops! A Blunt Canadian on NATO', *New York Times*, 11 July 1997.

APPENDICES

APPENDIX 1

The North Atlantic Treaty

Washington DC – 4 April 1949

The Parties to this Treaty reaffirm their faith in the purposes and principles of the *Charter of the United Nations* and their desire to live in peace with all peoples and all governments. They are determined to safeguard the freedom, common heritage and civilization of their peoples, founded on the principles of democracy, individual liberty and the rule of law. They seek to promote stability and well-being in the North Atlantic area. They are resolved to unite their efforts for collective defence and for the preservation of peace and security. They therefore agree to this North Atlantic Treaty:

Article 1
The Parties undertake, as set forth in the *Charter of the United Nations*, to settle any international dispute in which they may be involved by peaceful means in such a manner that international peace and security and justice are not endangered, and to refrain in their international relations from the threat or use of force in any manner inconsistent with the purposes of the United Nations.

Article 2
The Parties will contribute toward the further development of peaceful and friendly international relations by strengthening their free institutions, by bringing about a better understanding of the principles upon which these institutions are founded, and by promoting conditions of stability and well-being. They will seek to eliminate conflict in their international economic policies and will encourage economic collaboration between any or all of them.

Article 3
In order more effectively to achieve the objectives of this Treaty, the Parties, separately and jointly, by means of continuous and effective self-

help and mutual aid, will maintain and develop their individual and collective capacity to resist armed attack.

Article 4

The Parties will consult together whenever, in the opinion of any of them, the territorial integrity, political independence or security of any of the Parties is threatened.

Article 5

The Parties agree that an armed attack against one or more of them in Europe or North America shall be considered an attack against them all and consequently they agree that, if such an armed attack occurs, each of them, in exercise of the right of individual or collective self-defence recognised by *Article 51 of the Charter of the United Nations*, will assist the Party or Parties so attacked by taking forthwith, individually and in concert with the other Parties, such action as it deems necessary, including the use of armed force, to restore and maintain the security of the North Atlantic area.

Any such armed attack and all measures taken as a result thereof shall immediately be reported to the Security Council. Such measures shall be terminated when the Security Council has taken the measures necessary to restore and maintain international peace and security (**1**).

Article 6

For the purpose of Article 5, an armed attack on one or more of the Parties is deemed to include an armed attack:

- on the territory of any of the Parties in Europe or North America, on the Algerian Departments of France, (**2**) on the territory of Turkey or on the Islands under the jurisdiction of any of the Parties in the North Atlantic area north of the Tropic of Cancer;

- on the forces, vessels, or aircraft of any of the Parties, when in or over these territories or any other area in Europe in which occupation forces of any of the Parties were stationed on the date when the Treaty entered into force or the Mediterranean Sea or the North Atlantic area north of the Tropic of Cancer.

Article 7

This Treaty does not affect, and shall not be interpreted as affecting in any way the rights and obligations under the Charter of the Parties which are members of the United Nations, or the primary responsibility of the Security Council for the maintenance of international peace and security.

Article 8

Each Party declares that none of the international engagements now in force between it and any other of the Parties or any third State is in conflict with the provisions of this Treaty, and undertakes not to enter into any international engagement in conflict with this Treaty.

Article 9

The Parties hereby establish a Council, on which each of them shall be represented, to consider matters concerning the implementation of this Treaty. The Council shall be so organised as to be able to meet promptly at any time. The Council shall set up such subsidiary bodies as may be necessary; in particular it shall establish immediately a defence committee which shall recommend measures for the implementation of Articles 3 and 5.

Article 10

The Parties may, by unanimous agreement, invite any other European State in a position to further the principles of this Treaty and to contribute to the security of the North Atlantic area to accede to this Treaty. Any State so invited may become a Party to the Treaty by depositing its instrument of accession with the Government of the United States of America. The Government of the United States of America will inform each of the Parties of the deposit of each such instrument of accession.

Article 11

This Treaty shall be ratified and its provisions carried out by the Parties in accordance with their respective constitutional processes. The instruments of ratification shall be deposited as soon as possible with the Government of the United States of America, which will notify all the other signatories of each deposit. The Treaty shall enter into force between the States which have ratified it as soon as the ratifications of the majority of the signatories, including the ratifications of Belgium, Canada, France, Luxembourg, the Netherlands, the United Kingdom and the United States, have been deposited and shall come into effect with respect to other States on the date of the deposit of their ratifications.

Article 12

After the Treaty has been in force for ten years, or at any time thereafter, the Parties shall, if any of them so requests, consult together for the purpose of reviewing the Treaty, having regard for the factors then affecting peace and security in the North Atlantic area, including the development of universal as well as regional arrangements under the *Charter of the United Nations* for the maintenance of international peace and security.

Article 13

After the Treaty has been in force for twenty years, any Party may cease to be a Party one year after its notice of denunciation has been given to the Government of the United States of America, which will inform the Governments of the other Parties of the deposit of each notice of denunciation.

Article 14

This Treaty, of which the English and French texts are equally authentic, shall be deposited in the archives of the Government of the United States of America. Duly certified copies will be transmitted by that Government to the Governments of other signatories.

APPENDIX 2

Protocol to the North Atlantic Treaty on the Accession of the Republic of Poland[1]

The Parties to the North Atlantic Treaty, signed at Washington on April 4, 1949, Being satisfied that the security of the North Atlantic area will be enhanced by the accession of the Republic of Poland to that Treaty, Agree as follows:

Article I
Upon the entry into force of this Protocol, the Secretary General of the North Atlantic Treaty Organization shall, on behalf of all the Parties, communicate to the Government of the Republic of Poland an invitation to accede to the North Atlantic Treaty. In accordance with article 10 of the Treaty, the Republic of Poland shall become a Party on the date when it deposits its instrument of accession with the Government of the United States of America.

Article II
The present Protocol shall enter into force when each of the Parties to the North Atlantic Treaty has notified the Government of the United States of America of its acceptance thereof. The Government of the United States of America shall inform all the Parties to the North Atlantic Treaty of the date of receipt of each such notification and of the date of the entry into force of the present Protocol.

Article III
The present Protocol, of which the English and French texts are equally authentic, shall be deposited in the Archives of the Government of the United States of America. Duly certified copies thereof shall be transmitted by that Government to the Governments of all the Parties to the North Atlantic Treaty.

In witness whereof, the undersigned plenipotentiaries have signed the present Protocol.
Signed at Brussels on the 16th day of December 1997.

---

1. The protocols on the accession of the Republic of Hungary and the Czech Republic, signed on 16 December 1997, use the same language as this protocol.

APPENDIX 3

Enlargement Protocols Ratification Dates

NATO Member States	Date Protocols Were Approved	Individual or Body that Approved Protocols
Canada	2 Feb. 1998	Foreign Minister
Denmark	3 Feb. 1998	Parliament
Norway	3 March 1998	Parliament
Germany	26 March 1998	Bundestag
	27 March 1998	Bundesrat
France	20 May 1998	Senate
	10 June 1998	National Assembly
Greece	14 May 1998	Parliament
Luxembourg	27 May 1998	Parliament
Spain	21 May 1998	Congress of Deputies
	23 June 1998	Senate
United Kingdom	17 July 1998	House of Commons
	31 July 1998	House of Lords
United States	30 April 1998	US Senate
Iceland	4 June 1998	Parliament
Belgium	9 July 1998	Senate
	16 July 1998	House of Representatives
Italy	13 May 1998	Senate
	23 June 1998	House of Representatives
Portugal	16 Sept. 1998	Parliament
Turkey	21 Oct. 1998	Parliament
The Netherlands	6 Oct. 1998	Second Chamber
	1 Dec. 1998	First Chamber

APPENDIX 4

Open Letter to President Clinton

26 June 1997

We, the undersigned, believe that the current US-led effort to expand NATO, the focus of the recent Helsinki and Paris Summits, is a policy error of historic proportions. We believe that NATO expansion will decrease allied security and unsettle European stability for the following reasons:

In Russia, NATO expansion, which continues to be opposed across the entire political spectrum, will strengthen the non-democratic opposition, undercut those who favor reform and cooperation with the West, bring the Russians to question the entire post-Cold War settlement, and galvanize resistance in the Duma to the START II and III treaties;

In Europe, NATO expansion will draw a new line of division between the 'ins' and the 'outs', foster instability, and ultimately diminish the sense of security of those countries which are not included;

In NATO, expansion, which the Alliance has indicated is open-ended, will inevitably degrade NATO's ability to carry out its primary mission and will involve US security guarantees to countries with serious border and national minority problems, and unevenly developed systems of democratic government;

In the US, NATO expansion will trigger an extended debate over its indeterminate, but certainly high, cost and will call into question the US commitment to the Alliance, traditionally and rightly regarded as a centerpiece of US foreign policy.

Because of these serious objections, and in the absence of any reason for a rapid decision, we strongly urge that the NATO expansion process be suspended while alternative actions are pursued. These include:

Opening the economic and political doors of the European Union to Central and Eastern Europe; developing an enhanced

> Partnership for Peace program; supporting a cooperative NATO–Russian relationship; and continuing the arms reduction and transparency process, particularly with respect to nuclear weapons and materials, the major threat to US security, and with respect to conventional military forces in Europe.

Russia does not now pose a threat to its western neighbors and the nations of Central and Eastern Europe are not in danger. For this reason, and the others cited above, we believe that NATO expansion is neither necessary nor desirable and that this ill-conceived policy can and should be put on hold.

List of Signatories

Ambassador George Bunn (IIS Consulting Professor, Center for International Security and Arms Control, Stanford University)

The Honorable Robert Bowie (Former Director, Policy Planning Staff, and Counselor, Department of State; former Deputy Director for Intelligence, CIA)

Senator Bill Bradley (US Senator (1979–96))

Professor David Calleo (Director of European Studies, Nitze School of Advanced International Studies, Johns Hopkins University)

Ambassador Richard T. Davies (Former Ambassador to Poland (1973–78); Political Officer, NATO International Staff; Deputy Assistant Secretary of State for European Affairs)

Ambassador Jonathan Dean (Former Ambassador heading US Delegation to NATO Warsaw Pact Negotiations on Mutual and Balanced Force Reductions; Deputy US Negotiator, Four Power Agreement on Berlin; Adviser for International Security Issues, Union of Concerned Scientists)

Professor Paul Doty (Emeritus Director, Center for Science and International Affairs, John F. Kennedy School of Government, Harvard University)

Susan Eisenhower (Chairman, Center for Political and Strategic Studies)

David M. Evans (Former Senior Adviser to Helsinki Commission (1990–95); President, Integrated Strategies International)

Ambassador David Fischer (President, World Affairs Council of Northern California)

Ambassador Raymond Garthoff (Former Ambassador to Bulgaria (1977–79); Senior Fellow, Brookings Institution)

Dr Morton H. Halperin (Former National Security Council and Department of Defense Official)

Owen Harries (Editor, *The National Interest*)

Senator Gary Hart (US Senator (1975–87))

Ambassador Arthur Hartman (Former Ambassador to the Soviet Union (1981–87))

Senator Mark Hatfield (US Senator (1967–87))

Professor John P. Holdren (Chairman, National Academy of Sciences Committee on International Security and Arms Control; Professor, Harvard University)

The Honorable Townsend Hoopes (Former Under-secretary of the US Air Force)

Senator Gordon Humphrey (US Senator (1979–91))

The Honorable Fred Ikle (Former Under-secretary of Defense for Policy (1981–88))

Senator Bennett Johnston (US Senator (1972–96))

Professor Carl Kaysen (Professor of Political Economy, Harvard University)

The Honorable Spurgeon Keeny (Former Deputy Director Arms Control and Disarmament Agency; Senior Staff Member, National Security Council; President, Arms Control Association)

Ambassador James Leonard (Former Assistant Director, Arms Control and Disarmament Agency; former Deputy Permanent Representative to the United Nations)

Dr Edward Luttwak (Senior Fellow, Center for Strategic and International Studies)

Professor Michael Mandelbaum (Professor, Nitze School of Advanced International Studies, Johns Hopkins University)

Ambassador Jack Matlock (Former Ambassador to the Soviet Union (1987–91))

The Honorable C. William Maynes (Former Editor, *Foreign Policy*; Former Assistant Secretary of State for International Organizations Affairs (1977–80))

Ambassador Richard McCormack (Former Under-secretary of State for Economic Affairs (1989–91))

The Honorable David McGiffert (Assistant Secretary for International Security Affairs (1977–81))

The Honorable Robert S. McNamara (Secretary of Defense (1961–68); President of the World Bank (1968–91))

Jack Mendelsohn (Former Senior Foreign Service Officer; Deputy Director, Arms Control Association)

Philip Merrill (Former NATO Assistant Secretary General)

Ambassador Paul H. Nitze (Former Special Adviser to President Reagan and Secretary of State Shultz for Arms Control; former Deputy Secretary of Defense; former Secretary of the Navy)

Senator Sam Nunn (US Senator (1972–96))

Ambassador Herbert S. Okun (Ambassador to East Germany (1980–83); Ambassador to the United Nations (1985–89))

Professor W.K.H. Panofsky (Emeritus Professor, Stanford University)

Major General Christian Patte (ret.) (Former Director of NATO Logisitics (1990–96))

Professor Richard Pipes (Director, East European and Soviet Affairs for National Security Council)

Lt. General Robert E. Pursley (ret.) (Lieutenant General, US Air Force)

Professor George Rathjens (Professor, Massachusetts Institute of Technology)

The Honorable Stanley Resor (Former Secretary of the Army; Ambassador to the Mutual Balanced Force Reduction Negotiation)

The Honorable John B. Rhinelander (Former Legal Adviser to US SALT I Delegation; Deputy Legal Adviser, Department of State)

Vice Admiral John J. Shanahan (ret.) (Former Military Advisor to the US Ambassador to NATO; Director, Center for Defense Information)

The Honorable Marshall Shulman (Professor Emeritus, Columbia University)

Dr. John Steinbruner (Senior Fellow and former Director, Foreign Policy Studies, Brookings Institution)

Admiral Stansfield Turner (ret.) (Former Director of the CIA)

Ambassador Richard Viets (Former Ambassador to Tanzania and Jordan)

The Honorable Paul Warnke (Former Director, Arms Control and Disarmament Agency; Assistant Secretary of Defense for International Security Affairs)

Admiral James D. Watkins (ret.) (Former Secretary of Energy; former Chief of Naval Operations)

Notes on Contributors

Vinod K. Aggarwal is Professor in the Department of Political Science, Affiliated Professor of Business and Public Policy in the Haas School of Business, and Director of the Berkeley Asia Pacific Economic Cooperation Study Center (BASC) at the University of California at Berkeley. He is also founder and Editor-in-Chief of the journal *Business and Politics*. His research focuses on international relations, international political economy and theories of institutional change. Most recently, he has edited *Institutional Designs for a Complex World* (Cornell University Press), co-edited *Asia-Pacific Crossroads* (St Martin's Press), and is the author of *Debt Games* (Cambridge University Press).

Ronald J. Bee is a senior analyst at the University of California Institute on Global Conflict and Cooperation, based at UC San Diego. A specialist on NATO, US–Russian relations and nuclear proliferation, he is the author of *Nuclear Proliferation: The Post-Cold War Challenge* (1995) and co-author of *One Nation Becomes Many: The Access Guide to the Former Soviet Union* (1992). His co-authored book, *Looking the Tiger in the Eye: Confronting the Nuclear Threat* (1988) won a Christopher Award and received notable book of the year honours from the *New York Times*.

Beverly Crawford is a teacher of Political Economy at the University of California at Berkeley and is the Associate Director of UC Berkeley's Institute of European Studies. She is co-editor of *The Myth of Ethnic Conflict: Politics, Economics and Cultural Violence* (1998) and has written policy papers and articles on the causes of conflict in the former Yugoslavia and ethnic conflict in the post-Cold War era. Her current research interests focus on the 'new' economy and most recently she served as a co-principal investigator on a Ford Foundation project entitled 'From Promising Practices to Promising Futures: Job Training for the Information Age'.

Ernst B. Haas is Robson Research Professor Emeritus of Government and Professor of the Graduate School at the University of California at

Berkeley. His most recent work is *Nationalism, Liberalism and Progress*, 2 vols. (Ithaca: Cornell University Press, 1997 and 2000). Previously he contributed to the literature on international relations theory, international organization, regional integration and science/technology and international relations.

Charles A. Kupchan is Associate Professor of International Affairs at Georgetown University and a Senior Fellow at the Council on Foreign Relations. He is currently writing a book about American grand strategy and managing the transition from unipolarity to multipolarity.

Gale A. Mattox is Professor in the Department of Political Science at the United States Naval Academy and President of Women in International Security (WIIS), an educational, non-profit located at the University of Maryland and the largest international organization for women in the fields of foreign and defence policy.

Robert W. Rauchhaus is a Ph.D. candidate in Political Science at the University of California at Berkeley. His research focuses on international relations, foreign policy, and security studies. His dissertation, *Third-Party Intervention in Militarized Disputes: Primium Non Nocere*, examines and evaluates the effectiveness of various conflict management techniques employed by individuals, states, and international institutions.

Kenneth N. Waltz is Ford Professor, Emeritus of the University of California at Berkeley, and Research Associate at the Institute of War and Peace Studies and Adjunct Professor at the Department of Political Science at Columbia University.

Steven Weber is Associate Professor of Political Science at the University of California, Berkeley. His recent research focuses on the reorganization of political and economic institutions in the 'new' economy, with special attention to knowledge-based industries and open-source software models. His publications include *Cooperation and Discord in U.S.-Soviet Arms Control* (Princeton University Press) *Globalization and The European Political Economy* (Columbia University Press); numerous articles and chapters in the areas of U.S. foreign policy, the political economy of trade and finance, politics of the post-Cold War world, and European integration.

Abstracts

Marching NATO Eastward: Can International Relations Theory Keep Pace? *by Robert W. Rauchhaus*

In 1997 NATO decided to admit three new members. Why did the alliance offer membership to its former Cold War adversaries? What are the likely consequences of this decision? Which countries should be admitted in the future? This essay addresses these questions, places them in their substantive, theoretical, and methodological contexts, and outlines the volume's purpose and organization.

NATO Expansion: A Realist's View *by Kenneth N. Waltz*

The collapse of the Soviet Union left the United States as the world's dominant power. The author views NATO's expansion as an American policy designed to maintain and extend America's grip on European foreign and military policies. Instead of demonstrating the resilience and strength of international institutions, NATO's expansion shows how institutions are shaped to serve what strong countries believe to be their interests. Realist theory, however, leads one to expect that other countries will work to restore a more even balance of power in the world.

The Bosnian Road to NATO Enlargement *by Beverly Crawford*

The author argues that the decision to expand NATO was solidified through experience of the Yugoslav wars. Institutions that included Russia, the UN and the OSCE, failed to resolve the conflict; perceptions of Russian weakness and obstructionism led Western decision-makers to conclude that NATO, an alliance that excluded Russia, was the only institution that could ensure security in Europe. This argument supports the central claim of the realist theory of international relations: that power balances. Post-Cold War efforts to build a new 'security architecture' in Europe were bound to fail, because, in their effort to advance a new definition of security, harking back to old visions of 'collective security', they ignored this central feature of the international system.

Analysing NATO Expansion: An Institutional Bargaining Approach *by Vinod K. Aggarwal*

Traditional 'reflectivist' and 'realist' theories do not adequately explain why NATO is enlarging. Based on an institutional bargaining game approach – focusing on the goods involved, the individual situations of key actors and existing institutions – the author shows how the highest expected utility for the US would come from limited widening and some modest institutional co-ordination. The essay then examines how the Clinton administration tried to alter goods, bolster domestic support in Russia and modify institutions to reduce potential Russian opposition. In conclusion, based on this analysis, it is suggested that expansion may not be as detrimental as predicted by many analysts.

Organization Theory: Remedy for Europe's Organizational Cacophony? *by Ernst B. Haas*

Major theories of public organizations neither explain nor justify the eastward expansion of NATO. In addition to particular national hopes in Europe, the main reason for that expansion is found in US political attitudes concerning leadership in bringing about an American-defined vision of a post-Cold War world. NATO is seen as a core component in this vision. It is preferable that Europe assumes sole responsibility for its own defence and that NATO, far from expanding, be progressively eliminated, and other multilateral European organizations be adapted in proportion.

A Modest Proposal for NATO Expansion *by Steven Weber*

The argument in favor of NATO expansion is a modest one. Major theories of international politics are indeterminate about the middle-

and long-term effects of this policy decision. Practical political concerns exist on both sides of the expansion debate, but it is not possible to know at this point which of those concerns will be most important. Much of the political rhetoric around NATO expansion is overblown. This unfortunately creates a cycle of self-fulfilling prophecies where a decision comes to be, in a political sense, more important than it is in a purely strategic sense. This article challenges the premise of the debate. My alternative premise is that the stakes are not quite so high. NATO expansion will probably make a modest contribution to security, stability, successful transitions in at least some parts of Eastern Europe, and continued cohesion among the Western allies. And it will do that at a moderate cost – to national budgets and more importantly to the Russians. Russia has very little to fear from NATO expansion and might, under certain circumstances, stand to gain a few modest benefits from the process.

NATO Enlargement: A Step in the Process of Alliance Reform
by Gale A. Mattox

NATO enlargement was the right decision at the right time both for the candidate countries and for the alliance objective of stability and security in Europe. However, enlargement is only justifiable in the context of a broader reform of NATO and of the European security structure. This will require significant political will on the part of all parties and major readjustments of traditional security perceptions of Europe. NATO has taken a step down this road to reform in launching the New Strategic Concept, but the transformation of the broader European security architecture needs to include the OSCE, UN, EU/WEU as well as other institutions.

The Origins and Future of NATO Enlargement
by Charles A. Kupchan

Despite the clear strategic risks it entails, NATO enlargement proceeded because a small, but powerful, group of enthusiasts within the Clinton administration vigorously pushed the policy forward and overcome widespread opposition within the bureaucracy and the broader foreign policy community. Now that enlargement has begun, it should proceed. But if NATO enlargement is to be a vehicle for uniting, rather than redividing Europe, the West has only one viable option: opening NATO to Russia. The pacification of Russia and its inclusion in the West will reduce the need for a dominant US role in managing European security and necessitate a transatlantic security pact that becomes less Atlantic and more European.

Boarding the NATO Train: Enlargement and National Interests
by Ronald J. Bee

NATO enlargement required a convergence of US, western and eastern European national interests. The US, *inter alia*, wanted to maintain its leadership of NATO; Germany to secure its eastern border with an eye toward expanding eastern export markets; and France to acquire more leadership at less cost. Central and eastern Europeans wished to join NATO as a hedge against Russia and a door to the European Union. Russia remains viscerally uncomfortable with NATO enlargement, yet Putin's need for Western foreign aid has moderated his views. Kosovo complicated future NATO enlargement, serving to decelerate rather than accelerate the process.

Explaining NATO Enlargement *by Robert W. Rauchhaus*

A combination of international and domestic factors help explain NATO enlargement. America's current status as the world's only remaining superpower and its dominant position in NATO are key to understanding why the alliance is expanding. A number of domestic factors also play an important role, including the dominance of internationalist ideology. However, although many factors point in the direction of NATO enlargement, the decision was not inevitable. Whereas the Clinton administration used the Partnership for Peace framework as a fire-ladder that facilitated the entry of eastern European countries, other administrations may have used it as a firewall to keep them out.

Index

Books of Related Interest

Turkey: Anglo-American Security Interests, 1945–1952

The First Enlargement of NATO

Ekavi Athanassopoulou

> 'This extraordinarily interesting book focuses on a critical moment in Turkey's quest for a Western anchor to windward – the negotiations that resulted in not only Turkey but also Greece becoming members of the North Atlantic Treaty Organisation. ... This account of the statecraft of the 1940s and 1950s has a distinctly contemporary ring, for today Turkey is knocking at another Western door – that of the European Union'.
>
> **Richard H Ullman, *Princeton University***

288 pages illus 1999
0 7146 4855 8 cloth

NATO Enters the 21st Century

Ted Galen Carpenter (Ed)

NATO has sought to reinvent itself as a 'crisis-management' organisation to suppress conflicts on Europe's periphery – and perhaps beyond. Is NATO suited to playing such a role, or is the alliance a Cold War anachronism? How will Russia react to an enlarged NATO focused on out-of-area peacekeeping and conflict-prevention missions? Are there alternative security institutions that might better address Europe's security needs in the post-Cold War era?

200 pages 2000
0 7146 5058 7 cloth
0 7146 8109 1 paper

FRANK CASS PUBLISHERS
Newbury House, 900 Eastern Avenue, Ilford, Essex, IG2 7HH
Tel: +44 (0)20 8599 8866 Fax: +44 (0)20 8599 0984 E-mail: info@frankcass.com
NORTH AMERICA
5824 NE Hassalo Street, Portland, OR 97213 3644, USA
Tel: 800 944 6190 Fax: 503 280 8832 E-mail: cass@isbs.com
Website: www.frankcass.com

Culture and Security
Multilateralism, Arms Control and Security Building
Keith R Krause (Ed)

With the growing multilateralisation and regionalisation of the security-building process, the cross-cultural aspects of security-building dialogues have assumed a prominent place in contemporary policy debates. The case studies in this volume examine how and when cultural factors affect the elaboration and implementation of arms control and security-building policies.

264 pages 1999
0 7146 4885 X cloth
0 7146 4437 4 paper

Stability and Security in the Baltic Sea Region
Russian, Nordic and European Aspects
Olav F Knudsen (Ed)

This book emphasises the Baltic Sea region and its complex security challenges, seen in a longer-term perspective. Security is conceived of in the classical sense yet with a clear understanding of the links to the broader aspects.

304 pages illus 1999
0 7146 4932 5 cloth
0 7146 4492 7 paper

Preventing the Use of Weapons of Mass Destruction
Eric Herring (Ed)

The bulk of the literature on weapons of mass destruction (WMD) concentrates on preventing their spread. While that is an important subject, these studies contribute to the literature on preventing their use. A common argument runs through them: that, while complacency must be avoided, much of the post-Cold War focus among Western Governments on the threat posed by WMD is excessively alarmist.

200 pages 2000
0 7146 5044 7 cloth
0 7146 8097 4 paper

FRANK CASS PUBLISHERS
Newbury House, 900 Eastern Avenue, Ilford, Essex, IG2 7HH
Tel: +44 (0)20 8599 8866 Fax: +44 (0)20 8599 0984 E-mail: info@frankcass.com
NORTH AMERICA
5824 NE Hassalo Street, Portland, OR 97213 3644, USA
Tel: 800 944 6190 Fax: 503 280 8832 E-mail: cass@isbs.com
Website: www.frankcass.com